Daughter of Destiny
Kathryn Kuhlman...her story

Daughter of Destiny

Kathryn Kuhlman...her story

by Jamie Buckingham

DAUGHTER OF DESTINY
Copyright © 1976 by Bridge Publishing Inc.,
All rights reserved.
Printed and bound in Great Britain by
Forsyth Middleton & Co. Ltd.
Library of Congress catalog card number: 76-12034
International Standard Book Number: 0-88270-318-8
Bridge Publishing Inc., South Plainfield, New Jersey 07080
Valley Books, Gwent, U.K.

Contents

FOREWORD

The task of writing a biography is similar to that of performing an autopsy. The biographer can, if he is only doing a job, simply line up the facts, talk to people, read what others have said, and draw his own impersonal conclusions. But to perform that kind of operation on Kathryn Kuhlman whom God himself had anointed? Never. The task would have to be done by someone not only who knew her, but who knew her God also. It would have to be done by someone who would tell the truth, as the Bible writers told the truth of David's adultery, Elijah's insecurities, and Paul's bad temper. Yet it must be done by someone who would magnify the healthy parts even more than the diseased ones. To write her story is literally to touch God's anointed. Thus it would have to be done by someone with tears in his eyes. In truth, yes. But far more, in love.

Having worked closely with Kathryn Kuhlman, writing eight of her nine books, I had already drawn a number of positive conclusions about her life. After her death, however, as I talked to her critics—and they were legion—my own attitude became harsh and critical. I would hear myself, in discussing her life and ministry, focusing in on some character flaw, some shadow from her past or the mystery surrounding her death—rather than the good she did. In performing my own post mortem I was becoming like the pathologist who refers to the body of a loved one as "the heart attack," or "the breast cancer," while the husband grits his teeth in anguish and says, "She's not 'the breast cancer,' she's my wife of forty years."

Love makes the difference.

Two nights before I went into seclusion to write the final draft of this book, I had a dream. In the dream I was with Kathryn. We were lovers, not in a sexual sense, but in an intimate heart relationship. She was as I remembered her just before her death—frail and aging, not beautiful to look upon. Yet as we cavorted through the field, walked down a tree-shaded lane holding hands, and stood in a deep embrace, I not only loved her, I was in love with her.

She had been dead four months and the dream frightened me. It was not natural.

The next night I dreamed again. This time I was dressed as a deputy sheriff. Kathryn was with me, in some kind of protective custody. Then, from somewhere, other deputies appeared, all in uniform. But instead of helping me, they began ridiculing Kathryn, strutting around imitating her voice and mannerisms. Mocking her. All the while she sat quietly on a little stool beside the dirt road, head bowed, receiving the shame but making no move to defend herself. Angry and frustrated, I rose to protect her.

I shared the two dreams with my wife and two close friends. All agreed the dreams came from God—given that I might have the one ingredient absolutely necessary to write and interpret the life of Kathryn Kuhlman—love.

PUBLISHER'S PREFACE

During the last years of her life, Kathryn Kuhlman realized that her work was coming to an end. She wanted her whole story told, and without hesitation she selected Jamie Buckingham to write her biography. Her directions to him were very simple: "Tell it all, Jamie; tell it all!" Jamie complied with her wishes, and in "telling it all," this book reveals Kathryn's humanity along with her deep spirituality.

It was my privilege to be present at several of Ms. Kuhlman's miracle services. Whenever miraculous healings took place in her meetings, she was always careful to give the glory to God. She realized that her calling was not based upon her own abilities but, as she liked to say, "God chooses the foolish things of this world to confound the wise."

Before every service, she would pray, "Take not your Holy Spirit away from me," and this approach helps to explain the phenomenon of Kathryn Kuhlman and the supernatural wonders that accompanied her ministry. To have heard her speak, to have seen her pray for the sick, to have watched her dispense the love of God to laity and clergy alike was to realize that you were in the very presence of God. At the Full Gospel Business Mens Fellowship International Convention in Washington, DC, in 1969, for example, I watched as Kathryn called forward the ministers and priests who were present. Hundreds of men responded, representing many religious traditions, including Protestant ministers, Roman Catholic priests, Greek Orthodox clergymen, and Jewish rabbis. Ms. Kuhlman would go up to each one, look them straight in the eyes, and say, "Brother, you are hungry for God," While Kathryn touched their foreheads and prayed for these men of God, they would "fall under the power," conscious only of God and His great love. One had the feeling that each one would return to his congregation with renewed zeal and commitment.

The book's original publisher wrote, *"Daughter of Destiny* is an accurate and loving account of Kathryn's life as we knew her. It tells of a woman who was derided by some, really worshipped by others and who will surely have a unique place in God's Hall of Fame."

While *Daughter of Destiny* raises many questions, it also provides clear answers about the motivation and the power behind Ms. Kuhlman's uniquely blessed ministry. We believe this book will minister to you as it provides you with new insights and objective information concerning the life and ministry of Kathryn Kuhlman. We pray that the special anointing that was on her life will continue to flow from the pages of this book, touching you with God's healing love and power.

Lloyd B. Hildebrand
Executive Editor
Bridge Publishing, Inc.

CHAPTER I

RED TAG MYSTERIES

In death, as in life, she remained shrouded in mystery. She appeared on our TV screens and the faraway platforms as a fantasy figure—gutsy in her preaching yet tender to tears as she proclaimed healing to the sick multitudes. The world, from the Fifth Avenue fashion models to Hollywood's stars to the hard-hat mill workers in Pittsburgh flooded to her miracle services. On a planet ravaged by disease and spiritual darkness she represented that one ingredient without which mankind is doomed—hope. Many were healed. Others, seeing in her the glory of God, committed their lives to the Christ she proclaimed. In her speech and life style she seemed to epitomize the health, love and prosperity of the God she so reverently served. To many she seemed almost immortal. In fact, Maggie Hartner, Kathryn's personal secretary and alter ego, once told

1

me: "Miss Kuhlman will never die. She'll be right here until Jesus comes again."

But she did die. On February 20, 1976, in a strange hospital, in a strange city, surrounded by people she hardly knew, with a man she once disdained standing in the wings ready to preach her funeral. The woman whom *Time* magazine called a "veritable one-woman Shrine of Lourdes" was dead at the age of sixty-eight.

When she died there were more than fifty invitations waiting on her desk in Pittsburgh, begging her to conduct miracle services in communities across the world. A U.S. army official in Thailand had written inviting her to the Far East. There was an invitation from New Zealand. Two from Australia. Five from Europe. And dozens representing the major cities of America. The most touching was from the First Lady of Wyoming, Mrs. Ed Herschler—a victim of multiple sclerosis—asking her to come to Cheyenne.

Although Kathryn's death canceled all her invitations, it only intensified the mystery and intrigue surrounding her life.

All was not well. For almost four months Kathryn had been a virtual prisoner in two hospitals—one in Los Angeles and the other in Tulsa. D. B. "Tink" Wilkerson, a Tulsa automobile dealer and regent at Oral Roberts University, had moved mysteriously into her life eight months before. A virtual stranger before that, he and his wife, Sue, had left their business, their home, and their family to travel with Kathryn constantly. In her weakened condition she confided in no one else. The Wilkersons handled all her personal needs, including her finances.

The day after she died, Wilkerson, his wife, and Oral Roberts' personal bodyguard accompanied Kathryn's body from Tulsa to Los Angeles. Sunday morning at 10:00 A.M. the Wilkersons and the bodyguard, a Mr. Johnson, arrived at Forest Lawn cemetery with Kathryn's clothes and makeup case. They gave strict orders that "no one, absolutely no one" was to see the body. Forest Lawn, calling it a "red tag" funeral, put Kathryn's body on the second floor in a room with one entrance and windows which were locked and barred. Mr. Johnson sat outside the door in the hall guarding the entrance. No one, not even Maggie Hartner or Kathryn's other close friends, was allowed to see her body. Only the Wilkersons.

After the funeral it was revealed that two months before she died Kathryn had made out a new will. Although she left $267,500 to be divided among twenty employees and three relatives, the remainder of her more than two-million-dollar personal estate was left to the Wilkersons. All over the nation front-page newspaper stories read: "Kathryn Kuhlman, the evangelist, who solicited millions of dollars in contributions from her followers, has left none of her estate to her foundation or the church."

Her followers were hurt, and angry. But the changing of her will was only the tip of the iceberg. Each day following her death, new and disturbing facts came to light. I called Gene Martin, a longtime associate of Kathryn's, who had handled her mission outreach. He was attending an Assemblies of God convention in San Diego but agreed to see me if I would fly out to California. We were to meet in the lobby of the El Cortez Hotel on April 22 at two-thirty in the afternoon. When I arrived, after flying all the way from Florida and then renting a car to drive from Los Angeles to San Diego, I found only a note waiting for me at the front desk of the hotel. Martin had mysteriously changed his mind and now refused to talk.

I flew back to Tulsa where the plot thickened. Oral Roberts, who had spoken so glowingly of Kathryn at her funeral (which had been arranged by Tink Wilkerson),

3

refused to see me. Word had leaked out of Hillcrest Hospital in Tulsa that all those news releases put out by Tink Wilkerson prior to Kathryn's death, saying she was making steady improvement, were false. Nurses had testified she not only remained on the "critical" list following her surgery the last of December, but she had virtually died three times and had to be restored to life. Now, I discovered, pressure had come from sources "outside the hospital," and the nurses were forbidden to talk. The conspiracy of silence intensified the mystery. The intrigue grew deeper when a number of people in Tulsa told me of a dream each of them had the night before Kathryn died, saying they had dreamed it was not Kathryn's time to die. I left Tulsa wondering why everyone refused to talk, and who was telling them to shut up.

Back in Pittsburgh, David Verzilli, Kathryn's associate pastor for twenty-two years in Youngstown, Ohio, a man who had been (in the words of his own wife in a vitriolic letter to Maggie Hartner) "stripped of all self-confidence" by the domination of women in his life and ministry, also refused to talk to me.

I contacted Dino Kartsonakis, Kathryn's former pianist. A year before, when his public denunciations of her had appeared on the front pages of the nation's newspapers, he had told me he would be willing to "expose" Kathryn. Now though, he clammed up.

Of all those involved in the plot besides her loyal staff, only Tink Wilkerson, a quiet likable yet shrewd man, volunteered to talk. I spent more than three hours with him in Kathryn's once beautiful home in the Fox Chapel suburb of Pittsburgh. The home was now surrounded by armed security officers. Tink was accompanied by two bodyguards. The movers were stripping the house, removing all the priceless paintings and antiques to put them in storage.

Tink said he was telling me the truth, and I really wanted to believe him. Yet some of the things he told me I found hard to swallow. Among them was his contention that he would clear only $40,000 from his part in the will. The other had to do with the will itself. He said he was "just as surprised as anyone" when he discovered Kathryn had made out a new will and named him as the chief beneficiary—even though it was his lawyer from Tulsa, on his instruction, who flew to Los Angeles and made out the will for Kathryn to sign while she lay critically ill.

What was being hidden? What strange powers did these people—who had come into Kathryn's life during her final year—have over her? Why were so many people hiding, even shading, the truth? Was there some kind of foul plot, as many suspected? Had God, as others suggested, removed Kathryn from this earth much as He removed Moses— because her ministry was over? Or, and this was most intriguing of all, had the thing Kathryn feared most come upon her? Had the Holy Spirit departed, leaving her powerless to continue even with life itself. What was the truth surrounding her death?

The answers to all these questions seemed to center in Kathryn herself, rather than in those around her. To get them I knew I would have to go all the way back to the beginning, to the roots of her heritage, and start there.

CHAPTER II

I CAN'T
GO HOME AGAIN

In the central Missouri farmlands, when the winter whips across the prairies in a howling blue norther, driving snow and sleet before it like stinging, numbing nettles, they say the only thing between Concordia and the North Pole is a barbed wire fence—and even that's fallen down.

Summers are equally bad, for there is nowhere on all the earth as hot as Missouri in August—unless it's Kansas in July. But in between, when the earth blossoms fresh and green in the spring, or the high corn is shocked and ringed with yellow pumpkins in the fall, Missouri can be the most beautiful spot on all the earth.

Kathryn was born here, five miles south of Concordia on a 160-acre farm, on May 9, 1907. Her age—right up until the time she died—was one of the best kept secrets in the world. "It's nobody's business but mine," Kathryn told Dr.

Carl Zabia in St. John's Hospital in Los Angeles when he came into her room to inquire about her age. "Just put me down as 'over fifty.' "

"I'm sorry, Miss Kuhlman," the Jewish doctor smiled. "But I need to know your exact age in order to prescribe the correct dosage of medicine."

"Nobody," she half-whispered, peering up at him from her pillow, "nobody knows how old I am. But, dear doctor, if you'll hand me a slip of paper I'll write it down." She was chuckling now. "But don't you dare breathe it to a living soul."

Kathryn was almost right. A few people knew her age. Maggie Hartner was one of them. But when I tried to get the information from Maggie, she gave me the same look Kathryn once gave me and said, "Why, I wouldn't reveal my correct age either. What woman would?"

Unable to combat that kind of female vanity, I decided to wait until I could get my hands on Kathryn's passport, or could check the records back in Concordia.

Kathryn enjoyed keeping people guessing. She told the Canadian journalist, Allen Spraggett, back in 1966, that she was 84 years old—then was horrified when he quoted her in his book, *The Unexplained.* When she died, the banner headline on the front page of the morning final of the *Los Angeles Times* shouted: "Kathryn Kuhlman Dies at 66." They missed it by two years. She must have chuckled, even in heaven. She dearly loved putting things over on the press. And to have second-guessed the prestigious *Los Angeles Times* was one of her greatest scoops—especially when it was discovered that the *Times* got their information from the hospital officials. She had, even though she was dying, fibbed to the doctor about her age. Her vanity prevailed, even at the end, and along with it her sense of humor and the satisfaction of having carried to her grave the secret of her age.

Of course the records in Concordia gave the true date, and at the same time cleared up another mystery—the riddle of where she was born. Kathryn had always maintained she had been born in the large, two-story house at 1018 St. Louis Street in Concordia, a tiny community of 1,200 huddled along the railway which connected St. Louis to Kansas City. Exactly why she insisted she was born in town, rather than on the farm, no one seems to know.

In a taped interview with me she said, "When papa married mama, he promised her that if she would move out to the country with him until the farm was paid off, he would build her the biggest house in Concordia. When the supper dishes were washed, mama would draw a picture of the big house that papa had always promised her when the farm was paid off. Well, the day came. The farm was paid off. Papa built mama the kind of house that mama wanted. I came with the house. It was a big house. And you know something? From the time I was born in that house until this very day, everything has to be big. There was no inferiority complex with me because I knew I was loved. I knew I was a wanted child. It's a great satisfaction to a child to know that. I've always known that. I always knew that I was the apple of papa's eye."

No one disputed that. But everyone disputed that she was born in the big house in Concordia.

Joseph A. Kuhlman was a tall, curly-headed farmer of German extraction—as were nearly all the people in Concordia, a small Lutheran farming community about sixty miles east of Kansas City. He was twenty-five years old when he married Emma Walkenhorst, who was only seventeen at the time. They immediately moved out to the Kuhlman farm, a large tract of land about five miles south of Concordia in Johnson County. Kathryn's older sister, Myrtle, was born there, as well as her older brother, Earl. Myrtle was fifteen and Earl ten when Emma Kuhlman gave birth to her third child.

Aunt Gusty (Augusta Pauline Kuhlman Burrow), Joe Kuhlman's older sister, came by that same afternoon. It was Thursday, about four o'clock. She was driving a roan mare hitched to the whiffletree of a surrey. Looping the reins over a hitching rail beside the gabled, two-story house which sat in the middle of the north forty acres of the farm, she made her way up to the bedroom where Emma was nursing the newborn baby girl. Gusty, who had four children of her own, was a soft-spoken woman who had never interfered in her brother Joe's affairs. But this time, if what she had heard from her twelve-year-old daughter Fanita was correct, she felt it was necessary to speak up.

"Emma, I've heard you're going to name the baby Kathryn."

"That's right. Just before your mother died, Joe and I talked to her. We told her we'd name the baby for her if it was a girl—although we're changing the spelling." (Katherine Marie Borgstedt had been born in the province of Westphalia, Germany, in 1827. She married Johannes Heinrich Kuhlman in 1851 and the young couple moved to the United States two years later, settling in the German-speaking community of Concordia, Missouri. She had died, at the age of eighty, just three months before her daughter-in-law gave birth to her namesake.)

"It's a fine German name," Gusty said softly, "but you need to remember that none of mama's girls were called Katherine."

"Then it's time one of the grandchildren carried the name."

"Don't you understand?" Gusty continued. "The name doesn't sound right in Missouri. Every mule in the state is called Kate. In fact, the mule that kicked our sister Mary

Magdalena's son, Jason, to death was named Kate. A name like this will disgrace the entire Kuhlman family."

Emma bristled. "Well, it wouldn't disgrace the Walkenhorst family. Besides, her name is not Kate, it is Kathryn Johanna—Johanna after my mother. And she'll not disgrace the Kuhlmans either. That I promise."

It was a promise which, in the years to come, Emma Kuhlman often feared would not be kept. But nothing was going to change her stubborn German mind. Turning to fifteen-year-old Myrtle who was standing on the far side of the room, Emma said, "I think it has a nice ring to it, Kathryn Kuhlman. Don't you, Myrtle?"

Myrtle nodded vigorously and the argument was settled.

Gusty said nothing else. She paid her respects to the tiny baby which was nestled against Emma's breast, and then retreated down the steps to the carriage. "It's going to be bad enough growing up redheaded," she said to her horse as she unhitched her, "but to have to go through life with a name like Kate is more than any child should have to bear."

It was two years later when Joe Kuhlman, his farm now paid for and with cash in his pocket, approached William H. Petering, the local mail carrier, and closed the deal for the large lot on St. Louis Street in Concordia. The purchase was made on February 23, 1909, and the price of $650.00 was duly recorded at the Lafayette County Court House. Building was begun the next year, but it was 1911 before the Kuhlmans—Joe and Emma—and their three children, Myrtle, Earl (who was called Kooley), and four-year-old Kathryn moved in.

Exactly why Kathryn always maintained she was born in

11

the big, white, two-story house is another of the many mysteries surrounding her life. Yet she never backed down from the myth. In 1972, shortly after she received an honorary Doctor of Humane Letters from Oral Roberts University in Tulsa, Oklahoma, a devoted Kathryn Kuhlman admirer in Concordia, Rudi Plaut, started a local campaign to have a permanent historical marker erected along the highway in her honor. The marker was to read, in part:

> "The birthplace of Kathryn Kuhlman; she was a
> member of the Baptist Church, an ordained minister
> of the Evangelical Church Alliance, known for her
> belief in the Holy Spirit."

The town didn't like it. Kathryn was not without honor except in her hometown. Reports had trickled back that she was enormously wealthy. It seems that many of Kathryn's phone calls to her mother, while Emma was still living, were monitored by the local telephone operator. When Kathryn would brag to mama about the size of a particular offering or the number of people who came to the meetings, it immediately became public information in the little town. Since most of the folks in Concordia were in the lower or lower-middle income bracket, there was a general feeling that anyone doing better than that, especially if he or she was involved in religion, was to be despised. Some of the members of the local Baptist church felt that Kathryn should have helped them with their building program, since she had never moved her church membership. There were other factors which caused the conservative little community to think less than kindly about their most famous citizen: she was known to consort with Pentecostals, she practiced divine healing, and she had once refused to give an audience to an old school chum when she came to

Kansas City for a miracle service. All of which roused the jealous ire of some of the citizens. Then, when the small group, headed by Rudi Plaut, proposed the historical marker, stating that Kathryn was born in Concordia (when all the old-timers knew she had been born on the farm in Johnson County), it was too much.

On July 31, 1972, Kathryn wrote Harry R. Voight, a local historian and professor at St. Paul's College in Concordia: "This letter gives you my permission to have the proposed sign placed on the highway stating that Concordia is the birthplace of Kathryn Kuhlman."

A group of irate citizens called a town meeting in which there was a great deal of debate and some shouting. Sadly, the people of Concordia had forgotten the name of their little town meant *harmony*. Gary Beizzenherz, editor of the local newspaper, *The Concordian*, decided to try to settle the matter. He wrote Kathryn asking her to give the specific date and place of her birth. Of course Kathryn ignored the first request, but as to the place of her birth she wrote:

> "Be assured that I feel greatly honored to have the people of 'my hometown' honor me by erecting an historical marker noting Concordia as my birthplace!
>
> "I have always been proud of the fact that I was born in Concordia where the people are still 'the best in the world' and they continue to remain the very salt of the earth. . . ."

When the letter was made public in Concordia, the salt of the earth lost its savor. The folks whom Kathryn called "the best in the world" rose up in anger and refused to let the sign be placed on the road. If there was to be a sign anywhere, it should be out on State Road 23 in Johnson

County. There were some things Concordia might be proud of, but this "handmaiden of the Lord" was not one of them.

Although the people of Concordia may have wanted to disown Kathryn after she became famous, she never expressed anything but kindness and appreciation for the town where she was raised. Joe Kuhlman went into the dray business, operating the livery stable and running a delivery business. He was known as the wealthiest person in the community. Even though he was a backslidden Baptist who detested all preachers, he was still elected mayor in a town that was ninety-percent Lutheran.

Kathryn was only six years old when her older sister, Myrtle, married a young student evangelist, Everett B. Parrott, and moved to Chicago. That was three years before Emma gave birth to the last of the Kuhlman children, Geneva. But during that interim, Kathryn and her brother managed to twist their father around their fingers. Papa gave them everything they ever desired—and left the discipline up to mama. It was an unbalanced situation which was to affect Kathryn's personality the rest of her life.

When sixteen-year-old Kooley (whom the Kuhlman family called "Boy") had an attack of appendicitis while the family was at Grandpa Walkenhorst's for Christmas dinner, Joe almost went out of his mind with anxiety. Emma's mother had died at an early age of appendicitis, which was considered an almost fatal condition in the early 1900s. Joe turned one bedroom of the big house on St. Louis Street into a hospital room, brought in a doctor and two nurses from Kansas City, and spent a small fortune nursing Boy back to health. One afternoon he had the two nurses lift Boy out of bed and help him to the window so he could see the new toy he had bought him. It was a brand new, high-speed Dusenberg racing car—the same kind that was being used on the brick track up in Indianapolis. After Kooley got well, his father also bought him a stunt plane which he learned to fly, traveling all over the Midwest barnstorming. When he wasn't flying, he was racing his car at county fairs. Mama didn't approve, but papa's heart was soft and generous. Kooley got everything he asked for. According to those who knew Kooley, he was "wild." One report says he belonged to the "Midnight Tire Company," a group of men who roamed the countryside at night stealing tires for resale. Later he married Agnes Wharton, whom the folks in Concordia described as a "wonderful woman," who helped him get over his spoiled ways. He went to work for Heinie Walkenhorst (no relation to his mother) as an automobile mechanic.

Kathryn idolized her father. He would sit quietly while she teased his curly hair or ran a comb through his bushy mustache. Often, even after she was a long-legged teenager, he would hold her in his lap and let her lean her head against his shoulder. "Papa lived and died never having punished me once," she told me. "He never laid his hands on me. Never. Not once. Mama was the one who disciplined me. I got it down in the basement so the neighbors could not hear me scream. Then when papa came home I would run to him, sit on his lap, and he would take away all the pain."

"I can never remember, as a child, having my mother show me any affection. Never. Mama was a perfect disciplinarian. But she never once told me she was proud of me or that I did well. Never once. It was papa who gave me the love and affection."

After Kathryn became famous she used to get on the

phone at night and call her mother back in Concordia, talking for hours at a time. According to the telephone operator, Kathryn was constantly trying to prove to her mother that she had succeeded. "She would giggle and giggle," the former operator told me, "and of course we'd sit there listening, and giggle too. Then she would tell her mother all she had gotten. 'Mama, I've got the biggest Christmas tree in the city. It's sooooo tall, and has more than five thousand lights on it.' She would talk about the size of the offering at her miracle services as if she was trying to convince her mother that she was a success."

There seems to be ample proof that Kathryn deserved all those spankings she got as a child. When she visited her Grandpa Walkenhorst on his farm, he showed her his watermelon patch, explaining that even though the watermelons were green on the outside, they were always red on the inside. Kathryn, to the day she died, didn't like to take anybody's word for anything. Her inquisitive nature demanded she check it out for herself. So, after Grandpa Walkenhorst returned to the house, nine-year-old Kathryn took a butcher knife and plugged every watermelon in the patch—more than a hundred of them—just to be sure they were all red on the inside. When she got home, mama was waiting at the top of the basement steps.

Mama's birthday was August 28, which, when Kathryn was nine years old, just happened to fall on Monday. Monday was washday for Emma Kuhlman. It was, as Kathryn later said, "part of her theology." She washed clothes on Monday and ironed on Tuesday—just like she went to church on Sunday. Kathryn thought the nicest thing she could do for her mama, who was always whipping her, was to give her a surprise birthday party. She knew how her mama loved to entertain. She loved to dress up in her high-necked floor-length dress with the long sleeves and lace cuffs, fix her hair in a tight upsweep, don her hat with the tiny veil, and serve tea to her Methodist Sunday school class or the members of the "King's Herald"—a missionary organization in the church. Nobody, it seems, had ever seen Mrs. Joe Kuhlman dressed informally or with curlers in her hair. Kathryn later said, "I do not ever remember seeing my mother coming down to the breakfast table with a robe on. When mama came to breakfast she was always fully dressed. She wanted to be prepared in case a visitor came by the house."

But washday was another matter. On washday, mama locked the door and spent the day laboring and sweating over hot tubs of boiling water. Using a ribbed washboard, she would scrub the clothes, rinse them in a galvanized tub, run them through a hand wringer fastened to the side of another tub, and finally hang them on the line behind the house. As Kathryn said, washing clothes on Monday·was part of mama's theology. Even on those blistering days in August, when the sunflowers along the fence wilted in the heat, Emma Kuhlman would be bent over the steaming washtubs, scrubbing clothes.

Little Kathryn failed to take this into account when she set out, the week before, to surprise her mother on her birthday. She went from house to house through the community and invited thirty of the town's most prominent women citizens to come to a surprise birthday party for her mama. It was to be at two o'clock, Monday afternoon. Without telling any of the other women, she asked each one to bring a cake.

After lunch on August 28, Emma told Kathryn she was exhausted. "I'm going upstairs for a few minutes to lie down before finishing the laundry." Kathryn scurried out onto the porch to await the coming of the ladies.

At precisely two o'clock there was a knock on the front door. Emma, who had dozed off, jumped out of bed. Forgetting how she was dressed, she hurried down the steps. Her hair, at least that part which was not held up in awkward kid curlers, was hanging in straggles over her face. Her long dress was wilted from the steam and splotched with water. Her face was dirty and streaked with perspiration. Her arms, exposed from her elbows where her sleeves were rolled up, were red from having been plunged into the scalding water. She was wearing old button-up shoes, loose at the ankles, with no stockings.

She was horrified as she saw two ladies at the door. Realizing how she was dressed, she started to turn and rush back up the stairs. But it was too late. They had already seen her through the screen door. She had no choice but to let them in.

"Happy birthday, Emma," Mrs. Lohoefener said. Emma Kuhlman stood in the door, staring. There stood Mrs. Lohoefener and Mrs. Heerwald, two of the town's social leaders, dressed like they had just stepped out of a bandbox. Both were holding white layer cakes, superbly decorated. She let them in and barely had time to close the screen door when she heard more footsteps on the wooden porch. There stood Mrs. Tieman, Mrs. Shryman, and Hilda Schroeder—all carrying cakes—and all dressed like Easter Sunday morning. By then the ladies were arriving so rapidly Emma didn't even have time to close the door. She just stood there while they all streamed in. But between ladies, she got a peek at the grinning, freckled face of her mischievous redheaded daughter who was peering through the ferns that filled a huge earthen planter on a white stand near the porch steps. Emma gritted her teeth. "Just wait, young lady," she muttered. "Just you wait."

Emma Kuhlman had the rest of the afternoon to plan her punishment. However, she had to do her thinking while she worked feverishly to get the washpots off the stove, fix the water for tea, and serve it to the socialites—all of whom seemed to enjoy the party immensely. But that evening, as soon as the last woman departed, mama grabbed the guilty culprit by the arm and yanked her down the cellar steps. Kathryn later said that even though they had enough cake to eat for two weeks, she had to do most of her eating standing up, so great was mama's wrath.

Joe Kuhlman never understood Emma's harsh disciplinary treatment. Boy, in order to escape, had already left home. Myrtle had married. When Joe tried to interfere with Emma's spankings and negative criticism of Kathryn's behavior, she would turn on him. As a result he, too, began spending more and more time away. He fixed up a small room in the back of the livery stable where he often spent the night. When Joe Kuhlman was home, he spent his time with Kathryn, seeking, and receiving, the love he did not feel from his wife. In return, Kathryn developed an adoration for her papa which was close to idol worship—an adoration which was so strong that every time she talked about him—even after he had been dead for thirty-five years—it brought tears to her eyes.

Papa began to take Kathryn with him when he collected bills. The merchants grew accustomed to seeing her. They called her "Little Joe." Later she enjoyed the responsibility of going into places like Brockman's Poultry Produce, Rummer's Grocery Store, the drug store, the department store, the meat market, and collecting freight bills for papa on her own. Joe was a competent businessman, and he had taught Kathryn a great deal about business principles— teachings which she leaned on for years to come. In fact, even after the Kathryn Kuhlman Foundation was well es-

19

tablished, Kathryn would often refer to some business principle she had learned from her father. She was seldom wrong.

Despite all the time they spent together, however, Joe Kuhlman never really understood his mischievous red-headed daughter. It was easier to give her money, or clothes, than it was to try to guide her through her problems. His failure to understand the depth of her spirit was demonstrated, most forcefully, in the way he responded to that deep spiritual experience she had in the Methodist church—the church where Emma found so much of her own satisfaction.

Joe Kuhlman was not a religious person. He despised preachers, saying they were all "in it for the money." He had been deeply troubled when Myrtle had left town to marry her traveling evangelist, predicting the marriage would not last. (He was right.) The only times he attended services at the Baptist church, where he belonged, were at Christmas or if Kathryn was giving a recital or a reading. Other than that, he was never known to pray, read the Bible, or otherwise express religious sentiments. Yet perhaps he had more understanding than the church people gave him credit for. Sometimes the nonreligious are able to see things from a much clearer perspective, since their minds are not cluttered with the chaff of traditional religion. Kathryn seemed to think so. And all her life she had a tender spot for people like her papa, those who were disenchanted by organized religion but hungry for God.

Reverend Hummel, a Baptist evangelist, was in Concordia for a two-week revival meeting at the tiny Methodist church. There had been some excitement in the meetings. One of the town zealots, Grandma Kresse, who attended all the revival meetings in all the churches, had been extremely active in this one. While the Lutherans and the United

Church of Christ people frowned on her zealous activities, the Methodists, who were much more in the revival tradition in the early 1900s, did not think it out of the ordinary for someone to go up and down the aisles "seeking out the lost" during the traditional altar calls. Grandma Kresse was of this bent, and as soon as the evangelist finished preaching she would start up the aisle from her seat on the front row, talking to the children, urging them to "go forward" and seek the Lord at the altar rail.

Kathryn, who had just experienced her fourteenth birthday, had attended all the services that week. Sometimes she sat beside her mother, but more often she sat with a group of giggling girls her own age. Throughout the week she had watched Grandma Kresse going up and down the aisles. At first the teen-age girls giggled at her. But as the week wore on, and they saw some of their friends answer the altar call, they began to get scared. What if Grandma Kresse got hold of them?

But it wasn't Grandma Kresse who got hold of Kathryn. Sunday morning, standing with her mama at the close of the service, as the minister gave the invitation, Kathryn began to cry. It wasn't until years later, when she was able to evaluate that experience in the perspective of time and additional experiences, that she was able to understand she had been touched by the Holy Spirit. The sobbing was intense, so intense she began to shake. Emma looked over at her tall, gangly fourteen-year-old daughter, but was helpless to give any kind of encouragement. Like so many in the church, her relationship with God had been a social one. It was limited to bake sales, missionary society meetings, afternoon teas (when she was properly dressed, of course), and attendance at church meetings. But there had never been any teaching on how to respond to a dynamic encounter with the Holy Spirit. Indeed, no one in memory

21

had ever had a dynamic encounter—at least not with these results. Emma turned back to the hymn book, riveting her eyes on the words and notes, incapable of understanding the impact of what was going on beside her.

Kathryn dropped her hymn book into the rack in the back of the varnished pew in front of her and staggered out into the aisle. Her classmates, two rows in front of her, stared, wide-eyed, as she ran down the aisle and collapsed into the front pew. Dropping her head into her hands, she sobbed so loudly she could be heard all over the church.

Martha Johannssen, a crippled lady who, like Grandma Kresse, was considered "too religious" since she believed in a literal hell, leaned over the back of the pew and handed Kathryn a handkerchief. "Don't cry, Kathryn. You've always been such a good girl."

Even the "religious" people, it seemed, were unable to understand the convicting power of the Holy Spirit as He fell sovereignly on a young woman. Yet Kathryn's experience was not too different from those described in the Bible. Samuel, Isaiah, Paul, Mary the mother of Jesus, and scores of other biblical personalities had meetings with God that were deeply emotional, often unnerving events. And, as in Bible times, so in Concordia in 1921, no one seemed to understand.

For the rest of her life, Kathryn enjoyed relating what happened that morning after the services were over. "Walking home with mama, I felt the whole world had changed. I was aware of the flowers that grew along the street. I had never noticed them before. And the sky: it was azure blue with white, fluffy clouds that looked like swirls of angel hair. Mr. Kroenoke had gotten a new paint job on his house. But the house hadn't changed! Kathryn Kuhlman had changed. It was the same paint, the same street, the same town. But I was not the same. I was different. A soft breeze blew against my cheeks and sifted through my hair. I think that Kathryn Kuhlman floated all the way home that Sunday."

Papa was standing in the kitchen when Emma and Kathryn came through the front door. Kathryn ran to him, throwing her arms around his waist. "Papa, something's happened to me. Jesus has come into my heart."

Joe Kuhlman looked down, staring deeply into the face of his daughter. His face showed no emotion. "I'm glad," he said. That was all. He turned and walked away. Kathryn later said, "Whether he understood or not, I'm not sure. I never knew."

One thing Kathryn was sure of, however, was that her life had taken on a new dimension. The change was not instantaneous, but the added scope of having access to God through Jesus Christ was going to bring about that change. Until it came, however, things would continue as they were—getting worse by degrees.

The next night at the revival meeting, the evangelist asked all the young people who had made professions of faith during the meeting—and there were several—to come to the front.

"Now tell the people what you plan to do with your lives," he said.

Without changing the expression on her face, Kathryn answered: "i'm going to find me a good-looking preacher and marry him."

Then she brought down the house by turning to Reverend Hummel, who was single, and giving him a broad wink. Everyone remembered that her older sister, Myrtle, had married the young evangelist who conducted a revival in that same church eight years before.

But Emma Kuhlman didn't laugh. She knew Kathryn was a flirt. She also knew that if she set her heart on some man, any man, she could win him over. She saw the church as

23

Kathryn's only hope. Thus she began to urge Kathryn to join the church and become active in its organizations.

Kathryn, though, chose to join papa's Baptist church rather than mama's Methodist. She had a mind of her own.

"I don't know what to do with Kathryn," Emma Kuhlman told a close friend when Kathryn was sixteen. "She failed her math last year and had to take it over. She's just like Boy. I can't seem to control her."

Since papa felt that Kathryn could do no wrong, Emma had no one to turn to but Kathryn's older sister, Myrtle, who was visiting home for a few days at the beginning of the summer. The year was 1923, and the flapper rage was sweeping the nation. Liquor was illegal, but it seemed that every farm in Lafayette County hid a still. The speakeasies in the county were going full blast. The young people were dancing the Charleston, driving up and down the muddy Main Street in roadsters with rumble seats shouting "twenty-three skidoo," and drinking moonshine by the barrel. Emma knew that unless something happened to further change Kathryn, she wouldn't have the strength to endure the temptations of the day.

Secondary school in Concordia ended with the tenth grade. At sixteen Kathryn had all the formal education available unless she entered the Lutheran academy. Myrtle asked mama to let Kathryn join her and Everett for a series of tent meetings in the northwest. They would keep her for the summer and let her return in the fall.

It was an ideal solution, but Emma hesitated. Myrtle had married Everett Parrott who had come to Concordia to preach a revival service at the Methodist church. He was finishing his course of study at Moody Bible Institute in Chicago, and he was young and good-looking. A week after the revival was over, he wrote Myrtle, asking if she would come to nearby Sedalia, where he lived, to play the piano in a weekend meeting. She could stay with his parents.

Neither Emma nor Joe were in favor of it. Emma didn't want to see her daughter go off with a strange young man. Joe didn't want to see her go off with a preacher. They finally gave their consent and the Parrotts sent a carriage to take Myrtle the twenty-five miles from Concordia to Sedalia. She never did play the piano. Everett just wanted his parents to look her over. He wrote her every day for the next three weeks, and then they were married by the district superintendent of the Methodist church in Sedalia on October 6, 1913. Later Myrtle confessed she had never loved her husband but, like most of the girls in the tiny community, figured she had better take the first offer that came along to leave town. After all, she might not have another chance.

It was a stormy marriage, fraught with problems from the beginning. After a brief stay in Chicago, the young couple struck out on the evangelistic circuit—riding, as they used to say, the "sawdust trail." Parrott had a tent. They traveled from one town to another, mostly in the Midwest, holding tent revivals. Occasionally Myrtle did some of the preaching. Mostly, though, she acted as her husband's business manager. When word came that Dr. Charles Price, a teacher and evangelist with an amazing healing ministry, had come down from Canada and was holding services in Albany, Oregon, the Parrotts made a special trip to the far west to sit under his ministry. Unlike many of the evangelists holding tent meetings through the west, Dr. Price's ministry was relatively low-key. He spent a great deal of the time teaching on the power of God. He also talked about an experience beyond salvation called "the baptism in the Holy Spirit." Once in Albany he took Everett Parrott aside and spent several hours teaching him the scriptures on this particular subject. Parrott listened intently. But even

25

Price's ministry didn't bring the needed change. Despite the adoption of a little girl, Virginia, years later, the marriage finally ended in a divorce.

However, before the final problems developed which led to her divorce, Myrtle returned to Concordia for a brief visit.

"Mama, I have to leave day after tomorrow. Let me take Kathryn with me. Just for the summer. I'll send her back in case you want her to go to school in the fall."

"Papa and I will talk it over," Emma said, her face sober. "We'll try and decide as soon as possible."

Myrtle prayed throughout the night. Somehow it seemed imperative that Kathryn accompany her.

The next morning, early, she cornered her mother. "Have you decided?"

Emma turned her face away, not wanting to look directly at her grown daughter. "She's so young, Myrtle. She's only sixteen."

"Mama," Myrtle's voice had a touch of desperation in it. "She must go. I know God wants it. Do you want to stand in God's way?"

"How can you be so sure? How can you know what God has for Kathryn?"

"I just know," Myrtle said, breaking into tears. "I just know."

"Papa and I will talk about it again at lunch," Emma said. "We'll let you know before the day is over."

It was exactly four o'clock. Myrtle remembered because she heard the clock on the living room wall chime, when Emma came down the stairs, her face serious. Myrtle was standing near the deacon's bench in the front room, polishing her wire-rimmed glasses.

"We've decided," Emma said slowly, "to let her go. But it's with great reluctance on my part." Somehow, Emma

Kuhlman suspected that if Kathryn left, she would never return.

She was right.

The next afternoon Joe and Emma put their two daughters on the train to Kansas City. Kathryn was serious. She, too, suspected there were other forces at work in her life. Conflicting forces, fighting against one another. One force was urging her to stay, to "enjoy" her freedom. The other force was pulling her upward, and away. She had tried, God knew how hard she had tried, to run away from that upward call. But each time He had brought her back to the place of repentance. Each time she had sinned— and there had been enough times during the last two years—she had found herself back at her bedside, on her knees, asking God to forgive her. Now God was doing something else. And she had a feeling, as the train pulled out of the station, that it would be wrong if she even looked back over her shoulder. She waved goodbye at her mama and papa through the dusty window of the train, then settled back in the seat—looking straight ahead. Like her mother, she knew Concordia would never again be her home.

CHAPTER III

TENTS AND
TURKEY HOUSES

The conviction that it was God who had called her away from Concordia, and not necessarily her sister Myrtle, grew stronger after Kathryn arrived in Oregon. For this reason she felt guilty for having intruded into her sister's shaky marriage. To compensate for her guilt, she refused any favors, insisted on sleeping on the floor in the apartment living room, and spent at least two days of every week doing the laundry. Washing on Monday and ironing on Tuesday. It was her first experience with the regular chores of house-keeping. It helped convince her that while companionship with a man might be exciting (although the two examples she knew best, mama's and Myrtle's, were not very attrac-tive), having to care for a man who expected a woman to cook his meals and wash his dirty laundry was enough to give her second thoughts on marriage as a career.

Mondays were spent over the scrub board, arms deep in scalding water, as they moved from apartment to apartment following the sawdust trail. Tuesdays, of course, were ironing days. Parrott's heavily starched white shirts were enough to test the loyalty of any wife—much less a kid sister-in-law. Kathryn had watched mama and knew the procedure. Heat the heavy metal irons directly over the flames on the gas stove. While they were getting hot, sprinkle the starched shirts with water and roll them loosely so the entire shirt would be slightly damp. Lay the ironing board on the kitchen table and spread the shirt flat. Lay the molded metal handle of the iron using a quilted hot pad to keep your hand from getting burned, lick one finger and quickly touch the bottom. If it gave off a steamy hissss, the iron was hot enough to use. But keep it moving. With no money to buy extra shirts, a bad scorch would mean Parrott couldn't take off his coat during the sermon, no matter how hot it was under the canvas tent, because he had a hole in his shirt.

All the time was not spent washing and ironing. The northwest during the summer of '23 was pleasant. Myrtle and Kathryn did a lot of window shopping, going through the stores in the little towns in Washington and Oregon where Parrott would set up his tent. Myrtle needed Kathryn's joyful presence and Kathryn needed the stern maturity, yet sisterly kindness, which Myrtle provided. It was a good combination.

At night they attended the revival services where Kathryn got her first initiation to tent preaching. Everett Parrott had but one message: "Repent and be saved." He was a shouter. A pulpit thumper. He preached his one message over and over, using a variety of texts. By the end of the summer, Kathryn had heard all his sermons several times and was beginning to understand why Myrtle was reluctant to attend the services, even though her husband insisted, often angrily, that he needed her there to help take up the offering and play the piano.

Parrott's independent spirit bothered Kathryn. She quizzed Myrtle why he refused to cooperate with the local churches. It seemed better, she thought, to work with the churches and the pastors rather than to come into town, set up his tent, and begin to preach.

Myrtle looked at Kathryn wearily. "Honey, we've been doing it this way for years. We tried, in the beginning, to work with the pastors. But they were afraid of us. The Baptists wanted to know if we immersed. The Methodists quizzed us about sanctification. And the Nazarenes wanted to know if we preached holiness. But it seemed everybody was building their own kingdom and somehow we just didn't fit in. So, Everett decided to build his own kingdom—centered around that tent. And he's dragged me from town to town until I'm so weary I can hardly stand it."

"But wouldn't it be easier," Kathryn insisted in her naivete, "just to come into a town and settle down with a revival center. You don't have to have a membership which would threaten the pastors. Just preach salvation. Get them saved and if they want to join the local churches, let them go. That's the way I'd do it."

Myrtle smiled sadly and said, "You don't understand, sister. Everett feels his job is to evangelize—to light the fire of salvation in the hearts of the lost. The job of the churches is to keep the fire burning after we've gone. If we settle down somewhere we'd simply become another church. They criticize us all the time now because we take up an offering. And they aren't happy about the people we reach for Jesus. In fact, many of the people who are saved in our

31

tent try to join local churches after we leave, and they're not accepted. The only ones who really appreciate our ministry are the little skid row mission churches."

Kathryn was learning, quickly, the inner machinations of the "kingdom." She also began to understand why papa had always felt more comfortable staying home on Sunday. Yet deep within, before she went to sleep at night, curled up on her pallet in the living room, she would lie awake and think of a society where people of all denominations would gather together, not fighting, but praising God in harmony and unity—standing shoulder to shoulder against the darkness of the world. "I know it's possible," she thought. "I know that's the way God intended for it to be—like it was in the Book of Acts when they were all with one accord in one place. I'll bet if that ever happens we'll have another Pentecost right here on earth."

There was no way for Kathryn to have known, at that early age, that the dreams and visions she was having were part of God's plan to pour out His Spirit upon a hand-maiden who would become a spiritual Joan of Arc, leading the army of the Lord into new freedom and power as the world approached the end of the age.

On occasion Kathryn and Myrtle would sing or sometimes play a piano duet. Twice that summer Parrott asked the sixteen-year-old redhead to come to the platform and give a "testimony," which consisted of her story of being "saved" in the little Methodist church in Concordia. Both times she closed the testimony by reciting a lengthy poem, complete with dramatic gestures. The people responded heartily. They loved her drama and the way she pronounced her words. Parrott quickly concluded that if Kathryn were not restrained, she could become to him what David was to Saul. (Remember how the women sang, "Saul hath slain his thousands, and David his ten thousands," and enraged Saul to jealousy?) Yet he also knew that if he let Kathryn help take up the offering immediately after she spoke, the people gave more generously.

"If you decide to stay with the Parrott Tent Revivals," he kidded with her, "I'll even let you do some of the preaching."

That excited Kathryn, for during many of her "alone" hours she would read her Bible and prepare sermon outlines—just in case. But the time never seemed to come. As the summer drew to a close, and the Parrotts began to make their plans for the fall, Kathryn was not included.

Papa sent money for her return trip and Everett went down to the train station in Portland, Oregon, checked the schedules back to Concordia, and purchased her return ticket.

On Friday before Labor Day, Myrtle helped Kathryn pack her clothes. The battered old suitcase was sitting on top of the radiator in the small apartment. Everything had been neatly folded. Only the lid remained to be closed. Myrtle was standing in the middle of the room, watching sadly. Kathryn, straightening the last of her clothing with her back to her sister, began to cry.

"I don't want to go back," she sobbed.

"You don't have to go back!" Myrtle was startled. It was Everett Parrott who had just come in.

It was too good to be true. "But what about the train ticket?" Myrtle stammered.

"We can get the money back," Parrott said calmly. "I inquired about it yesterday when I got the ticket. I thought she might want to stay, but I was going to leave it up to her. She can be a big help in the ministry."

There was more conversation, but Kathryn heard none

of it. She was too choked on the tears of happiness and relief. Years later she said she often dreamed of that suitcase, and the radiator. "Sometimes in my sleep," she told me, "I still see it. I can see every item of clothing, and that bent clasp on the lid. It haunts me, for it was the big turning point of my life. Had I gone back to Concordia, I would have been stuck there. No telling what would have happened. But even then the Holy Spirit was working in my life, directing my footsteps. From that moment on I was in the ministry—and I've never regretted a single moment of it."

Those first few years were hard, traveling with Myrtle and her husband, whistle-stopping from one community to another. They would go into town, find a vacant lot and set up their tent. Then Kathryn and Myrtle would walk through the town ringing a hand bell, inviting people to the service that night. In the evening services Kathryn occupied a place on the front row of benches, while Myrtle often joined her husband on the platform. Myrtle was constantly warning Kathryn about things which would disgrace "the ministry."

"Kathryn, don't cross your legs like that. Your legs are so long that everyone notices. Just cross your ankles—and be sure and keep your knees together."

Myrtle's influence was good. Although she was stern and unbending, like mama, she was still a sister and not a parent. The next five years, although they were difficult ones, were the best years in Kathryn's early life.

During this time Parrott enlisted the services of Dr. Price's pianist, an extraordinary keyboard musician named

Helen Gulliford. Although Helen was eleven years older than Kathryn, they became fast friends. Many people thought they were sisters, they looked so much alike. While Helen at 5'6'' was two inches shorter than her slender young friend, the two were able to wear the same clothes. They enjoyed being with each other. Gradually Kathryn's affections changed from Myrtle to this single woman who was to play such a profound role in her life. She was the one woman who would stand between Kathryn and disastrous heartbreak, yet find herself unable to stop the headstrong young evangelist from eventually destroying her ministry.

Things were not going well with the Parrott Tent Revival team. Myrtle and Everett were fighting much of the time. She accused him of consorting with other women, becoming more and more like her mama, hard and unyielding. By the time they got to Boise, Idaho, things had gone from very bad to terrible. Parrott didn't even show up for the meeting, choosing to take his tent and travel on to South Dakota. In Boise, services were held in the Women's Club, and Myrtle did the preaching. The offerings were so low they didn't even make their expenses for renting the building—much less pay the rent on their tiny apartment. For two weeks their meals consisted of bread and canned tuna fish.

Since Parrott controlled the funds, Myrtle's only hope was to join him in South Dakota. Helen balked. She had been through enough. A concert artist, she never felt comfortable playing on tinny pianos in little community halls before fifteen or twenty people. Kathryn, too, was badly disillusioned. Although she enjoyed helping with the preaching, she couldn't see any hope for the future as long as she stayed with the Parrotts.

After the final service, the night before they were scheduled to leave—Myrtle to return to her husband and Helen and Kathryn still undecided—a Nazarene pastor approached them outside the Women's Club.

"Don't leave," he said to Myrtle. "I realize things have been pretty bad, but we need you here."

Myrtle shook her head. "We can't afford to stay. We have run out of money."

"Well, let the girls stay then," he offered. "I pastor a small mission church near here. They can come in and, at least, play the piano and sing."

Myrtle looked over at Helen and Kathryn, who had been following the conversation. They both nodded their heads. "All right," Myrtle said with a note of resignation. "Kathryn wants to preach anyway. Why not give her a chance and see what she can do."

"Fine," the little pastor beamed. "They can start tomorrow night."

And that's how it all started. It was Kathryn's first sermon on her own, in a dirty little mission church which used to be a pool hall in a run-down section of Boise. A few old chairs had been pulled in and the piano, which belonged to the bar next door, had been wheeled through the back door, occupying a place near the rickety pulpit in the corner of the room.

As a last request, Kathryn asked Myrtle to loan her ten dollars. "I want a new yellow dress for my first sermon."

"Kathryn," Myrtle said, shaking her head and sounding for all the world like mama, "you can't buy the kind of dress you want for ten dollars. It will take twice that much. Besides, I don't have it. I'm not sure we have even ten dollars in the Parrott Tent Revival bank account in Sioux City."

"Do you still have some of the signed checks that Everett made out?" Kathryn asked.

Myrtle nodded.

"Then give me one of those. Make it out for ten dollars.

I'll not cash it until I'm sure you have enough money to cover the check."

"But you still can't buy the kind of dress you want for ten dollars," Myrtle argued. "You're never satisfied with cheap clothes. You always want the best."

"I have it all planned," Kathryn said. "I may not get it in time for the first service, but I'll have it before I leave town. I'll buy the material for ten dollars. Then I'll take it to a dressmaker and have her make it for me. I know just how I want it made. Then after I get my first offering from the mission, I'll pay the dressmaker. How does that sound?"

Myrtle shook her head. "I would never do a thing like that. Never!"

But she wrote out the check and left it with Kathryn. Before the week was out, Kathryn had her dress—a yellow pulpit dress with fluffy sleeves and a hem that came just to the top of her ankles. Not only that, but she had convinced the merchant where she purchased the material to let her pay him out of her first offering, and talked the dressmaker into sewing the dress for nothing—a "ministry unto the Lord." She held onto the check for three months and finally cashed it in Sioux City, Iowa, when she made a brief visit to see Myrtle and assure her that she could make it on her own.

And make it she did. One bleak day Kathryn and Helen arrived in Pocatello, Idaho. The only hall available for her services was an old opera house, so long fallen into disuse that there was some question whether it would stand up after a cleansing; its dirt seemed to be its strongest reinforcement. But it took more than a little dirt to cool the combined fervor of Kathryn and Helen, who were billing themselves as "God's Girls." "Even then," Kathryn told me, "I knew what God could do if only the gospel—in its simplicity—were preached." Before the two young women left town, after six weeks of holding nightly services which often lasted past midnight, the main floor and both balconies were filled.

Their welcome in Twin Falls, Idaho, was as warm as the weather was cold on the January day they arrived. On the second night, just as Kathryn was leaving the building following the preaching service, she slipped on the ice and fractured her leg. Helen took her to a doctor who had his offices near the civic hall where the services were being held. He put her leg in a heavy cast and told her to stay off it for at least two weeks. The doctor, though, didn't know anything about the fierce determination of this young woman who was beginning to sense her direction in life. No broken leg was going to keep her from doing what God had called her to do. She never missed a single service, preaching for the rest of the month—every night—leaning on crutches with her leg encased in the heavy cast.

A trained nurse, veteran of World War I, who attended the services, wrote a letter to the editor of the Twin Falls paper saying: "I have seen courage and determination on the battlefields of France. I saw that same courage and determination last night in a young lady who stood on the platform preaching salvation."

Her critics, and she was beginning to collect them even in the early 1930s, said that Kathryn was selling a mixture of "sex and salvation." To some extent they were correct. The two single women were quite attractive, and part of their appeal lay in their unique presentation of the gospel. They would linger after the services as long as someone needed help—and often those needing help were lonely men who were unable to differentiate between the love of a heavenly Father and the sex appeal of a young woman who was totally uninhibited in her dealings with men and women alike. Fortunately, Helen Gulliford was far more conservative than Kathryn, and often cautioned her about becoming too friendly with any of the male admirers who flocked to the altar rail for her prayers. Kathryn did seem to be more wary than in the first days of her ministry and, thanks to Helen's constant warnings, endeavored to remain discreet—even when she felt she should remain until the early hours of the morning helping some skid row bum "pray through" to salvation.

It was during one of these "after meeting meetings" that she had her first experience with the phenomenon of speaking in tongues.

Kathryn and Helen had come to Joliet, Illinois, for three months of services in the second floor of an old store building. (It was here, by the way, that a group known as the Evangelical Church Alliance persuaded the young evangelist she needed to be ordained. She agreed. It was the only ecclesiastical authorization she ever had.) Kathryn's only message was salvation, and her message that night was simple and to the point. The crowd, which had numbered several hundred, had gone, and Kathryn stayed on with the half dozen people who were still kneeling at the altar rail. One of those was Isabel Drake, a teacher who commuted from Joliet into Chicago on a daily basis. Kathryn was sitting with Isabel's mother on one of the front benches while the young teacher crouched at the altar, sometimes sobbing, sometimes praying. Suddenly Isabel rose to a full kneeling position, lifted her face toward the ceiling, and began to sing. Kathryn said, "I had never heard such music. It was the most beautiful singing with the most beautiful voice I had ever heard. She was singing in a language I had never heard, but it was so ethereal, so beautiful, that I felt the hair on my skin begin to rise.

"Her mother, who was sitting beside me gripped my hand and almost broke my fingers. 'That's not my daughter singing,' she said, her voice coming in tiny gasps. 'Isabel can't even carry a tune. My daughter can't sing a note.' "

Kathryn said the mother was almost hysterical. It was all she could do to keep her from jumping up and rushing around the room. Instead they sat quietly together, listening to the beautiful music and the supernatural flow of words that came from the mouth of the young teacher. Sometimes her voice would range up to a high C, and then float off in a minor key, only to drop down to a whisper before picking up on the theme again. Although the words sounded like it might be some ancient Greek or Phoenician chant, Kathryn knew their origin was not earthly.

The music continued for almost fifteen minutes. The young teacher then dropped her head and remained quiet at the altar before turning and embracing her mother. Although Kathryn had sat under the teaching of Charles Price and knew of Pentecostal groups (they were called "holy rollers" in those days) who spoke in tongues, she had never heard it before. However, something in her heart registered that this was from God. Isabel had never heard of the "gift of tongues," nor had she dreamed that her praying would lead her into this dimension of the Spirit. All she had been doing was asking God to fill her with more of Himself—not knowing that her prayer would be answered by a visit from the Holy Spirit.

Many years later, Kathryn witnessed a similar experience in Portland, Oregon. It was during a huge miracle service in 1973. Kathryn had been there for a service on Saturday and then returned Sunday afternoon for a final meeting. The Civic Auditorium was packed. Thousands had been turned away. During the service a Catholic nun, dressed in her habit, came forward having just been healed of a tumor in her thigh. She was very timid when Kathryn quizzed her about the nature of her healing. Finally, in a bare whisper, she told how she had been sitting on the main floor with six other nuns and two priests when she felt the burning in her leg. She squeezed the area where the large tumor had been, and it was gone. The two priests insisted she come to the platform to testify of the healing.

"Oh, honey, that's so wonderful," Kathryn said. "I'm so glad."

Kathryn was weeping. She often wept when someone of this nature—a quiet priest or nun, an older pastor or perhaps wizened missionary who had spent his life in God's work—came forward to testify of healings. She had a special place in her heart for the old, the poor, little children, young couples, and especially the servants of God.

"I thank God for you," Kathryn said softly as the nun smiled shyly and turned to walk off the platform.

The little nun took only two or three steps and then turned back to where Kathryn was standing at the microphone. Speaking barely above a whisper, she said, "Miss Kuhlman, I'm so hungry to be filled with the Holy Spirit."

Then, before Kathryn could reach out to touch her, before she could utter the first word of a prayer, the nun just collapsed to the floor. Ordinarily there were men around to catch those who had this experience which she called "going under the power" or being "slain by the Spirit." This time, though, there was nobody close enough to catch the nun. She just slipped to the floor, and at the same time she began speaking in a beautiful, unearthly language.

"A holy hush came over that great congregation," Kathryn said in describing the incident. "Thousands had filled that Civic Auditorium. No one spoke. I stood there completely transfixed, awed by what was going on as this precious Catholic sister, who knew practically nothing of the baptism of the Holy Spirit, spoke in tongues. Her eyes were

41

closed, and coming from those lips was a language as perfect as that which years ago came from the lips of Isabel Drake. It was not babble, for the Holy Spirit does not babble. It was a perfect language, as the Holy Spirit within her used her lips to offer praise and adoration to the heavenly Father above."

It has bothered many theologians and religious commentators that Kathryn Kuhlman, herself, did not give a clear-cut testimony of her own personal experiences. Although her conversion at fourteen was a definite experience, it was not the life-shattering, character-changing experience that many felt was necessary in order to be qualified to preach. Her conversion, rather, only seemed to start at this experience—maturing, with many ups and downs, as a lifelong process of salvation. There were many flaws in Kathryn's life which, because she was constantly in the public eye, were over-accentuated. Even in the final year of her life the Christian world discovered some character traits about Kathryn which were far from perfect.

Yet she never claimed to be anything but an artless, unadorned, common person. "I am the most ordinary person in the whole world," she often proclaimed. Very few of her fans took her seriously, though, looking upon her as some kind of a super saint. Even when she told them she was not to be worshiped, they worshiped the way she said it. Her critics, on the other hand, never had to labor to discover her faults. Like the miracles which followed her ministry, her faults were always hung out in the open, exposed to the world.

She had far more critics inside the church than she did outside. The people of the world, hungry for reality, flocked to her services, eager to see with their own eyes what other preachers had been only talking about. These "people of the world," as Kathryn called them, had looked everywhere for reality and supernatural power. Many had gone deep into the occult, spiritism, and witchcraft hoping to find there the answers to their inner thirst. If anything, they could probably recognize a miracle a lot faster than those blinded by the churchy tradition of false and dead religion which preached that the age of miracles was past— in an effort to defend their own powerlessness. Kathryn was never swayed by this kind of empty rationalism. Over and over she preached, "We have got to stick with the Word of God. Stay with it. Nothing else and nothing added. The very second you go beyond the Word of God, you go off into fanaticism, and we no longer have the respect of the unregenerated. At that point we bring reproach on the most beautiful person in the world, the Third Person of the Trinity—the Holy Spirit."

Kathryn knew that every man on the face of the earth was built with a God-consciousness inside. A hunger for God. She recognized human nature as yearning, longing to come into fellowship with God—a fellowship which had been broken through Adam's sin and was even now blocked by the sin of mankind.

Speaking to the International Convention of the Full Gospel Business Men's Fellowship in Dallas, Texas, in 1973, Kathryn laid it on the line. "We have got to keep respect, for we represent God the Father, we represent Jesus Christ the great High Priest, and in this hour of the great charismatic movement, we represent the great unseen person, the Holy Spirit. We represent Him in this hour, the church's greatest hour. The eyes of millions of people are on us. The eyes of the organized church are upon us who are in this great charismatic movement. The eyes of the unregenerated world are upon us. Call it whatever you will, we have got to keep their respect. We have got to stay with the Word of God."

Still her critics attacked her. "She preaches the necessity of being 'baptized in the Holy Spirit,'" they said, "but she never tells us when she had this experience." But Kathryn was not experience-oriented. She insisted that a man's theology must be built around the person of Jesus Christ and ignited by the fire of the Holy Spirit, rather than being built around some experience—either their own or someone else's. Thus when she actually had her experience, which she defined as "the baptism in the Holy Spirit," was incidental. She believed in it. She coveted it for other people. She lived it. But Kathryn, herself, was unique.

At that same convention at the Hilton Hotel in Dallas in 1973, Kathryn said, "I believe in speaking in an unknown tongue. I have declared myself before the whole world. I have to declare myself because it's scriptural. It's in the Word of God. But remember, the Holy Spirit does not babble. The Holy Spirit is perfection. Know that! We need some good old-fashioned teaching in this charismatic movement. We've got to come back again to the Word of God. If we don't, we're going to lose the respect of the millions that are watching us and the thousands who are on the borderline waiting, watching, inside hungry, hungry.

"This is the church's greatest hour. We are living in the closing moments of this dispensation. We've got to forget personalities. We have got to forget our own desire of wanting to get ahead. We've got to get away from trying to climb higher than the other, as though you've been given a greater revelation than someone else, trying to be more spectacular than the other, shouting louder than the other, being more emotional than the other. Beloved, we've got to be careful. We're in an hour of crisis. Yes, I believe in tongues. I believe it is for the church today. I believe every church in the nation should have tongues and interpretation—all the gifts of the Spirit. For I believe God is restoring to the church today all the gifts and all the fruit, just as it was in the Book of Acts. And when the restoration is complete, we'll all experience the great 'catching up' when Jesus comes again. . . ."

Yet, none of Kathryn's associates ever heard her pray in tongues, not even Maggie Hartner, who was closer to her than any other living human being.

And so her critics, from Pentecostal and non-Pentecostal circles, continued to rage at her. The Pentecostals because she never talked about her baptism in the Holy Spirit and because she refused to allow the expression of tongues in her miracle services, and the non-Pentecostals because she testified that she believed in all the gifts, including tongues, and encouraged the people to exercise them within their churches. While Kathryn, seeming oblivious to all the criticism, continued on in her unique way.

For that matter, there is no evidence that Kathryn ever experienced a miraculous healing—although she ministered healing to millions of sick persons. Those closest to her knew that for several years before she died she suffered constantly from an enlarged heart and, during the last year, never went anywhere without her medicine. When she had to undergo radical heart surgery in Tulsa in November 1975, she was ridiculed in the secular press and in some fundamentalist magazines for preaching healing but not being able to heal herself. The only explanation her friend Tink Wilkerson could give was, "God didn't elect to give her a miracle that way."

Perhaps Tink, in his simple, non-theological way, was boring in at the very heart of Kathryn's theology. Most of us have our own personal interpretations of how God should run the universe—based on our own limited personal experiences. Kathryn, on the other hand, defied all tradition. She defied the boxes men tried to fit her into. When asked why many who were sick left her service unhealed, she would just shake her head and say, "I don't know. I don't know." In fact, she once said that the very first question she wanted to ask Jesus when she got to heaven was, "Why were some not healed?"

The theologians had answers. Hundreds of them. But the theologians never saw miracles. Kathryn, who was one of the greatest instruments of the miracle power of the Holy Spirit since the days of the apostles, had no answers.

"I have no healing virtue," she said over and over. "I cannot heal a single person. All I do is preach faith. God does the healing. Whom He heals and whom He chooses not to heal is His business. I am but His handmaiden."

Thus those who criticized her position, or who criticized her because she was not perfect, or who pointed out she was not qualified to minister because she was a woman, or hadn't been to seminary, were on dangerous ground.

There was a time, Myrtle recalls, when, she feels, Kathryn was "called to preach." It came soon after Kathryn had joined the Parrotts in Oregon during the summer of 1923. They had attended one of Dr. Price's meetings and when they came out into the cool air of the evening, Kathryn began to weep. Myrtle found a bench near the church building, and Kathryn, unable to control her weeping, put her head in Myrtle's lap and sobbed for long minutes.

"All those people," she finally choked out. "All those people who did not receive Jesus as their Savior."

"What do you mean?" Myrtle asked tenderly.

"He gave the invitation for men and women to accept Christ, and no one came. They just stood there. Dying in their sin. Didn't you feel it too?"

"Feel what, Kathryn?"

"Feel that burden for the lost. I must preach, Myrtle. I'll never be satisfied until I am doing my share."

Kathryn never referred to that night again. She didn't like to hang her theology on a peg in time. She worshiped a God of the now, whose Holy Spirit was doing far more exciting things today than He ever did yesterday. She once told me that she was so busy trying to keep up with what God was doing today, she didn't have time to recall her yesterdays. For that reason she seldom answered her critics. She knew where she was, even if they didn't, and to stop and try to explain would take too long. If they didn't like her experiences—or lack of them—if they were negative about the way she dressed, acted, spoke, or spent money—well, that was their problem. She felt she was under a divine mandate. Like Nehemiah building the wall around Jerusalem, she was too busy to come down and argue with the enemy.

In one of her rare moments of nostalgia, Kathryn did talk about her theology. "When word got back to Myrtle that we were having great services in Idaho, she sent me a telegram from Spokane, Washington. It was terse but profound: 'Be sure you have your theology straight.'

"I didn't even know what theology was," Kathryn chuckled. "I'm glad I was stupid, stupid enough to believe that all I had to do was preach the Word and God would take care of my theology."

But there was more involved than "preaching the Word." There were posters and handbills to be printed. And meetings to be organized in every new community. It seems she hit them all, following the Snake River all the way from Payette to Pocatello and on up to Idaho Falls. Caldwell, Nampa, Mountain Home, Twin Falls, Burley, Blackfoot, Basalt, and Bone. "Name any little town in the state of Idaho," Kathryn later told reporters, "and I worked at trying to evangelize it."

In Rexburg, up near the Montana border, Kathryn and

47

Helen found a little Baptist church which had been closed for almost two years. Asking around, they found one surviving deacon who still had the keys to the old building. He scratched his head and looked wonderingly at the two pretty young girls who asked if they could hold services in the little church.

"Well, young ladies," he said slowly, "it's closed up now so I don't reckon you could hurt us any more than we're already hurt."

Kathryn and Helen opened the building, cleaned it themselves, and then went through the little community announcing the services. A widow, who took in boarders but had no extra beds, had her son scrub out the turkey house. Kathryn and Helen spent three nights there before another family gave them a room in which to sleep, and a bed.

Idaho winters were cold, and sometimes there would be no heat in the guest rooms. To keep warm, Kathryn would snuggle under a huge pile of quilts and lie very still until she got one part of the bed warm. Then she would turn over on her stomach, take her Bible, and for hours at a time study the Word of God until it became a part of her.

"I got my schooling at the feet of the greatest teacher in the world," she later said. "It wasn't in some great university or theological seminary. It was in the school of prayer under the teaching of the Holy Spirit."

"Sometimes," Kathryn chuckled, "I read the Bible all night because I was afraid to turn off the light and go to sleep. For some reason, those people in Idaho liked to hang huge pictures of their ancestors on the walls of the guest rooms. There would be grandma in her high lace collar and grandpa with his long beard. They were always so stern looking, staring down at me from their high perches. And sometimes I just felt more comfortable keeping the lamp on all night long, reading the Bible."

Moving south from Idaho through the wasteland of Utah, Kathryn and Helen arrived in Pueblo, Colorado, where they rented the old Montgomery Ward building on Main Street. They remained there for six months.

"I was so conscientious," Kathryn said, "that I was afraid of being criticized for having more than one dress. So I had three dresses cut out of the same bolt of yellow material. At my last service in Pueblo, heads were bent in silent prayer. Suddenly the stillness was broken by a drunken voice from the back, bellowing, 'My God—can't I ever get away from that yellow dress? I see it when I sleep at night. I see it all day long. It haunts me!' "

It was a good time for Kathryn to leave, for the service barely survived the unscheduled interruption.

Denver, a hundred miles to the north, was beckoning. It was there she would begin to build her own kingdom, and get her first taste of national acclaim, only to find that the chastising hand of God was mightier than her own rebellious ways. For it was there that she would experience the bitterness of humiliation and failure, leaving in her mouth the taste of ashes for having drunk from the heady cup of human passion.

CHAPTER IV

"PREACH, AND DON'T EVER STOP"

Everything Kathryn did was big. When she preached, even if there were only a handful of people in the building, she preached like there were ten thousand. She never let up. At the invitation, she assumed everyone in the congregation needed to repent and give their lives to Christ—even if they were all ministers and missionaries. Many years later, when she met with all the pastors in a major city prior to a miracle service, she gave an invitation asking them to repent and be "born again." Many came forward, in tears, asking her to pray for them. She never took anything for granted. She was often criticized for gushing over some Hollywood movie star or famous political personality. But she also gushed over some obscure priest who had taken a vow of poverty, or over a highway construction worker who had been healed in one of her meetings. She treated taxi drivers and senators just alike—both were equally important in God's sight, and therefore in hers also.

I remember two instances, and find them perfect to compare. The first time I met Kathryn was in her suite of offices on the sixth floor of the Carlton House in downtown Pittsburgh. The offices are plush, taking up the entire end of the hotel wing. To get through the door with the gold embossed name of the Kathryn Kuhlman Foundation on the outside, you must ring a doorbell, which in turn sets off a Westminster chime in the office. Therefore no one ever just walks in, they are escorted in. Inside, the atmosphere is homey, warm, and inviting—even though every desk is filled with worker bees buzzing diligently. The decor is feminine—a reflection of Kathryn herself. The walls are cream colored and beige, the deep pile carpet is aqua, and flower arrangements—real and artificial—seem to fill the room.

One end of the room is dominated by a champagne colored sofa which is cluttered with books and magazines—gifts which have come through the mail. The end table near the sofa is piled high with small gift boxes containing gold Cross pens which Kathryn is sending to some special friends for Christmas.

The rooms are filled with mementos. There is a beautiful, hand-carved wooden jewelry box given her by Madame Thieu in gratitude for her work in Vietnam. There are antique lusters which Kathryn herself picked out from a small gift shop in Rome. A huge, brooding portrait of deaf Beethoven hangs over Maggie Hartner's desk, reminding the busy secretary, perhaps only on a subliminal plane, that handicaps should never cause a person to give less than her best—the thing that Kathryn demanded of all who worked for her.

Everywhere are photographs: the rooftop school in Hong Kong which was built with money from the Kathryn Kuhlman Foundation; Kathryn standing with Vietnamese soldiers, dressed in full battle garb; Pope Paul and Kathryn, just inches apart, looking intently at each other; standing arm in arm with Teddy Kolek, the mayor of Jerusalem; and her favorite photo, preaching in Stockholm before 16,000 with her translator, Joseph Mattson-Boze, standing by her side. A small Swedish boy stands in front of her all by himself, staring intently as if in a trance.

On one of the desks, under the glass, is a cancelled check for $10.00, drawn on the Security National Bank in Sioux City, Iowa. It is made out to Kathryn Kuhlman, signed by Everett B. Parrott of the Parrott Tent Revival, and dated July 14, 1928. Kathryn never forgot from whence she came.

When she entered that afternoon it was like a combination of the Queen of England and the rushing mighty wind of Pentecost. She literally swept into the room, stood for a moment in a hip-out stance as she stroked one thigh with her hand, and then, leaning forward, grabbed both my hands in hers. "Aw . . . and you've come all the way from FLAW-ree-daa." Then, just as quickly, she said, "Com'on, there's somebody in here I want you to meet. Com'on, com'on, she's verrrrry special."

Kathryn had hold of my arm now, her slender fingers biting gently into the flesh, pulling me along with her as she leaned against me. At sixty she was the perfect combination of sex, showmanship, spirituality, and a domineering mother. She quickly guided me into her small, personal office. There, sitting in the oversized leather chair looking terribly uncomfortable, was a stout old woman dressed in a cotton print dress. Her hair was wrapped in a bandana and her fingers nervously handled an old cotton handbag.

"This is Mrs. Romanaski," Kathryn gushed. "She's one of my favorite people. She's Polish, lives over on Northside, doesn't speak English very well, but she never misses one of her services at Carnegie Hall. She wasn't able to put anything in the offering this morning at the miracle service because her husband is sick. Soooo, she came all the way up here just to let me know she loves me and is praying for me."

Kathryn stood for a long moment, looking down at the little Polish woman who sat with her head humbly bowed, fingering a loose thread on her stained old handbag.

"That's the kind of people God has given me in this ministry," Kathryn said, nodding her head. She continued nodding, as though she were drawing out her approval beyond the ordinary. "That's the kind of people He has given me."

She was crying now, wiping the tears away with the back of her hands. The little Polish woman was crying. And so was I. I felt I had opened the door and walked into the heart of a woman I had never met, but had known all my life—for her heart beat, it seemed, with the heartbeat of God.

The other scene took place almost seven years later. I was with Kathryn backstage in her dressing room at the Shrine Auditorium in Los Angeles. She had just finished a four-and-a-half-hour miracle service, having stood on her feet the entire time. She was sixty-seven years old (though none of us then were exactly sure about her age), and she was exhausted. I was just getting ready to leave when there was a knock at the door. Naurine Bennett, the wife of a wealthy real estate broker from Palos Verdes Peninsula, who had been healed a number of years earlier of scleroderma and now worked as a volunteer at the stage door entrance, stuck her head into the dressing room.

"Miss Kuhlman, there is someone here who would like to see you."

I looked at Kathryn. She had wilted into a chair, every ounce of strength seemed wrung from her almost emaciated body. But she knew that Naurine would not come to the door unless there was a need. She never asked who it was. She just sat up and motioned, "Of course, send them in. Send them in."

The door opened wider and in walked an old man—well into his eighties—with an erect military bearing. A companion said, "Miss Kuhlman, I'd like to introduce General of the Army Omar Bradley."

Instantly Kathryn was again the Queen of England and the Rushing Mighty Wind. She rushed to the door and went into her routine. All the exhaustion had fled, and in its place was exuberance and life. Taking both his hands in hers, she stepped back and looked down her arms in admiration at the great hero of World War II who had stood shoulder-to-shoulder with Dwight Eisenhower and Douglas MacArthur.

"Aw, God love you! And you were *here* for the MIR-a-cle service!"

"He sat through the entire service," the companion said. "And insisted on coming back here to meet you."

I stood to one side, thinking of Mrs. Romanaski sitting in that big brown leather chair, nervously twisting her cloth handbag in her gnarled old fingers. Kathryn treated the distinguished five-star general no differently than she had that poor little Polish woman from Northside in Pittsburgh. Both were children of God. Both souls for whom Christ had died.

They talked about spiritual matters for a few minutes. Then the general mentioned a specific need in his life.

"Dear Jesus," Kathryn intoned, closing her eyes and reaching out to pray for him.

It was as far as she got. His legs buckled under him and he crumpled backwards—"slain in the Spirit." Don Barnard, who traveled with Miss Kuhlman as her bodyguard, had entered the room with the general. He caught him as he fell and eased him to the floor where he lay for a few moments as if he were asleep. When he began to move slightly, Don helped him to his feet and gently held his arm. He was still unsteady.

"Our wonderful Lord can meet your every need," Kathryn said deliberately, her face glowing with faith. "I know how much He must love you right this minute."

She made no move in his direction, but the general's knees buckled once again and he slipped back into Don's strong arms.

After he was gone, Kathryn paced the small room, back and forth, going all the way to one wall and then turning and marching back to the other, her arms raised in prayer and praise. "Blessed Jesus," she said over and over. "I give you praise! I give you glory!"

There were no "little people" around Kathryn. Everyone was important. Everyone was big. It was one of the secrets of the success of her ministry. People knew they were important around her, and knowing this, began to understand that they were important to God also. Everything Kathryn did was big. "Think big. Act big. Talk big," she told her associates. "For we have a big God."

It was this same philosophy which helped her get established in Denver in the year 1933. Earl F. Hewitt, a businessman, had joined her shortly before she came to Pueblo as her business manager. This was depression time. Many of the banks across the nation had closed. Every city had bread lines. Unemployment was at the highest peak in the nation's history. Hundreds of thousands of businesses had closed; and the business that seemed to suffer most was God's business—the church. Only those in the dedicated minority, those who made up the membership of the genuine kingdom of God, gave to the Lord during those days of want. All the rest, that vast army of the "Sunday religionists," waited until times of abundance to begin giving again. The churches were struggling. And Kathryn, who wasn't even a part of the institutional church but was out on the fringes ministering to those who had been rejected by both society and church, had to be content with whatever dregs were available. Nothing seemed to daunt her spirit, however, or cause her to believe in anything less than a God of abundant plenty.

"You go up there to Denver like you've got a million dollars," she told Hewitt. "We're going to take that city by storm."

Hewitt gave the young woman a crooked smile. "But we don't have a million dollars. We have only five dollars. That's all."

Kathryn just laughed. "If we serve a God who is limited to our finances, then we're serving the wrong God. He's not limited to what we have or who we are. If He can use somebody like me to bring souls into the kingdom, He can certainly use our five dollars and multiply it just as easily as He multiplied the loaves and fishes for the people on the hillside. Now go on up to Denver. Find me the biggest building you can. Get the finest piano available for Helen. Fill the place up with chairs. Take out a big ad in the *Denver Post* and get spot announcements on all the radio stations. This is God's business and we're going to do it God's way. Big!"

The building Hewitt found was almost a duplicate of the building she had used in Pueblo. It, too, was a Montgomery Ward warehouse and was located at 1733-37 Champa Street in downtown Denver. Using a combination of faith, brass, and credit, Hewitt rented 500 chairs and a grand piano, telling the people he would pay for them in two weeks, at the end of the revival campaign. The two weeks revival, however, stretched into five years. From the very first night, Kathryn was an institution in Denver.

Helen arrived a few days early to arrange the music for the campaign. She enlisted help from the three daughters of A.C. Anderson—Mildred, Lucille, and Biney—who made up the Anderson Trio. The girls worked with Helen and sang for the opening service in the old store building. They continued singing for nearly all the services for the next five years. Helen also planned the Saturday night services, which were great musical concerts.

The people of Denver were hungry for the type of fare served up by Kathryn and Helen. The churches, like the economy, were sick and dying. Many had closed down. Of those that remained open, most were sparsely attended and the services were dry and lifeless—a reflection of the era in which they lived. In contrast, Kathryn did not reflect the depression. She reflected the greatness of God. Instead of talking lack, she talked plenty. Instead of talking about empty pockets and empty stomachs, she encouraged the people to come and feast at the marriage supper of the Lamb. And the miraculous happened. The people brought their loaves and fishes, their small offerings, and they were multiplied a thousandfold. Instead of sending the people to the degrading soup lines run by the state and federal governments, she encouraged those who had food to bring it and share it with those who had none.

"We're saints, not beggars," she told her poor congregation. "God has promised in Psalm 37:25 that the righteous shall not be forsaken nor shall His seed have to beg for bread."

And the people believed her. There were only 125 persons present that first night of the campaign, August 27, 1933. But she preached as though there were twelve thousand in the congregation. The improvised warehouse was hot and steamy, but the signs on the front windows carried in bold letters the announcement that Kathryn Kuhlman, the young evangelist, was beginning a special series of services. From the first notes of the piano as Helen ran her gifted fingers up and down the keyboard, the people knew this was no ordinary meeting. They believed God had sent this woman into their midst to give them hope in a time of desperation, love in a time of hate, and trust in a time of disbelief and doubt. She had come to restore in them their God-given human dignity. To remind them who they were. The following night there were more than 400 persons, and from then on the old warehouse could not hold the crowds.

They came from the gutters and ghettos, from the slums and the rat-infested flats. They came from the apartment buildings and the rescue missions. The services lasted long into the night, with Kathryn, Helen, Hewitt, and a dozen others who had been hand-picked, praying with those who remained for ministry.

All who came were not "down and outers." Others, from the fashionable suburbs of Denver, who had wanted to help in ministry but had no opportunity in their churches, came also. Services were held every night with the crowds spilling out onto the sidewalks.

But Kathryn was growing restless. She had remained in Denver longer than she had stayed any other place since she had begun to preach. To stay longer would mean she might have to get involved in the administration of a church— something she didn't want. After five months of continuous services she announced to the congregation on a Friday night that she had fulfilled her task and was going to leave.

The announcement was met by loud protests. People jumped to their feet shouting, "No! no!" Then a man whom

Kathryn knew only by sight, a man who had been attending the services for only a few weeks, stood to his feet.

Over the din he shouted, "Young lady, it's time you stopped running. We need you here. If you'll agree to stay in Denver, I will personally finance the down payment on the biggest building you can find. We'll call it the Denver Revival Tabernacle, and we'll put a huge neon sign on the top that says, 'Prayer Changes Things.' "

The shouting, applause, and promises of other pledges from the congregation convinced Kathryn she needed to stay. A search was begun for a place to build the tabernacle. In the meantime, since Montgomery Ward needed their warehouse, the meeting place of the church shifted to the warehouse for the Monitor Paper Company at 1941 Curtis Street. A sign was erected naming the building the KUHLMAN REVIVAL TABERNACLE. The ministry was in full swing.

Helen Gulliford had formed a choir of more than a hundred voices, composing much of the music they sang. A number of outside speakers were invited in for special services. Kathryn knew her limitations. She was not a teacher. She had but one message, "Ye must be born again." She knew that in order to keep the people, she would need to feed them. This was done through the musical program and the outside speakers who gladly accepted her invitations to come and preach at the fastest growing assembly in the West.

Favorite teachers were Evangelist and Mrs. Howard W. Rusthoi, who had pastored independent churches in California, Oregon, and Missouri. Alternating each night for two months of straight meetings, one would preach while the other would direct the singing. Joining them in several of their meetings was the young evangelist Phil Kerr, an extraordinary song composer and radio preacher.

A typical week of the campaign was that of January 11, 1935:

> Sunday, 11:00 A.M. Kathryn Kuhlman, "Ye Must Be Born Again."
>
> Sunday, 3:00 P.M. Phil Kerr, "Mountain Moving Faith."
>
> Sunday, 7:30 P.M. Mrs. Rusthoi, "Barriers to Hell."
>
> Monday, 7:30 P.M. Howard Rusthoi, "Why I Married My Wife."
>
> Tuesday, 7:30 P.M. Phil Kerr, "The World's Greatest Prayer Meeting."
>
> Wednesday, 7:30 P.M. Mrs. Rusthoi, "Bringing Up Father."
>
> Thursday, 7:30 P.M. Howard Rusthoi, "Is Mussolini the Anti-Christ?"
>
> Friday, 7:30 P.M. Phil Kerr, "What the Bible Says about Divine Healing."
>
> Saturday, 7:30 P.M. Special All-Musical Service.

It was while the group was meeting in the paper warehouse on Curtis Street that Kathryn was exposed to the concepts of divine healing. Phil Kerr often preached on the subject, as did other evangelists who came in. "Healing services" were often held at the close of the evangelistic meetings, and the preacher would ask all the sick to come forward for special prayer. On some occasions they would be anointed with oil. On other occasions they would be asked to go to a back room for special prayer. In some instances, there would be dramatic healings and the people would come back the next night to testify. This thrilled Kathryn, for although she seldom prayed for the sick herself, she was always amazed—and gratified—when people were healed.

Unfortunately, many of the people began to identify

Kathryn with Aimee Semple McPherson, the flashy Pentecostal preacher from Los Angeles. Sister Aimee, as her followers called her, built her five-thousand seat Angelus Temple in Los Angeles in 1923—the year Kathryn left home to join the Parrotts on the West Coast. If Kathryn was a showman, Aimee was a super-showman. Her incredibly dramatized sermons—presented on a stage complete with changes of scenery, colored lights, sound effects, and casts of hundreds—were called the "best show in Los Angeles." She later founded the International Church of the Four Square Gospel.

In 1926 Aimee was the number-one topic in America. For five weeks—May 18 to June 23—she was missing. She was last seen at the beach and was believed to have drowned.

After a frantic search which involved several police forces, an army of private detectives, and even included the president of Mexico, Aimee reappeared and said she had been kidnapped. However, the police doubted her story and accused her of hiding out in a love nest in northern California with a former Angelus Temple radio operator. She was finally dragged into court to face charges of corrupting public morals and manufacturing evidence. All the charges were eventually dropped.

Kathryn's ministry grew up during the midst of this scandal. Helen constantly cautioned her about using discretion. "There are enough people bringing a reproach against the kingdom of God without you getting involved," she warned. Kathryn, although she later conducted a giant miracle service at Angelus Temple in the winter of 1968, never met the famous "faith healer," Sister Aimee. As close as she ever got was when she visited her grave some twenty years after she died. In a report to *Christianity Today* magazine, Kathryn said, "I never met her (Aimee Semple McPherson). But several years ago Maggie Hartner and I visited her grave. There we found a young man and a woman, who was probably his mother, viewing the monument erected to the memory of Miss McPherson. The woman was telling how her preaching had made Jesus so real. 'I found Christ through her life,' the woman said. At that point Kathryn Kuhlman thought to herself that if after I am gone, just one person can stand by my grave and say, 'I found Christ because she preached the gospel,' then I will not have lived in vain."

That's the way Kathryn was. If she had any misgivings about the garish showmanship and ostentatious life of the famous evangelist, she never voiced them in public. For while Kathryn despised all purported faith healers and the wreckage they left behind, she did her best to speak kindly of them and do everything possible to keep unity in the kingdom. Thus even though there were some in the Denver area who likened Kathryn's ministry to that of Sister Aimee, there was no resemblance other than both were women and both were trying to serve God in their own way.

One of Kathryn's greatest disappointments was that her father, whom she loved so deeply, never heard her preach. She always contended that papa's dislike for preachers grew out of the fact they seldom, if ever, preached the pure Word of God. She was so certain that man was created to have fellowship with God, and that once he heard the true Word of God he would commit himself to the Author of the Word. Therefore she just knew papa would respond favorably to her ministry. Not just because she was his "baby," but because she was preaching truth.

Papa never got that chance, and the fact that he died

without Kathryn knowing whether or not he had ever accepted Christ as his Savior remained one of the great frustrations of her life. In fact, in 1973 when I made a special trip to Pittsburgh to interview Kathryn for a cover story to appear in *Guideposts* magazine, she said, "There is but one story I want to talk about—and that's about the time papa died."

It was one-thirty P.M. on the Sunday after Christmas—December 30, 1934, that the twenty-seven-year-old girl received the phone call. She had just come in from the Sunday morning service. "Kathryn, your father has been hurt. He was in an accident."

The caller, an old friend, had been trying to reach Kathryn for two days, but the lines were down because of heavy snow. Joe Kuhlman had been working late the Friday night of December 28, catching up on all the billing following the Christmas rush. Mama called him, asking him to bring home a dozen eggs. Joe, who was sixty-eight years old, started out into the night to go by Buffman's Poultry House for the eggs. The streets were icy and he was partially blinded by the driving snow. He got less than a block on his way toward home when he fell, breaking all the eggs in the brown paper "poke" (sack). Picking himself up, he decided it would be less dangerous to brave the ice and go back after more eggs than to try to explain his clumsiness to mama. Gingerly he made his way back to Buffman's. He wished he had an extra pair of socks, like many of the people he passed, so he could pull them over his leather shoes to give him some traction on the thick ice.

Entering the store, he said to Seckle Buffman, "Seckle, I need another dozen eggs. I fell, and Emma would be most unhappy if I came home without them."

Carrying his new paper sack, he started out again down Main Street. He got as far as Ninth Avenue, near his dray business, when he started across the street. From that point on, there is still confusion as to exactly what happened. The story the witnesses told was that just as Joe Kuhlman reached the center of the street, Mr. Katze, of Topsy's Cafe, was coming down the street in his Buick automobile. Katze had asked his college-age son to drive because he felt the boy was more sure of himself on the icy roads. Katze's brother-in-law was sitting in the back seat. Suddenly the boy saw Joe Kuhlman standing in the middle of the road. In order to avoid hitting him, he swerved sharply, went into a skid, and slid into the front yard of Dr. Sholle. Jumping out of the car, they saw Joe Kuhlman lying in the street. His skull was fractured, but there were no other marks on his body. No one in the car felt an impact, nor were there any marks on the car. Still, no one could say for sure whether the car hit him or whether he slipped on the ice and hit his head. He remained in a coma for two days and died on December 30.

Kathryn, driving a V-8 Ford, started out across Colorado in a blinding snowstorm. She recalled, "Only God knows how fast I drove on those icy roads, but all I could think about was papa. Papa was waiting for me. Papa knew I was coming."

About a hundred miles from Kansas City, she stopped at a telephone station and called ahead. Aunt Belle, her mother's sister, answered the phone.

"This is Kathryn. Tell papa I'm almost home."

There was a pause, then Belle answered back. "But, didn't they tell you?"

"Tell me what?" Kathryn answered, feeling panic clutching at her throat.

"Papa is dead. He died early this morning."

The next miles were like a nightmare to her. There were no other cars on the road as her headlights stabbed into the

65

snowy whiteness and her windshield wipers battled vainly against the freezing rain as it fell in piercing needles.

Arriving home in the wee hours of the morning, she found the family all in the living room, surrounding the open casket of her beloved papa, keeping the traditional "wake" practiced by those in mid-America. Kathryn refused to look at the face of the man she idolized. She had been home many times since she had left ten years ago. Nothing had changed. Only this time everything had changed. She knew she would never come home again and find papa waiting. She knew that mama would sell the big house, that place which had been her security in those early years. And hate surged in her like a volcano. Hate towards those she felt had taken her father's life.

When she told me the story, thirty-seven years later, she still wept. We were sitting in her personal office in the Carlton House in Pittsburgh. She was seated on the floor, leaning back against the wall, and I was near her in the brown leather chair.

"I can still remember it," she said, wiping the tears from her eyes, "as vividly as if it were yesterday. We were all seated on the front row of the little Baptist church. I simply could not accept papa's death. It couldn't be. After the sermon, the people got up and filed past the casket, looking solemnly down into papa's face. When they had all gone by, the funeral director came and stood beside the family, motioning for us to get up and go by. Uncle Herman was the only one of his brothers left. Aunt Gusty had died the year before. Mama, Myrtle, Boy, and Geneva moved slowly out into the aisle and down past the open casket. I was the only one left, and I didn't want to get up.

"Then, I don't know how, I was suddenly standing at the front of the church, looking down. But I couldn't bear to look at his face. Instead I fixed my eyes on his shoulder. It was that same shoulder where I had often laid my head when I had an earache. Papa had no healing power. No healing virtue. I wasn't even sure he was a Christian. But he had love. And that love would make all the pain go away.

"I reached down and gently touched my fingers against his shoulder. As I did, though, something happened. It was as though I were brushing my fingers over a sack of flour. That was not my papa. That was just a black wool coat covering something which had been discarded, something once loved, now laid aside. Papa wasn't there."

Kathryn returned to Denver, having learned a lesson which can come only through hatred and loss. The lesson on forgiveness. Her family, over her mother's objections, insisted on bringing suit against the persons they felt responsible for papa's death. Kathryn, however, said she could have no part of it. She left before the case was settled—out of court.

"Vengeance," she told me later, "must always be left in God's hands. To have held a grudge, to have taken vengeance against that boy, would have hurt me infinitely more than it would have hurt him. That's the reason I would never sue anybody, regardless of how they hurt me or took advantage of me. I am God's person. I belong to Him. I'll trust Him to do what's best to me—and to those who hurt me."

It was a lesson which would be severely put to the test many times—especially on an occasion when some of her most trusted associates would turn on her and commit public slander. But she never backed down on her way of forgiveness. She left it in the hands of God.

In early 1935 the group of men who had been searching for a building in Denver reported they had found the ideal spot for the tabernacle. It was the old truck garage, formerly the livery stable, for the Daniel and Fisher Department Store. The building was located on the corner of West Ninth and Acoma Streets, and renovation work was begun on February 5 of that year. Four months later the huge building, complete with two thousand seats, was filled to overflowing for the dedication service on May 30. A seventy-two-foot neon sign, running the length of the building, said "Denver Revival Tabernacle." Under it, in smaller letters, was another sign: "Evangelist Kathryn Kuhlman." On top of the building at one end, in more neon, was a sign with three-foot letters which said "Prayer Changes Things."

The services, though, remained the same. The Anderson Trio sang at most of the meetings. Helen Gulliford played the piano. During the altar calls she roamed up and down the aisles looking for people who held up their hands for prayer and inviting them to the front. Kathryn preached. At the close of each service—from 10:00 until 10:15 P.M.—Kathryn went on the air, live, over KVOD radio for her program, "Smiling Through."

Wearing a flowing pulpit dress, Kathryn would enter from the back of the building and come down a side aisle, waving to her audience and shaking their hands. People would reach out to try to touch her. She would respond by saying, "Aw, God love you, God love you." Smiling, waving and chuckling, she would come to the stage while Helen played the piano in the background. She often opened the meetings by saying, "Isn't it just great to be a Christian! If you agree, give me a big, hearty 'AMEN!'" The building would roar with amens. Then while they were settling down, Kathryn would tell them a homey little story.

"You know, just this morning I was up in my little room in the St. Francis Hotel. Room 416. It's such a tiny little room.

Mrs. Holmquist, God love her, does the best she can. But the wallpaper is peeling off the walls and the elevator is nearly always stuck—yet for four dollars a week it's like heaven to me."

She would pause here for laughter as the people identified with her and her life style.

"And while I was lying across my bed, studying the Word of God, there was a tiny little knock at the door. I asked God to excuse me, told Him I'd be right back, and went to the door. There was this little man . . . are you here, sir? If you are, wave your hand. Oh, oh, there he is. Way back there. Stand up, sir, let all the people see you. I want them to know that this is an absolutely true story. You know, ministers love to exaggerate. In fact, some of the stories I've heard ministers tell are better than the real thing. That's right."

There was more laughter. The little man in the back waved his hands and sat back down. Kathryn continued.

"Guess what," she said, leaning on the pulpit in a down-to-earth fashion, like she was talking to just one person. "This precious little man told me that he's been drinking three bottles of wine each night for the last thirteen years. But three nights ago he came to the altar at the close of the service and Brother Hewitt knelt with him and they prayed through. It took until one o'clock in the morning, but when he got up from his knees he was delivered from alcohol. He came by this morning to tell me. And now he's here tonight to prove to all the world that Jesus Christ sets men free from slavery."

Her voice, which had begun in a raspy whisper, had now built to a shouting crescendo. The people were already on their feet applauding as Kathryn pointed again at the man and said, "Let's give him a real big God Bless You."

Even before the people had stopping clapping, Helen

was back on the keyboard and the choir was singing. Another revival service was underway.

It was during one of these revival services that Kathryn received what she later described as the greatest thrill of her life up until that time. Like papa, Mama Kuhlman had never heard her daughter preach. Now that Kathryn was established in the huge building with her name on the side in large letters, she felt she should invite mama to come up for a service. The night Emma came to the services, Kathryn preached on the subject of the Holy Spirit. When she finished the sermon, she gave an invitation. "All those who want to be born again, and to know the third person of the Trinity, the Holy Spirit, can come to the prayer room behind the pulpit. I'll be back there and so will some others. We'll be praying for you."

Kathryn made her way directly to the large room behind the platform and found it almost full. She went from one kneeling person to another, praying for them. Almost fifteen minutes later, while the prayer time was still intense, the side door opened. In walked Emma Kuhlman. Kathryn spotted her and motioned for her to come stand beside her.

"What do you think of all this, mama?" Kathryn whispered. "Did you ever think your little girl would amount to this?"

Emma Kuhlman reached out and took Kathryn's hand. "Baby, I'm not here to brag on you. I'm here because you spoke truth tonight and I want to know Jesus as you know Him."

Kathryn started to laugh, then realized her mama was serious—dead serious. Before she could say anything, mama was kneeling on the floor, her head bent over the back of a chair. Kathryn, now choked with tears, reached out and laid her hand on the back of her mama's head. The moment her fingers touched, mama began to shake, then cry. It was the same kind of shaking and crying that Kathryn remembered as a fourteen-year-old girl when she had stood beside mama in that little Methodist church in Concordia. But this time there was something new. Mama lifted her head and began to speak, slowly at first, then more rapidly. But the words were not English, they were the clear, bell-tone sounds of the unknown tongue.

Kathryn fell to her knees beside her, weeping and laughing at the same time, mixing her deep alto voice with that of her mama's as they, each in her own way, praised God together.

When Emma opened her eyes, she reached out for Kathryn and held her tightly. It was the first time that Kathryn could ever remember being embraced by her mother. "Kathryn, preach that others might receive what I have just received," mama wept. "Preach, and don't ever stop."

Kathryn said, "Mama did not sleep for three days and two nights after that experience, so great was the joy of the Lord upon her. She was a new person. The love of God radiated from her. His joy and His love filled her to overflowing. She returned to Concordia, and for the rest of her life she had a wonderful, sweet communion with the Holy Spirit."

Ina Fooks, a member of the Denver group, wrote about Kathryn's ministry saying: "Miss Kuhlman held fixedly to the idea that God can and will use a great evangelistic center where the gospel is preached in its glorious fullness and where all are cordially welcome. While church membership is an important part of the religious life of many, there are thousands of others, she feels, who have no church affiliation and will make none. The members of the various

71

churches find occasion to visit the tabernacle when there are no services in their home church, as services are held every night of the week at this tabernacle with the exception of Monday night. The non-churchman feels entirely welcome and thoroughly enjoys the services because he is asked to do nothing but join Jesus. The only interest of the tabernacle work is the salvation of souls and the deepening of the spiritual experiences of those who attend the services."

The ministry rapidly expanded beyond that, however. A Sunday school grew up. Three busses brought the children in from outlying districts. A children's church developed on Sunday for kids under twelve. Many of the people joined in outside ministry, going with groups to the jails, correctional institutions, and old folks homes. The women formed a "Woman's Society," and Kathryn was invited throughout the city to preach in schools and other churches. Baptismal services were held in the borrowed baptistry of a local Baptist church with Miss Kuhlman doing the immersing. And although she never called herself a pastor, preferring to be referred to as an evangelist, she conducted funerals and presided over the marriages of many of the people in the congregation.

Work on the Denver Revival Tabernacle was never really completed. The brick walls, the heating plant, the wiring and plumbing—all needed constant care. During the week the men who were without jobs would show up at the tabernacle in work parties. The women, with Kathryn and Helen leading the way, brought in food. That which was left over each day was carried home by the men who had no money to buy food of their own.

Visiting preachers came and often stayed for months at a time. Wilbur Nelson came from California for a series of meetings. Harry D. Clarke, who used to direct the musical program for Billy Sunday after the death of Ira Sankey, came for several appearances. Canadian evangelist Norman Greenway and opera star Harry Parkes Bond both spent time ministering at the tabernacle, preaching and singing. Phil Kerr returned several times, sometimes to raise money for his nationwide radio ministry. Kathryn was very generous with these men, encouraging the people to give as much as they could. Raymond T. Richey came up from Texas with a healing campaign and preached from the same text, Jeremiah 33:3, every night for three weeks. Kathryn even invited Everett and Myrtle Parrott to hold a series of meetings.

But nobody thrilled the people, and Kathryn, more than the handsome evangelist from Austin, Texas, Burroughs A. Waltrip. Nor could anyone imagine, when he first came to preach at the tabernacle early in 1937, that in less than eighteen months he would have become the person through whom the most promising young woman evangelist in the world would destroy her career.

CHAPTER V

THE SLAYING
OF THE EGYPTIAN

In 1970, newspaper columnist Lester Kinsolving (an ordained Episcopal priest) "exposed" that thirty-two years before Kathryn Kuhlman had married, then divorced, Burroughs A. Waltrip. The writer failed to realize, however, that while Kathryn had tried to keep that unhappy chapter of her life buried in the past, she was not ashamed of it.

"Once a mistake has been confessed, then it is under the blood of Jesus," she told me after the column came out. "But sadly, Mr. Kinsolving knows nothing of the forgiveness of Jesus."

It was about as close as Kathryn ever came to speaking out, even in private, against someone who attacked her. Kinsolving, besides exposing his biblical illiteracy by calling her gift of the word of knowledge "psychic," sneered at her oratorical style, calling it "unbelievable corn."

Kathryn quickly penned a letter of forgiveness, even though the renegade priest had made no offer to apologize:

"Two things I shall always remember—your kindness in taking the time to send the personal note, and your hearty laughter (just once) during our interview in the office. Remembering these two incidents, I can forgive you for anything.

"The article was *not* offensive—and I only regret my inability to use the human vocabulary as you do. Mine is still and will always remain in the 'corn stage.' "

Kathryn's openness and love had a way of disarming even those who attacked her. While *MS* magazine—an organ for the women's lib movement—treated her with scorn, other periodicals like *Time* went deeper and recognized the touch of God.

In reply to her critics, Kathryn enjoyed recalling one of her "papa stories." One time, she said, papa was coming through a revolving door. A drunk staggered up and pushed him aside. A man, standing close by, said, "Are you going to let him get away with that?" And Joe Kuhlman, who was the mayor of the town and its richest citizen, said quietly, "I can afford to."

That was Kathryn's attitude. "I can afford to let them get away with it. Just as Jesus never answered His critics, I have absolute confidence that my heavenly Father is big enough to handle every situation."

But for a while, back in 1938, it seemed like even God was not big enough to handle His headstrong, redheaded handmaiden. For once in her life she was determined to do things her own way, regardless of what God—or His people—thought about it.

Kathryn's marriage to Burroughs Waltrip, who left his

wife and children for her love, was more than a horrible mistake. It was sin—rebellion against God. At the same time, it became the crucible—as Moses' slaying of the Egyptian guard earned him exile in the wilderness of Midian— which would bring her to the place of total surrender to God's perfect plan for her life.

It is impossible to write about Kathryn Kuhlman without writing about God. Her life was not her own. In a very real way, she was a daughter of destiny. Chosen. Ordained to be His special handmaiden. If she chose, because of some character trait that made her stubborn, to rebel against God's plan for her life, then God simply tightened the checkrein until she was forced to comply with His command. In fact, God has a way of taking our rebellion, our sins, our flagrant disobedience, and molding it into our future tensile strength. So while Kathryn later realized she had sinned she also realized that because she had walked through her dark valley, she could better comprehend the cross, and the meaning of her own redemption. For through it all, even when she was "killing the Egyptian" and wandering in the cruel wilderness created by her disobedience, God's hand was upon her.

Everybody in the church in Denver tried to talk Kathryn out of marrying Burroughs Waltrip. None succeeded. Waltrip made his first trip to the Denver Revival Tabernacle in 1937. He came on the recommendation of Phil Kerr, the radio evangelist, and stayed for almost two months. At thirty-eight, he was eight years older than Kathryn. He was, as Kathryn later described him, "the best-looking guy that ever was." Good looks and good preaching made a good combination, and Kathryn invited him back in the fall of the year. This time his wife, Jessie, and their two sons, aged six and eight, came along. There was some speculation at the time that Jessie was uncomfortable with her rangy, dark-haired husband who was spending time with the long-legged redhead. She wanted to be around to keep an eye on him—and them. The people in Denver found Jessie Waltrip to be quiet and unassuming, an ideal wife for the dynamic preacher.

But something happened during Waltrip's second visit to Denver. The facts are unclear. Mrs. Waltrip took the boys and returned to Austin. It was time to enter them in school. A month later Waltrip wrote his wife saying he was not coming home. The report he gave in Denver, however, was that Jessie had deserted him. He had pled, he said, for her to join him, but she refused. Charging her with desertion, he traveled north to Mason City, Iowa, near the Minnesota border. The people in Mason City were impressed with his preaching. They encouraged him to stay and begin a work similar to that which Kathryn had in Denver. It wasn't long before Waltrip had obtained a big building which he renovated and called the Radio Chapel—since he was also using it for daily broadcasts over KGLO.

In early 1938 Waltrip made a public announcement that he was going to fast until he received the $10,000 necessary to complete work on the chapel. To assist him in the fund raising he brought in a revival team to hold services in the nearly completed building. His guest ministers: Harry D. Clarke leading the singing, Helen Gulliford at the piano, and Kathryn Kuhlman preaching.

Kathryn, billed as "America's Greatest Young Lady Preacher," stirred the crowds. But it was her Friday night message, entitled "Wanted—A Man," which brought out the reporters from the *Globe-Gazette*. The next morning headlines greeted the early risers with, "Young Blond Evangelist Arrives at Radio Chapel." The subhead stated: "Takes Over Job as Waltrip Continues Fast to Get $10,000."

The newspaper reporters got right at the heart of the matter. "An attractive young woman, nearly six feet tall, with blond, permanent-waved hair and laughing eyes has come to Mason City to help Evangelist Burroughs A. Waltrip in his campaign at Radio Chapel.

"There is no permanent or romantic connection, however," the paper stated in the second paragraph, "but Miss Kuhlman did state that 'I don't like to leave as long as he needs my help in the work here.' "

The story continued: "When the reporter expressed surprise that such an attractive young woman should still be single at the age of twenty-five, she smiled and then pondered for a moment before answering.

" 'Perhaps a man would find it almost too strenuous being married to one with my schedule,' she laughed."

One has to assume, from reading the yellowed newspaper clippings from the January 1938, *Globe-Gazette,* that Kathryn had already started fibbing about her age. Actually she was almost thirty-one, but for some reason felt more secure if her followers thought her younger. It was an unexplainable trait which would stay with her until the day she died. Even after she was in her late sixties she still insisted her radio announcer sign on with "And now Kathryn Kuhlman, the young woman you have been waiting for." When reporters quizzed her about her age, she would laugh and say, "Just put down 'over fifty.' " When they pinned her down for an exact figure, she would avoid answers. Those closest to her justified her action as a "woman's prerogative."

Kathryn returned to Denver, but not until she and Burroughs had already formulated plans for their marriage—his divorce now final. Helen Gulliford had seen it coming for a long time.

"She was beginning to feel that life was passing her by," Helen told a close friend. "That she was going to miss the excitement of living with a man."

Helen could see that Kathryn was changing. Her preaching, once so dynamic, was becoming weak. It was, Helen lamented, as though God was leaving her to her own devices. She was strong enough, and had enough personal magnetism to make it on her own, to fool some of the people all the time. But the more discerning members of the congregation began to realize that "their Kathryn" was not the same. Headstrong, she was determined to have her own way—even if it meant the destruction of her entire ministry.

Kathryn couldn't see it that way. She often talked with A. C. Anderson, the wise father of Mildred, Lucille, and Biney—the Anderson Trio. In fact, Kathryn spent most of her holidays, Christmas and Thanksgiving, at the Anderson home. She had a special love for Mother Anderson and on several occasions remarked that Mr. Anderson played a big role in filling in after the death of her father. But when it came to Burroughs Waltrip, Kathryn listened to no one. She insisted that Waltrip's wife had deserted him and that meant he was free to remarry. Someone had given Burroughs a book, which he later passed along to Kathryn, putting forth a view that a man and wife were not married in God's sight unless they loved one another when they got married. On the basis of this strange doctrine, Waltrip was now justifying his divorce, saying that he had never been married in God's sight (even though he had two children) and was free to marry Kathryn. In fact, he said, since he had not loved his wife he had been "living in sin" and was just now repenting and getting his life straightened out. This way he could follow what he said had been God's plan for him all along—to marry the slim, young redhead from Denver.

"There's no good coming out of this," A. C. Anderson cautioned Kathryn after Burroughs had come down from Mason City. The two of them had eaten an evening meal at the Anderson home. But Kathryn heard no one, Anderson, Helen, or even E. F. Hewitt, who begged her not to get involved with Waltrip.

The Andersons made a special trip to Mason City to try to reason with Waltrip. They discovered that none of the people in Mason City knew he had been married before. Waltrip came down to the hotel where Mr. and Mrs. Anderson were staying and talked with them until two o'clock in the morning. At times the argument grew heated and hostile. "If I could convince the Anderson family," Waltrip finally stormed, "I could win Denver."

But neither the Andersons nor the people in Denver could accept the fact that the marriage was part of God's plan. All they could do was hope, and pray, that somehow Kathryn would come to herself before she did something which would destroy the ministry all of them had worked so hard to build.

Kathryn was a loner. She refused advice from those around her. Submission, especially to a man or a group of men, was a foreign concept. "Every Christian should hear directly from God," she said. "Religion puts you into bondage, but Christianity sets you free. Submission to men is bondage. I want to be free and let God speak to me directly."

If Kathryn had any one great weakness in her long and fruitful career, it was her refusal to submit herself to the godly people around her. Moses submitted himself to elders. And the Apostle Paul taught Christians to "submit one to another." But, for some strange reason, the whole idea threatened her.

Kathryn was never able to see that listening to another

would not take away her rights before God nor would it turn her into some kind of puppet who jumped only when another pulled her string. In submission she could have found the needed checks and balances for the decisions in her personal life. Had she been submissive in 1938, she would not have destroyed her ministry. But headstrong and independent, she plunged ahead, determined to have her own way.

All of this however, reveals an incomprehensible truth. Often God's best plan can be thwarted by man's disobedience, meaning a second plan has to be devised, which in the skillful hands of an Almighty God turns out to be even better than the original design. It took many years for the mills of God to grind the grist of Kathryn's rebellion into exactness, but when the work was done, when the great fish returned her to the shore, when the bush burned and the voice of God was once again heard directing her to return to the original commission, she was ready to move.

In the meantime, however, was the wilderness, the depths of the sea, the darkness of separation from God. Yet she deliberately ate the forbidden fruit.

Standing before her congregation in Denver, Kathryn announced at the Sunday morning service on October 15 that God had revealed a new plan. She and Waltrip had decided to combine their ministries. Headquarters would be in Mason City, Iowa. She and Waltrip would take turns commuting back and forth to Denver for the services—800 miles. "The two of us can accomplish far more than either of us separately," she proclaimed.

Although she had not mentioned marriage, everyone

seemed to know. A ghastly hush fell over the congregation. All the rumors they had been hearing about Waltrip divorcing his wife in order to marry Kathryn—it was all true. Women began to sob. Several got up from the choir and walked out. Men sat stony faced in their pews, looking at Kathryn in disbelief. How could she do it? This woman, who had preached such dynamic messages about purity and holiness. This woman who had been such a model of decency and divine compassion. Was everything she had said a myth? Was she unable to follow the Lord she had so diligently encouraged them to follow for the last five years? Where was the inner strength? The power? Others could sin and fall away from God, but not their leader. Because she had been given much, then much was required. It was a hard life she had chosen. No one doubted that. All knew what she had sacrificed. Marriage. Children. Just to build the work in Denver. But to give it all up? To throw it away for a divorced man who had left his wife and two children? It wasn't worth that.

"No, Kathryn, don't say it. Don't do it. Please!" It was Helen Gulliford, standing at the piano bench, her face ashen, her eyes brimming with tears.

Earl Hewitt, Kathryn's business manager and substitute preacher, dropped his head to his knees. Broken. Mr. Anderson sat. Silent. That which he feared had come to pass.

Kathryn waved her hands dramatically and tried to make light of the entire situation. "Don't you understand," she said almost gaily. "I'm not leaving you. I'll be back."

But it was Kathryn who did not understand. The people saw beyond her, to the ministry, and knew that if she followed through on her headstrong plan, all was lost. In that moment they saw her, standing before them stripped of God's anointing and knowing it not. She was like Samson who went out sheared of his hair to challenge the Philistines, but "wist not that the Lord was departed from him."

The meeting broke up in shambles. Kathryn left through a side door. Early the next morning she caught the train to Des Moines where Waltrip met her and drove her to Mason City. They applied for the marriage license and she stated she would be twenty-six years old on her next birthday—even though she was thirty-one at the time. On October 18, 1938, she was married in Waltrip's Radio Chapel by a Methodist minister, Rev. L. E. Wordle of nearby Swaledale.

Only two people from the Denver Revival Tabernacle attended the wedding—Ina Fooks and Earl Hewitt. Before the service Hewitt met with Kathryn and explained the situation. Helen Gulliford had resigned from the Kuhlman ministry. She would stay in Denver to work with one of the groups which had already pulled away from the tabernacle. Hewitt said Kathryn would never again be welcome in Denver. He offered to buy her share of the building. She accepted and handed him the keys to her kingdom. Like a person possessed, she could not stop what she had started, even though the weight of it was already more than she could bear.

Halfway through the service she fainted. Waltrip helped revive her. Clutching her arm, he helped her through the remaining vows. The Egyptian was slain and before her lay only the barren wastes of the backside of Midian—a desert through which she was to wander for the next eight years.

CHAPTER VI

THE BUSH BURNS

Like all of God's servants who have been driven into the wilderness for their sins, Kathryn was soon forgotten by those she left behind. The pain of remembering was too great for those who had loved and followed her. It was easier to put her out of mind. Therefore most of her old followers salted their memories and quickly filled the void with new activities.

Hewitt asked William Watson, one of the favorite evangelists who had held services at the tabernacle, to take over the next week. Sunday morning, however, it was discovered that Watson had fled town on Saturday night. Hewitt did the preaching but lacked strength. The flock scattered. Some stayed with Hewitt. Others recalled Watson and began their own church in Barnes Business School. Still another group eventually joined with a new young Pentecostal minister who was just getting started in Denver,

Charles Blair. But many, far too many, returned to the world—scarred, disillusioned, lost to the kingdom.

Kathryn returned to Denver several times after that. Always alone. Although she was welcome at the Andersons' house for meals, she never mentioned Burroughs Waltrip. It was as though she had never married him.

Ina Fooks, who had been one of Kathryn's strongest supporters, visited the Radio Chapel in Mason City on several occasions. "All Kathryn does is sit on the platform behind her husband and cry," she reported when she got back to Denver.

When the people of Mason City discovered that Waltrip had lied to them about his first marriage, they, too, drifted away. The Radio Chapel was closed. Burroughs and Kathryn packed their bags and stole away into the wilderness night. They were heard of in Kansas, Oregon, Arizona, and even spent some time visiting back in Concordia. But she was as forgotten to her public as Moses to the Egyptians while he served out his exile in the desert of Sinai.

Two occasions during this wilderness exile are worth mentioning, for they had a direct relationship on what was to follow. Kathryn began to feel she needed to test the water by accepting some invitations to preach on her own. This bothered Waltrip who wanted her to stay with him. However, realizing that she was a preacher first and a housewife second, he allowed her to take a few solo engagements. One of these was in Pittsburgh, Pennsylvania. Jack Munyon, the pastor of a large, interdenominational church, invited her to the rough-and-tough city for a six-week series of meetings in early 1943. It was Kathryn's first visit to Pittsburgh, and she was well received. Munyon felt it was better, though, if the people did not know about her marriage. Thus, even though Waltrip stayed with her part of the time at the William Penn Hotel, Kathryn agreed to keep him under wraps. Munyon's five-year-old son almost let the cat out of the bag one night, however. When someone asked his father where Miss Kuhlman was staying, the little kid piped up and said, "Oh, she's living in the hotel with some man." It took some fast explaining by Munyon to cover that one up.

During this trip to Pittsburgh, Kathryn became fast friends with a tall, willowy supervisor at the telephone company, Maggie Hartner, who would later play a large role in her life. Miss Hartner, who was living with her mother, was a member of Munyon's church. She continued to correspond with Kathryn after she returned to the West Coast and later became her secretary and closest friend.

The other instance took place in Portland, Oregon, shortly after Kathryn left Pittsburgh. The guilt of her marriage was weighing heavily upon her. On several occasions, when she was quizzed by newspaper reporters, she flatly denied she was married—saying it was a rumor emanating from old enemies in Denver. Her sister, Myrtle, had told her pastor in Portland, Oregon, of Kathryn's ministry. However, she, too, failed to mention that Kathryn was married to a divorced man. The pastor was impressed with Kathryn and after she paid a visit to Portland and preached in his large church, he invited her back for a series of meetings. Then, on Saturday before she was to open the series on Sunday morning, the pastor received an urgent telephone call from one of the leaders in his church.

"Did you know the woman evangelist you have invited to preach for us is married to a divorced man?"

The pastor was shocked. "Not only that," the informant continued, "the man left his wife and two small children in order to marry her. It destroyed her ministry in Denver and has caused problems everywhere she has gone."

That afternoon the pastor made a difficult phone call. Contacting Kathryn who had already arrived in Portland, he said, "Had I known the truth to begin with . . . now I have no choice but to cancel the meetings. It would destroy my ministry as well."

It hurt. Deeply. Kathryn got in her car and drove through the suburbs of the Oregon city, weeping. She was gone for almost six hours, driving and crying. Was this to be her lot for the rest of her life? Hadn't God called her to preach? How could she fulfill His mission if the rumors kept following her across the nation, causing her to be locked out of the churches? Over and over that dark evening she kept asking herself John Milton's searching question: "Doth God exact day labor, light denied?" Yet she knew, in her heart, that Milton's answer did not fit her situation. For to "stand and wait" would not rectify her situation. It would take more radical action than that. The burden of the guilt was becoming more than she could bear.

No one seems to know exactly when the separation took place. In a 1952 interview with the *Denver Post* she said, "He charged—correctly—that I refused to live with him. And I haven't seen him in eight years."

That would put the separation in 1944—which is probably accurate. This means they lived together for the better part of six years. She did tell me, in one of those rare times when she was willing to indulge in nostalgia, "I had to make a choice. Would I serve the man I loved, or the God I loved. I knew I could not serve God and live with Mister. [She called him "Mister" from the very first time she met him.] No one will ever know the pain of dying like I know it, for I loved him more than I loved life itself. And for a time, I loved him even more than God. I finally told him I had to leave. God had never released me from that original call. Not only did I live with him, I had to live with my conscience, and the conviction of the Holy Spirit was almost unbearable. I was tired of trying to justify myself. Tired.

"One afternoon," she continued, the rims of her eyes brimming with tears as she talked, "I left the apartment—it was in the outskirts of Los Angeles—and found myself walking down a tree-shaded street. The sun was flickering through the great limbs that stretched out overhead. At the end of the block I saw a street sign. It said simply, 'Dead End.' There was heartache, heartache so great it cannot be put into words. If you think it's easy to go to the cross, it's simply because you've never been there. I've been there. I know. And I had to go alone. I knew nothing about the wonderful filling of the Holy Spirit. I knew nothing of the power of the mighty third person of the Trinity which was available to all. I just knew it was four o'clock on Saturday afternoon and I had come to the place in my life where I was ready to give up everything—even Mister—and die.

"I said it out loud, 'Dear Jesus, I surrender all. I give it all to you. Take my body. Take my heart. All I am is yours. I place it in your wonderful hands.' "

Kathryn had known, for almost six years, that she had been fooling herself—seeking God's blessing without being willing to live under God's precepts. All those times she and Burroughs had stood together behind a pulpit, preaching repentance, yet knowing, deep inside, they were living in unrepentant disobedience. They had been the vessel through which others had drunk of the water of life, but their own mouths had been sealed, and they were unable to quench their thirst from that very water they carried to others. Many had been brought into a new relationship with Jesus Christ. Some had even been healed. For God had promised that "my word shall not return unto me void, but it shall accomplish that which I please, and it shall prosper in the thing whereto I sent it." But with infinite sadness Kathryn realized that she had become like those great stone lions she had seen pictures of in Europe—with the water

89

pouring out of their mouths. They were able to give water to all those who were thirsty, but unable to drink of it themselves—for they were made of stone. Her heart had become like that.

For months, it seemed, every time she opened her Bible her eyes had been drawn to the Book of Proverbs. It was as though this particular book had been placed in the natural opening place, so that almost every time she fell across her bed, weeping, and let her Bible drop open, there were the Proverbs.

"He that hath no rule over his own spirit is like a city that is broken down, and without walls."

"Bread of deceit is sweet to a man; but afterwards his mouth shall be filled with gravel."

"He that covereth his sins shall not prosper: but whoso confesseth and forsaketh them shall have mercy."

And Burroughs. "The just man walketh in his integrity: his children are blessed after him," Proverbs said. Yet his children, now in their teens, had been forced to grow up without their father.

Kathryn knew, from her study of the Word of God and her experience with Him as a loving Father, that God was able to take even an impossible marriage situation, one that was born in sin and rebellion, and turn it into something pure and holy—without dissolving the relationship. She had seen it many times among her friends. She had seen others do exactly what she and Burroughs had done, and had watched as God heard their cry of confession and their plea for forgiveness, and had granted them new hearts along with His allowance for them to remain together. It was because of these examples that Kathryn and Burroughs had forged ahead, hoping that God would treat them in a similar way. But they had made the universal mistake. They had looked at the way God had treated others, taking their cue from these examples rather than seeking God's perfect plan for their lives. Kathryn had forgotten she was a unique person. For unto whom much is given, much is required.

Kathryn had known, by the time she was fourteen, that she was destined to be different. Destined to be about her Father's business. It was a feeling she was never able to shake. How, then, could she continue on in a relationship that was not only displeasing to God, but literally preventing her from achieving all that God had planned for her.

She thought of all those times they had sat together across the breakfast table, the bed in the next room still warm and rumpled, and asked God to bless the food—knowing He could not bless them at the same time. For six years they had played their game. But she could play it no more. She had to choose.

To repent is to turn around. Kathryn Kuhlman did that on that Saturday afternoon on a tree-lined street in California. She died that afternoon. She became a seed willing to fall into the ground and be buried. Blinded by tears, she turned around and started back up the street whence she had come.

Three days later, standing in the train station in Los Angeles, now completely cried out, she took her final look at Mister. He stood quietly. His jet black hair was beginning to gray at the temples. His face, so dark and smooth when she met him, was now creased. Much of her life was behind her and she had nothing to show for it. All she knew was she had a one-way ticket to Franklin, Pennsylvania, where she had been invited to hold a two-week meeting. They stood on the platform, awkwardly holding hands, waiting for the conductor to shout "All aboard." Kathryn stared vacantly at the heavy wheels of the passenger car and remembered that day in Concordia when she and Myrtle had boarded the train for Kansas City. Only this time she did not have a loving sister who was sitting beside her. This time she was alone.

"After Franklin, where?" Burroughs said nervously, realizing he was interrupting a reverie in which he was no longer a part.

"I don't know," Kathryn replied, never lifting her eyes from the steel wheels on the tracks. "I just know I must go. I must follow Him."

Burroughs squeezed her hand. Gently. He knew, too. He knew they had been fooling themselves all along. He knew also that Kathryn was not his. She never had been. Now they had come to the moment of truth when they would once again set each other free. Kathryn's decision was made. It had been made three days before when she came home and told him she was leaving. But his? Could he return to Austin and start over with his family? Inwardly he shook his head. If it meant that he was destined to wander the land like some phantom ship, never touching shore, slipping into fog banks to escape detection, if that was his lot then he would steel his soul and walk into it. For despite everything else Burroughs Waltrip was, he was a man of God—and he recognized the hand of his Lord on the woman that days before had been his wife. He, too, knew she was different. He had known it all along. But he had hoped that somehow he could make his own rules and still win the game. Now the two of them, standing side by side on the dirty wooden platform of the Los Angeles railroad station, knew that they were not their own. They belonged to Another.

Now He was requiring of her that which she had promised Him on that tree-lined street. The train whistle sounded down the tracks. The young couple standing down the platform from them kissed and called caresses to one another as the man climbed up the gray-green steps of the car.

"All aboard!" The conductor was walking briskly down the platform toward the door. The white-coated porters were picking up the little stools beneath the train steps and swinging into the cars.

"If you get on that train, you'll never see me again," Burroughs said softly. "I will never interfere with your life or your ministry."

What Kathryn said in reply is known only to God, for no one knows to this day what became of Burroughs A. Waltrip, Sr. When she took the porter's hand and climbed aboard the eastbound train, Burroughs Waltrip disappeared. He kept his promise. To the letter.

To my knowledge she never heard from him again. Except once. I was in her office in the Carlton House in 1970, the week after Valentine's Day. She pulled the door shut and went over to her desk. Very slowly she pulled a Valentine card from the top drawer, holding it like sacred parchment. Leaning across the desk, she handed it to me.

"Look at this, will you?" she whispered hoarsely.

It was a simple "Be My Valentine" card with two red hearts fastened together with a golden arrow. Inside were two words, written in ink: "Love, Mister."

I looked up at Kathryn. Her face was raised toward the ceiling, her eyes tightly shut, tears squeezing from the lids and making tiny rivulets down her aging cheeks. "No one!" she whispered. "No one will ever know what this ministry has cost me. Only Jesus."

Had I stayed in that office I would have had to remove my shoes, so great was the power of God. I slipped out, through the outer office, into the hallway and down the elevator to the lobby. If that's what the cross meant for Kathryn

Kuhlman, what would it mean for me? I was not ready, at that time, to face that question in my own life.

But even though the California decision had been made, the path was anything but smooth. Traveling alone, Kathryn went first to Franklin and then set out trying to start over again. Ohio. Illinois. Indiana. Down into West Virginia. Almost every place she went she met the same resistance. They knew of Waltrip—and of the scandal in Denver. Once a person has shot an albatross, it seems, and has to wear the carcass around his neck, the stench remains for a long time. There is, as Thoreau once wrote, no odor so bad as that which arises from goodness tainted. She turned south. Virginia. The Carolinas. And finally, in late 1945, she wound up in Columbus, Georgia. Each place it had been the same. Her technique hadn't changed, only now as a middle-aged woman it was a little more difficult. She rented a hall, took out ads in the newspapers, purchased time on the radio and announced her meetings. The people in Columbus responded. By the third night the city auditorium was full. Then someone smelled the albatross. There was a phone call to Denver, and another to Mason City, Iowa. Someone called the newspaper and a reporter came out to interview the battle-weary evangelist. Kathryn balked, which was the worst thing she could do with the press. The newspaper, smelling a story, went to work. Two days later, after the story had been aired before the entire community, Kathryn was on a bus, heading back north. The hospitality in the south was not very warm that fall.

Yet her wilderness days were almost over. And although there were still battles to be fought, she was on the verge of a breakthrough that even Kathryn, with all her dreams and visions, never imagined possible. Like Moses in exile, tending sheep and goats, with all the pride and ego burned from his life by the heat of the desert, Kathryn's bush was about to burn. The time was just ahead when she would hear God from the flames of a miracle, giving her fresh instructions for the next phase of her life.

It happened back in Franklin, Pennsylvania, a town of about 10,000 in the northwest sector of the state between Pittsburgh and Erie. It was a blustery cold February day, with snow flurries whipping up the city streets, when Kathryn stepped off the bus and made her way to the phone booth to call Matthew J. Maloney. Maloney, who owned the Gospel Tabernacle, had been impressed with Kathryn when she visited Franklin before for the two-week meeting in the famous building where evangelist Billy Sunday had gained his notoriety. He headed up a board of trustees at the tabernacle and had invited her to return to Franklin for another series of meetings in the low, rambling building located at Otter and Twelfth near the center of town.

Exactly why Kathryn returned to Franklin remains another of the many mysteries surrounding her life. Perhaps it was because it was one of the few places she had preached and no one brought up the question of her marriage. Perhaps it was because the town was so remote that people were not likely to find out about it either. Or, perhaps God spoke to her directly. No one seems to know. But in early 1946, almost two years after she turned her back on Waltrip, she stepped off the bus in Franklin to begin the next chapter in her life.

Things went well. The old tabernacle seated 1,500, and it was filled from the very beginning. Encouraged by her reception, Kathryn started to branch out. Radio was the natural medium.

In the spring of 1946, wearing a smart black dress, long kid-leather gloves, and a Hattie Carnegie hat, Kathryn walked into the office of radio station WKRZ in nearby Oil

City. She told the receptionist she wanted to see the program director, Frank Shaffer. After being ushered into his tiny office, she told him, firmly but politely, she had come to buy air time. According to Clarence Pelaghi of the Oil City *Derrick*, Shaffer had an aggravating habit which tested the patience of his guests. Slowly and painstakingly he would take out his pipe, fill it, pack it, and slowly suck on it while he tried to get it lighted. While he was going through this routine he would remain totally silent, ignoring the person who had come into his office as he concentrated all his attention on his pipe.

Kathryn, standing across the desk from the nonchalant radio man, endured the ordeal for a moment and then spoke out, "Young man, do you want to sell time or don't you? I don't have time to waste. And don't do that test on me; it won't do you any good."

Shaffer was caught by surprise. He wasn't used to people talking to him like that, especially women, and most especially women wanting to buy time for a religious broadcast. Most of them were so intimidated they would either leave or agree to take time at some God-forsaken hour of the day. Shaffer lowered his pipe into the ash tray, pulled out his rate sheet, and got to work.

The staff at the radio station watched this exchange with some delight. Although they could not hear the conversation, since it was taking place in a control booth, they could see through the glass windows and knew immediately that Shaffer had met his match.

Kathryn asked a few relevant questions such as the power of the station, the geographic area it covered, and the number of listeners. She insisted on a certain time every morning. And she got it. She left without ever inquiring about the cost. If God had told her to broadcast and had given her the time, she'd let Him worry about the cost. It was a procedure she would follow the rest of her life.

Kathryn began making daily trips from Franklin to Oil City, eight miles away. The radio station was located on the third floor of the Veach Building. Before going on the air each day, Kathryn would chat with Ruth Lytle, the secretary and bookkeeper, and other members of the staff. But she was careful to keep her past hidden.

Kathryn was especially fond of her announcer, Ted Finnecy of Rouseville. She liked the way he handled her introductions, calling her "that young woman you have all been waiting for." She insisted that the radio station keep recordings of Finnecy's introductions on hand, and whenever he was unable to be present they would use the recording, rather than a substitute announcer. Finnecy, who was a Catholic, would always bless himself with the sign of the cross when he gave the introductions. But his seriousness stopped there, and often during the broadcast he would stand on the other side of the glass doing Kathryn Kuhlman imitations, playfully mocking her gestures and facial expressions, trying to make her laugh. Kathryn enjoyed it, and the other staff members would sometimes double up in laughter outside the soundproof studio as they watched Finnecy and Kathryn making faces at each other through the glass.

Kathryn's dramatics did cause some problems at the station, however. The only microphone available was a table mike. At times Kathryn would get excited during her presentation and would move so close to the mike it seemed she was biting it. This drove the engineer into frenzied action trying to level the volume. The problem was solved by moving the mike to the opposite edge of the table and screwing it down. Later the station got a mike with a boom, just to take care of the dramatic preacher from Franklin.

By midsummer, Kathryn's fame had spread and she

added a Pittsburgh radio station—with the broadcasts emanating from Oil City. The added fame caused problems, however. A number of people wanted to get close to her, and unable to do so at the tabernacle meetings, would come to the radio station instead. They would sit in the lobby and watch Kathryn through the large glass window. Soon the lobby was so packed with people the station personnel could not do their work. When some of the people began to react emotionally, even hysterically, crying out to God in confession or weeping as they fell under conviction, the radio station had to bar all visitors from the studio.

The other problem centered around the abundance of mail. The letters would come to the radio station by the bagful. Finnecy, who enjoyed kidding "Katie" about her good looking legs, telling her she should be on stage rather than in the pulpit, would often sort through the mail— much of which contained money. Finding an envelope with coins which jingled inside, he would throw it aside saying to Kathryn, "You don't want this small stuff, do you?"

When Kathryn happened to announce over the air that she had just ripped her last pair of nylon stockings (nylon was very scarce following the war), the station was inundated with packages of nylon stockings from grateful listeners. The same thing happened when she once let it slip that she had lost her umbrella. The staff at the radio station was glad when she finally made her move to Pittsburgh so they could get back to normal. But all of them knew they would never have another program as effective as Kathryn Kuhlman's.

However, before she was to move south to the big city, there were still hurdles to jump in Franklin, and miracles to experience. On several occasions Kathryn had preached on "healing." And things happened. She always closed her services with altar calls, inviting people to be "born again."

Invariably the altar around the front of the building would be filled with kneeling persons, crowding onto the platform and down the aisles. The response was just as great when she had a "healing line." Taking her cue from the popular "faith healers" who were moving about the country, she would ask all the sick to come forward, after which she would lay her hands on their heads and ask God to heal them. The results were not spectacular, but there were results. A few people were healed. And no one was more surprised, or perplexed, than Kathryn herself. She was determined to find out more about this physical manifestation of God.

"I knew in my own heart that there was healing," she said. "I had seen the evidence from those who had been healed. It was real, and it was genuine, but what was the key?"

Was it faith? If it was, what was faith? Was it something that one could manufacture, or work up in oneself? Was it something that could be obtained through one's own goodness or moral status? Was it something that could be procured in exchange for serving the Lord, or through benevolence? And in whom did the faith reside? The person who was sick? The one who was conducting the healing meeting? In the crowd of people surrounding them? Or in a combination of all three? Surely it was not left to the capriciousness of chance. If Jesus healed all those who were brought to Him as the Bible said, and if He commanded His disciples to do even greater things than He did, then why weren't there more healings?

When Kathryn saw an advertisement that a noted "healing evangelist" was scheduled to hold a tent meeting in Erie, she decided to go. Although Kathryn had strong reservations about the sensationalism that generally characterized such meetings, she knew she would never be satisfied until she attended a service. Perhaps, just perhaps, they had found the secret to releasing God's healing power to the sick and dying.

It was a difficult experience for Kathryn. One of the most difficult of her life. She drove to Erie alone, determined to remain incognito. The giant tent was located on the south edge of the city. The signs, as she entered the parking lot read. "MIRACLE REVIVAL. SIGHT FOR THE BLIND! HEARING FOR THE DEAF! POWER TO GET WEALTH!"

Taking a seat on the back row, she waited. When the evangelist came on the platform, he came on as though shot from a cannon. At one point he got up and walked on the back of the long bench behind the pulpit. At another time he leap-frogged over the pulpit itself. The audience was worked into a frenzy, screaming, wailing, almost beyond control. Kathryn later described it as a "nightmare come to life."

During the service, he auctioned off pieces of his old revival tent, to the highest bidders, which he promised would bring health and prosperity to those who wore them on their bodies or slept with them under their pillows. As the meeting grew more intense the preacher began to scream, saying he felt a "spell coming on," which he indicated was a "Holy Ghost unction" enabling him to lay hands on the sick and they would be healed. People in the congregation crowded into the aisles, swaying back and forth. When the meeting was at the peak of frenzy, a healing line was formed. This line belied the seemingly spontaneous nature of the meeting, for each person who wanted to be in it had previously been assigned a number at the gate. Thus, Kathryn noted with dismay, people had to wait, sometimes for days, to have their number come up. After all, the evangelist could only pray individually with so many people in one evening.

The people lined up by the scores. One by one the evangelist went down the line, checking cards and slapping people on the head and commanding them to "BE HEALED!" Many of them keeled to the floor. Others screamed and shook. But Kathryn could not help but notice that the more seriously ill patients were steered out of the healing line to an "invalids' tent" away from the prying eyes of the public. While some of the people did seem to be genuinely helped—perhaps even healed—the vast majority of those who had broken their crutches had to be helped out of the tent by sympathetic loved ones—still unable to walk. To those the preacher proclaimed that their faith was not strong enough yet; that they should come back the next night for more of the same.

In talking about that night, Kathryn said, "I began to weep. I could not stop. Those looks of despair and disappointment on the faces I had seen, when told that only their lack of faith was keeping them from God, were to haunt me for weeks. Was this the God of all mercy and great compassion? I left the tent, and with hot tears streaming down my face I looked up and cried, "They have taken away my Lord and I know not where they have laid Him."

Years later Kathryn wrote, "I could not see the hand of God in man's superfluity of zeal, and I saw the harm that was being done in attributing everything to 'lack of faith' on the part of the individual who had not received his healing. Inside myself, I was crushed: my heart told me that God could do anything; my mind told me that through ignorance and lack of spiritual knowledge, there were those who were bringing a reproach on something that was sacred and wonderful and accessible to all. No preacher had to tell me that the power of God was real . . . I was assured of these facts as I read the Word of God. The Word was there, the promise had been given: there was surely no changing of

God's mind, and certainly no cancelling of the promises. I think that no one has ever wanted truth more avidly than I—nor sought it harder."

Yet she had not found the truth she sought for in the healing tent. It had to be found elsewhere.

Fortunately Kathryn had learned a valuable lesson in her earlier days. She had learned that the only way to find truth was to come in sincerity and let the Lord give her the revelations from His Word. So, once again she turned to the Bible for her answers.

"When Jesus died on the cross and cried out, 'It is finished!' He not only died for our sins, but for our diseases too," she told me. "It took several months for me to realize that, for I had not been taught there was healing for the body in the redemption of Christ. But then I read in Isaiah where 'He was wounded for our transgressions, bruised for our iniquities, and by His stripes we are healed.' I had no choice but to accept that Jesus did not die just to open the way to heaven, but to provide healing as well.

"I knew that if I lived and died and never saw a single healing miracle like the apostles experienced in the Book of Acts, it would not change God's Word," Kathryn said. "God said it. He made provision for it in our redemption at Calvary. And whether I ever saw it with my earthly eyes did not change the fact that it was so."

Fortified with this new kind of faith—not a faith in healings, but a faith in God—Kathryn began preaching with a new kind of zeal, centering in on the doctrine of the Holy Spirit. Somehow, she realized, it was the Holy Spirit who was carrying on the work of Jesus.

On Sunday, April 27, 1947, Kathryn began her series on the Holy Spirit. She had tapped into a truth from which she would draw for the rest of her life.

"I see in my mind the three persons of the Trinity sitting down at a great conference table before the formation of the earth ever took place. God, the Holy Father, gave the others the news that even though He would create men to have fellowship with Him, that man would sin—and break that fellowship. The only way fellowship could be restored would be for someone to pay the price for that sin. For if another did not pay it, then man himself would have to continue to pay the price in unhappiness, disease, death, and eventual hell.

"After the Holy Father finished sharing, His Son Jesus spoke up and said, 'I'll go. I'll take the form of a man and go down to earth to pay that price. I'll be willing to die on a cross so that man can be restored to perfect fellowship with us.'

"Then Jesus turned to the Holy Spirit and said, 'But I cannot go unless you go with me—for you are the one with the power.'

"The Holy Spirit responded and said, 'You go ahead. And when the time is right, I shall join you on earth.'

"So Jesus came to earth, born in a manger, and grew to manhood. But, even though He was the very Son of God, He was powerless. Then came that magnificent moment at the River Jordan when Jesus, coming up out of the baptismal waters, looked up and saw the Holy Spirit descending upon Him in the form of a dove. It must have been one of the greatest thrills Jesus received as He walked in the flesh on this earth. And I can almost hear the Holy Spirit whisper in His ear, 'I'm here now. We're running right on schedule. Now things will really happen.'

"And they did happen. Filled with the Spirit, He was suddenly empowered to heal the sick, cause the blind to see, even raise the dead. It was the time for miracles. For three years they continued, and then, at the end, the Bible says He 'gave up the ghost,' and the Spirit returned to the Holy Father.

"After Jesus was in the grave for three days, that mighty third person of the Trinity, the Holy Spirit, returned. Jesus came out of the grave in a glorified body. He performed no more miracles during the short time He was here, but He gave His followers a great promise—the greatest promise of all the Bible. He said that same Holy Spirit who had lived in Him would return to live in all those who opened their lives to His power. The same things that He, Jesus, had done, His followers would do also. In fact, even greater things would be done because now the Holy Spirit would not be limited to one body—but would be free to enter all those everywhere who would receive Him."

Kathryn paused. She had never preached like that before. It was a new revelation. A new truth. Yet it came straight from the Bible. She was shaking as she continued, "The last words He said before He went away were, 'And ye shall receive power after that the Holy Ghost is come upon you.' God the Father had given Him the gift. Now He was passing it on to the church. Every church should be experiencing the miracles of Pentecost. Every church should be seeing the healings of the Book of Acts. The gift is for all of us."

Dumbfounded over what she had said, Kathryn left as soon as the service was over, leaving the ministry at the altar to a group of men who came forward to help. She was up all that night, in her little attic room on the third floor of the Business Women's Club where she lived, pacing the floor, praying, and reading her Bible. It was as though she had stood with Simon Peter when Jesus had said to him, "Flesh and blood hath not revealed this unto thee, but my Father which is in heaven."

The following night she was back at the tabernacle. The

room was packed with expectant faces. Every seat on the long wooden pews was taken. The huge open-beam rafters resounded with joyful singing as she entered the room. The people had come expecting. Expecting a miracle.

Just as Kathryn stood to preach there was a disturbance in the audience. A woman was coming forward. She had her hand up. "Kathryn, may I say something?"

Kathryn looked at her. Plump. About fifty. Dressed in a gray tweed suit and wearing a black straw hat adorned with a small white flower. She carried her handbag in her right hand, but was waving her left hand in the air. "Come on, honey, of course you can say something."

The woman came to the front of the building and stood facing Kathryn, separated only by the long pipe from which the altar curtain was hanging by little brass rings. She talked softly.

"Last night, while you were preaching, I was healed."

Twice Kathryn tried to say something, but nothing came out. She finally stammered, "Where were you?"

"Just sitting here in the audience," she smiled back.

"How do you know you were healed?" If it was of God it could stand examination.

"I had a tumor," the woman said shyly. "It had been diagnosed by my doctor. While you were preaching, something happened in my body. I was so sure I was healed that I went back to my doctor this morning and had it verified. The tumor is no longer there."

There had been no numbered healing line. No laying on of hands. No prayer. The miracle simply occurred while Kathryn was preaching about the power of the Holy Spirit.

It took a full week for Kathryn to grasp what had happened. Then, on the following Sunday, another miracle occurred, this one even more spectacular. In 1925, George Orr, a World War I veteran—and a Methodist by denomination—had been injured in an industrial accident.

A splash of molten metal so badly scarred the cornea of his right eye that he was declared legally blind. His ophthalmologist, Dr. C. E. Imbrie of Butler, Pennsylvania, said the eye was permanently impaired and the resulting scar on the cornea was too deep for surgery. If they operated, they would have to remove the eyeball.

In March 1947, Orr and his wife attended one of the tabernacle services in Franklin. Over the next two months they returned several times to hear Kathryn preach. On May 4 they drove up from Butler for the morning service, riding with a young couple who was also interested in Kathryn's ministry. Kathryn was still preaching about the power of the Holy Spirit and during the service declared, flatly, on the basis of the woman who had been healed earlier in the week, that physical healing was just as possible today as spiritual salvation.

Something happened inside George Orr. He prayed, "God, please heal my eye."

The next moment he felt a strange tingling sensation in his eye, as though something were passing through it. Then it began to steam tears. In fact, Orr was embarrassed since he couldn't control the watering. His eye overflowed and tears splashed onto his jacket.

After the service, afraid to tell anybody what had happened to him, he staggered out of the building to his car. On the way home he kept blinking the eye as it continued to stream tears. Then, just as they went over a hill, he said the sun seemed to suddenly burst forth in all its glory. Cupping his hand over his good eye, he shouted, "I can see! I can see everything!"

George Orr, who had long been drawing workman's compensation because of his blindness, returned to the service in Franklin on Tuesday night to testify.

Kathryn's bush had begun to burn.

CHAPTER VII

PITTSBURGH

It was obvious that Kathryn was going to have problems with M. J. Maloney, who owned the Gospel Tabernacle and was in charge of finances. Maloney wasn't just conducting a ministry, he was running a business. Operating the Gospel Tabernacle was a good business, especially if the owner got a cut of all the offerings.

No one in the history of the tabernacle, not even Billy Sunday, had drawn the crowds that Kathryn was drawing once the miracles began to take place. Of course the offerings increased as the crowd grew in size. Besides this, Kathryn's mail had more than tripled—thanks to the radio ministry and mailings. Susan Miller, a young secretary, had volunteered to help Kathryn with the mailings. This consisted of "prayer letters," pictures of Kathryn, and a copy of a little booklet she had put together called "The Lord's Healing Touch." Maloney insisted his contract called for him to get a certain percentage of all the revenue—including that which came through the radio ministry and the mailouts. Kathryn balked. Somehow it just didn't seem right. Maloney threatened to sue. The stage was set for a showdown.

"He's no different from Simon the magician," Kathryn said when told Maloney was threatening to sue her for more money. "As long as our offerings were normal he was satisfied. Now that they have increased, he wants a bigger piece of the action. Let him sue. We'll see whose side God is on."

But Maloney was too wise to sue in the beginning. He simply took down the signs advertising the Kathryn Kuhlman services and padlocked the doors of the tabernacle. Despite the fact he had given Kathryn a contract granting her exclusive use of the building, he was still the owner. When the word got back to Kathryn that her signs were down and some of Maloney's men were standing guard at the doors to keep her people out, she was furious.

"We have a contract," she said through tight lips to a small group of men who had brought her the news. "We are legally entitled to use that building. We're going to have a service tonight even if we have to break the doors down."

Northwest Pennsylvania is coal, oil, and iron country. The men who lived and worked there were the original blue-collar workers—Polish and Irish. Fighting was as natural as eating. In fact, a fist fight was never considered immoral—unless you backed down. When Kathryn's followers sensed that someone was trying to take advantage of their "preacher lady," their blood began to boil.

"Just give us the word, Miss Kuhlman," a burly, muscular wildcatter said. "We'll get that building open for you."

Kathryn was a master at handling men. She could read their moods. She knew when to be gruff, when to be the sharp business person, when to act soft and feminine, and when to play helpless.

"Listen, fellows," she said, "a woman has certain limitations. Now if I were a man. . . ."

"Say no more, little lady." The speaker was a man in his early sixties with a massive stomach and arms to match. "You just come on down at the regular time. That building will be open."

Kathryn stayed in her apartment until time to leave for the meeting—chuckling and praying. She only wished she could be there to see what was going on. What did go on was a bloody fist fight, with the Kuhlman gang clear winners over the Maloney gang. In fact, the Maloney gang fled after several of them were knocked to the floor during the scuffle. The Kuhlman gang then took crowbars and, while the great crowd of people who had gathered to watch the scuffle (and attend the meeting) cheered and waved handkerchiefs, broke the locks off the doors. They had a capacity crowd that evening, with a proud bunch of ushers who patrolled the building throughout the service—not only looking for miracles, but keeping a sharp eye to make sure the enemy had not infiltrated the camp.

Kathryn then had her men buy new padlocks, lock the doors, and take turns patrolling the building to keep Maloney's men out.

Maloney retaliated through the courts. On June 4, 1948, he posted a $500.00 bond and Judge Lee McCracken signed a preliminary injunction restraining Kathryn and her people from use of the Franklin Gospel Tabernacle. On Saturday, June 5, the Franklin *News-Herald* headlines read: "COURT ACTION TAKEN AGAINST MISS KUHLMAN. INJUNCTION TO BAR EVANGELIST FROM TABERNACLE GRANTED."

Kathryn was back on the front page.

The writ ordered the defendants, i.e., Kathryn Kuhlman et al. (named among the co-defendants was George Orr of Butler), to give the keys of the new locks to M. J. Maloney and the trustees for the tabernacle. They were also ordered to no longer hold services in the building until the court could study the case, and to call off their "agents who have with force, menaces, and threats occupied by patrolling the inside of said tabernacle."

"We'll obey the law," Kathryn said. "We used the building as long as we had a legal right to it. Now, until the courts say we can use it again, we'll stay out. But we're going to fight this thing."

And fight it she did. Kathryn retained two prominent Pittsburgh lawyers, J. R. Heyison and Jason Richardson, as her defense attorneys. Although she had once said she would not sue to get her rights, in this one case she did. Her lawyers filed a counter suit demanding that Maloney give an accounting of all gifts, tithes, and offerings made to the tabernacle and defendants from February 5, 1940, up until the present. Their case was to prove that he had not taken action against Miss Kuhlman until her offerings increased. The newspapers continued to carry the story on the front pages.

Meanwhile, more than two thousand of Kathryn's people gathered in the nearby Sugar Creek Auditorium and pledged in excess of ten thousand dollars toward the construction of a new tabernacle in Franklin. The figure did not include the $2,500 which had already been donated for a new Hammond electric organ. A new board of trustees was elected.

Maloney took out a full page ad in the *News-Herald* telling his side of the story. He stated that his records showed that the tabernacle had paid Miss Kuhlman $60,680.32 in "salary" over the two-year time she had ministered. The rest of the offerings, he contended, belonged to him.

In the ensuing court trial, which was frequently interrupted by noisy demonstrations, Attorney Richardson asked Mr. Maloney if it was true that he (Maloney) had asked Miss Kuhlman for twenty-five percent of the total offerings and that when she refused, he had locked the doors. Maloney swore loudly and said "No." The audience loved it.

Maloney then bought more newspaper space, stating the real reason he had locked the doors was that Kathryn—having made herself rich off the poor people of Franklin—was going to move to Pittsburgh. He had it on firm authority, he stated, that she was under contract to conduct a series of meetings in the Carnegie Auditorium in Pittsburgh's Northside.

Kathryn countered by issuing a press release. Since her radio broadcasts in the Pittsburgh area had brought such a great response, she felt obligated to conduct a series of meetings in that area from July 4 to August 1, she said. That did not mean she was leaving Franklin. In fact, she said, she was completing plans for the new tabernacle. She would continue to conduct services in Franklin even though her primary ministry during July would be in Pittsburgh. She went ahead to say that while she had been in Franklin she had received at least 150 invitations to establish herself elsewhere, but had instead bought a large dwelling formerly owned by Attorney John L. Nesbit at Liberty and Tenth Streets.

The battle continued to rage through the month of June. Maloney scheduled a meeting in the old tabernacle, but only seventy-five people attended. Kathryn's people, on the other hand, purchased the old roller skating rink at Sugar

Creek, three miles outside of Franklin. It was a well-built structure with a strong hardwood floor. The biggest problem was the roof. The rafters were old and showed signs of rot. But the men decided to leave that until later, and got to work turning the old building into a tabernacle. Only, since there was already a tabernacle in Franklin, they called the new meeting place "Faith Temple." The seating capacity was almost twice the size of the old tabernacle and from the first service it was packed—standing room only.

A week later there was a knock at the door of her third floor apartment. The sheriff, dressed in street clothes, was waiting in the hall. He introduced himself and asked to come in.

"This morning my office received papers which I am required to serve you. It is a divorce suit filed in Arizona by Burroughs A. Waltrip, Sr. You are named as the defendant."

Kathryn stood silently, her head bowed. The ghost of the past had reappeared just when it looked like everything was working out in her favor.

The sheriff reached over and touched her arm. "My office ordinarily releases the names of all divorce suits to the local newspaper. But I have been attending your services and am convinced God sent you to this crime-riddled county for a special purpose. That is the reason I am delivering these papers personally. There is no need for anyone but the two of us to know what has happened. God bless you in your ministry among us. I am at your service."

He turned to leave but Kathryn reached out and caught his arm. For just a minute their eyes met. He smiled, and she nodded. "I will be grateful to you for the rest of my life," she said softly.

He was gone. It would be almost seven years before a newspaper in Akron, Ohio, learned of her divorce and ran it as a front page story. But by that time Kathryn's ministry would be so firmly established that no slander from the past could hurt it. She knew, however, that nothing short of a miracle could have saved her if, in 1948, the story hit the papers in Franklin. Until he died, twenty-three years later, Kathryn sent flowers to the sheriff on his birthday. She never forgot.

When Kathryn moved to Franklin, she took up residence in the third floor attic room of the Business Women's Club. It wasn't long before she met two women who were to have a profound influence on her life. One was Jesse Vincent, the other was Eve Conley. Both were widows. Jesse worked at the bank in Franklin and Eve, whose pharmacist husband had recently died, lived with her. Neither were Christians, although both were fascinated by Kathryn's ministry and personality, attending as many of the services at the tabernacle as possible.

Eve was a terrific cook, and the two of them decided to invite Kathryn to their home for Thanksgiving, 1946. After the meal, Kathryn said, "You think you invited me here, but you didn't. I came on a much higher invitation than from two wonderful women. God sent me here to minister to you, and I am not going to be satisfied until the two of you are on your knees, confessing your sin and asking to be born again."

"Tell us about your Jesus," Eve said seriously.

For the next twenty minutes Kathryn took them through the Bible, pointing out the passages that proved Jesus Christ was the promised Messiah, the Son of God. "There is

113

no other way to God," Kathryn said softly, "except through Christ. Are you now ready to give your lives to Him?"

They both nodded, and slipped from their chairs to the carpeted floor. Kathryn joined them on her knees and was a witness as they entered the kingdom of God.

Shortly after that Kathryn moved in with them. When Jesse Vincent died, she left her estate to Kathryn—much of it in jewelry. It was the beginning of a large collection of precious jewels and antiques which years later would become the basis for another newspaper headline. Many people gave Kathryn large gifts, either in person or in their wills. One grateful woman summed up the feelings of thousands. "I would have paid it all out in doctor and hospital bills. Therefore, since I was healed in Kathryn's meetings, why shouldn't I give it to her?" It was a valid question, but it did not alleviate the many accusations made against Miss Kuhlman across the years for being "wealthy." Eve Conley continued on with Kathryn, working as her personal secretary and confidante, assisted by Susan Miller who was still giving part of each day to help with the various mailings.

During this time Kathryn had been corresponding regularly with another woman, Maggie Hartner, whom she had met in Pittsburgh several years before. Since Maggie was working at the telephone company in Pittsburgh, she was able to call long distance at a reduced charge. She called almost nightly, urging Kathryn to return to Pittsburgh for another series of meetings. "Everybody I know is listening to you over WPGH," Maggie said. "All you'd have to do is announce you're going to have a service and the place would be packed."

Kathryn finally conceded. She came down and looked over Carnegie Hall. The custodian, a Mr. Buffington, showed her through the building.

"Look," Kathryn said, "I want a lot of chairs up here on the platform. This place is going to fill up in a hurry."

"Aw, Miss Kuhlman, we'll never fill this auditorium," the custodian said. "Even them opera stars can't fill it."

"Well, I want the platform full of chairs," she said, turning to walk out the door. She whirled back and looked straight at the custodian. "Aw, God love you! You're concerned about me, aren't you? Well, just you wait and see. We're going to have the biggest and best service this building has ever seen."

She was right. The first service was the afternoon of July 4, 1948. The building was so packed she had to have another service that same evening. It too was jammed to capacity.

From the very beginning there were miracles. The Pittsburgh paper ran a full page feature story, complete with an artist's sketch of what Kathryn now called her miracle services. The reporter said:

> Miss Kuhlman comes from no recognized church; pretends only to be an emissary of the doctrine of faith in God. Yet, night after night, she has jammed the North Side Carnegie Music Hall to overflowing. Hundreds have crowded the outer corridors to hear a few fragments of her words, additional hundreds have been turned away. . . . She's the combination of the orator and the actress; the songstress and the evangelist. . . . When hymns are sung, her voice rises high and clear above the crowd. . . .

Ever since her association with Helen Gulliford, music had played a big part in Kathryn's ministry. Soon after she came to Franklin she made contact with Jimmy Miller, who had played the piano for Jack Munyon in Pittsburgh. Miller

115

eagerly accepted Kathryn's offer to be her pianist. Later Munyon's organist, Charles Beebee, also joined her. Both were at the instruments when she came to Pittsburgh for the first time in 1948—and both remained with her until she died.

Kathryn expanded her radio ministry after she returned to Franklin, beaming her half-hour programs into Ohio, West Virginia, Maryland, and the Washington, D.C. area. The services at Faith Temple continued on a regular basis, but because of the expanded ministry, Kathryn began holding services in many of the nearby cities: New Castle, Butler, Beaver Falls, and at Stambaugh Auditorium in Youngstown, Ohio. But more and more Kathryn was attracted to Pittsburgh, with regular services in Carnegie Hall.

Miracles continued to happen. Paul R. Gunn, a young Pittsburgh policeman, had been taken to a local hospital on September 28, 1949 with viral pneumonia. A lung ailment was diagnosed as cancer following bronchoscope, sputum, and X-ray examinations. In October he started attending the services at Carnegie Hall. During the fourth service he said he felt like a match had been stuck to a piece of paper inside his chest. In December a company doctor approved him for work and he started back on his job in January, 1950.

James W. McCutcheon was another miracle. Three years before he was standing on a timber which was struck by a bulldozer in Lorain, Ohio. He was thrown to the ground and the ball joint of his hip was crushed. Five operations failed. The last one, a bone graft, was equally unsuccessful because of decalcification. The doctors recommended still another operation. McCutcheon was on crutches when he entered Carnegie Hall on November 5, 1949. His daughter, sitting next to him with her hand on his knee, later said she felt something like electricity enter her arm from his leg while Miss Kuhlman was preaching. He arose from his seat and walked without the support of his crutches. Instantly healed.

The Pittsburgh paper reported many of these miracles. And although they also had a great deal to say about those who were not healed, in most cases they accurately reported the miracles as well.

"Each night a few rise above the physical world they've known," a reporter for the Pittsburgh *Press* wrote. "On Friday—the healing night—there was a young woman from Canton, Ohio, who came to pray for relief of a spine separation. She walked to the stage upright and knelt by the organ to pray in thanksgiving.

"A little boy about five, said to have been crippled since birth, tottered down the aisle on his own legs and held his arms on high for Miss Kuhlman to see.

"A woman who said she had been in a wheelchair twelve years walked to the stage and wept openly before the microphone. Her husband stood beside her, his face streaming with tears. . . .

"For everyone who has proclaimed a cure, a score more have faded off into the darkness, as miserable and heartsick as when they came. But most will be back."

One who kept coming back—for five months before he was healed—was Charles C. Loesch. Injured in an accident fourteen years before, his sacroiliac had become calcified, causing him to walk in a stooped position, bent forward from the hip in a grotesque manner. One leg was three and three-quarters inches shorter than the other, so he had to wear a special shoe with a built-up sole. He had been in constant pain ever since the accident.

Mr. Loesch's children encouraged him to attend the miracle services both in Pittsburgh and Franklin. Nothing happened to his body, but coming home from the first service he poured out all his liquor and threw away his cigars—never to return to them again. However, he did keep returning to the miracle services. The more he came, the more he forgot about his own problems, focusing his prayer on those in worse shape than he.

Then one afternoon at Faith Temple, sitting with a large group of men on the stage while Miss Kuhlman preached, his leg began to vibrate. The vibration caused his heel to hit against the floor like an air hammer. Miss Kuhlman immediately stopped preaching and turned around.

"What's this?" she inquired loudly.

Embarrassed, Loesch could only bend over and hold on to his wildly vibrating leg, trying to keep it from hitting the floor.

"You're being healed, sir," Miss Kuhlman exclaimed. Then turning to the audience, she said, "The power of God is on that man."

It was indeed the power of God. After the service Loesch discovered that not only had his leg grown out, but his back was loose and limber.

It was the beginning of a twenty-eight year loyalty to Miss Kuhlman in which he would give up everything else to follow her, becoming her maintenance man, chauffeur, and factotum.

During the week Kathryn and Eve Conley were staying at the Pick Roosevelt Hotel in Pittsburgh, traveling back to Franklin for the Sunday services. Maggie Hartner, who was now spending two days a week working for Kathryn (as well as holding down her job at the telephone company), kept the pressure on, begging Kathryn to move to Pittsburgh.

"I can't, Maggie," Kathryn replied. "I just can't. You don't understand. These people took me in, loved me, and accepted me when no one else in the world wanted me. I owe them my life. No, the roof on Faith Temple would have to literally cave in before I'd believe God wanted me to move to Pittsburgh."

The last week of November, western Pennsylvania experienced the biggest snowfall in its history—more than forty inches in a three-day period. A great Thanksgiving service had been planned at Faith Temple. But the traffic was stopped for hundreds of miles. Even if the roads had been open, though, there still would have been no service. The accumulated weight of snow on the roof of the old building was too much for the rotten timbers. On Thanksgiving Day, 1950, the roof of Faith Temple caved in.

Three weeks later, Kathryn bought a house in Fox Chapel, a suburb of Pittsburgh. It was to be her home until she died.

CHAPTER VIII

TENTS AND TEMPLES

Kathryn's penchant for stirring up controversy followed her to Pittsburgh. By the early spring of 1951, her meetings in the Carnegie Hall were being picketed by angry pastors and a few church leaders who claimed she was "stealing sheep" from the local churches.

She countered that she was not stealing sheep, just feeding a flock of starving lambs.

That made the ministers even more determined to deal with their "competition." They complained to the mayor's office that since Kathryn had held meetings in the city-owned auditorium every night for more than six months, she had actually turned their tax-supported property into a church. But Pittsburgh's mayor, David Lawrence (who was later elected governor of the state), turned out to be one of Kathryn's staunchest friends and supporters. A Roman Catholic, he issued instructions that Kathryn was to stay in

Carnegie Auditorium as long as she wanted. She remained for twenty years. But in the meantime the controversy grew more intense.

Redbook magazine assigned Pittsburgh reporter Emily Gardner Neal (who later helped write *I Believe in Miracles* for Miss Kuhlman) to look into the situation. The resulting story set Kathryn on the road to national prominence. In an unprecedented editor's foreword to their seven-page story, *Redbook* said:

> The amazing story of Kathryn Kuhlman was one which *Redbook* editors approached with misgivings. No amount of doubt regarding "faith healing" of any sort, however, could obscure the fact that startling things were happening at Miss Kuhlman's evangelistic services in Pittsburgh. For four months, writers and researchers investigated the healings and cures. If *Redbook's* investigators erred, it was on the side of skepticism. But as they questioned and studied, the editors' original incredulity gave way to a conviction that the facts demanded publication. . . .
>
> Physicians' statements, of course, have been difficult to obtain; although a doctor may not personally object to describing a patient's progress under such circumstances, he usually refuses out of deference to the medical profession's wariness of faith healing. . . .
>
> This magazine has in its custody the following confidential documents: twenty testimonials from persons claiming to have been healed; four statements from clergymen supporting Miss Kuhlman's ministry; two letters from public officials; four workmen's compensation reports; two statements from men in fields allied to medical work and six medical and X-ray reports. . . .

C. M. Clark, Pittsburgh hearing-aid expert, stated in a letter: "We actually saw God's miracle healing" of a deaf-mute who repeated words "using lip forms, throat tones and nasal sounds which she had never experienced."

This magazine therefore invites readers' attention to this report, the integrity of which has been checked in every possible way, confident that persons who have faith, or the hope of it, will find here a message of deep inner significance.

Despite *Redbook's* claim that they could prove many of those who attended the miracle services were healed, Kathryn's critics grew even more vocal. For the first time in her career she was being attacked theologically rather than personally. It was an entirely new war.

The most vicious attack came in the summer of 1952. At the invitation of Rex and Maude Aimee Humbard, a traveling evangelistic family from Arkansas, Kathryn went to Akron, Ohio, for a series of meetings in the huge tent erected by the Humbard family on Triplett Boulevard next to the Akron airport. The Humbards were well-known in Ohio, although their ministry had been a traveling one. With Rex and his wife were Dad and Mother Humbard, who had been preaching for more than forty years, and Rex's brother, Clement. Kathryn, of course, was already famous throughout the area due to her extensive radio broadcasts and the large services she had been holding on a regular basis at Stambaugh Auditorium in nearby Youngstown.

What Kathryn didn't know was she had invaded the lair of the most noted fundamentalist preacher in the North, Dallas Billington, of the million-dollar Akron Baptist Temple. Billington had been ordained a Southern Baptist minis-

ter at a small church in Murray, Kentucky in 1924. Shortly
after, the fiery preacher, in collusion with several other
Baptist ministers—including John R. Rice and J. Frank
Norris of the First Baptist Church of Ft. Worth, Texas—
began a devastating attack on the Southern Baptist Convention saying it had turned liberal. As the attack grew more
vicious, some of the pastors withdrew from the SBC and
formed a loose league of independent Baptist churches
whose primary purpose seemed to consist of attacking lib-
erals, Catholics, faith healers, and women preachers. In
fact, one of the most popular books making the rounds was
written by John R. Rice and entitled, *Bobbed Hair, Bossy
Wives and Women Preachers*. Billington, a former factory
worker who could never be accused of running from a fight,
was granted a church theological degree—Doctor of
Bibliology—from the First Baptist Church of Ft. Worth,
Texas. He moved to Akron in 1925 to establish the Akron
Baptist Temple. During his twenty-seven years, he had built
a dynasty over which he ruled as absolute monarch in the
thriving rubber city. The arrival of the huge Humbard
family tent, which had a seating capacity of more than
15,000, and "that woman faith healer" Kathryn Kuhlman at
the same time, was tantamount to waving a red flag in front
of an angry bull. Kathryn was in for the fight of her life, only
this time she was not throwing against a bush leaguer like M.
J. Maloney, but the king of swat, Dallas Billington.

Billington lost no time in getting out of the dugout. He
had every intention of belting her out of the park. Hopefully he'd be able to hit a grand slammer and get rid of the
Humbards as well. Like Casey, he eventually struck out, but
not until he hit a lot of screaming foul balls which had
everyone in Akron ducking.

On Sunday, August 10, 1952, Kathryn made her first

pitch, preaching to more than 15,000 people who jammed the huge tent. Many of the people arrived as early as five o'clock that morning in order to get seats for the nine o'clock service, which lasted until after noon.

On August 15 Billington struck back. In a news release which was plastered on the front page of the Akron *Beacon Journal,* the bombastic preacher offered $5,000 to anyone—man or woman—who could prove he or she could heal a person through prayer.

"I make my offer to emphasize my belief that there is no greater racket in America, whether it be horse jockeying, dog races, or the numbers racket, than the so-called divine healers of our day. I have a mute class in my congregation. If Kathryn Kuhlman will come out to the temple on Sunday and open their ears and loose their tongues so they can talk, I'll let her hold one service in my temple each month for twelve months free of charge."

Billington, who publicly accused Kathryn of having received her training from the writings of Aimee Semple McPherson, stated: "Nowhere was the power of divine healing ever given to be administered by any woman. Women have their rightful places but when you put one in the pulpit it is unscriptural."

Billington was following the straight fundamentalist line, a line he himself had helped make popular as one of the most powerful and successful preachers of his generation. There was never any indication that he was attacking Kathryn personally, although before the fight was over he did go to his pulpit and "expose" her as a divorcee. However, he felt he had a divine right to blow the trumpet and warn the sheep that there was a wolf prowling the outskirts of town.

Kathryn, remembering her victories in Franklin, flushed with the success of her ministry in Pittsburgh and

Youngstown, and encouraged by the thousands of people who rose to her support, wound up and fired her fast ball right down the middle.

"I have been in this vicinity seven years, and I feel that my life and ministry speak for themselves," she told the newspaper. "I have never at any time or place made a statement that I have ever healed anyone. It is the power of God. Go right ahead and publish anything Dr. Billington says. He's going to split his church wide open."

The response was instantaneous. The newspaper's circulation department reported that the demand for extra papers was second only to the annual requests which poured in from all over the country at Soap Box Derby time—an annual event for which Akron is famous. Letters by the thousands poured into the newspaper office as well as into Kathryn's offices in the Carlton House in Pittsburgh.

Rex Humbard, who never expected this kind of battle from one he called a "brother in the Lord," was aghast over what was happening. He called Kathryn, releasing her from her obligation to preach the following Sunday, if she wished.

"No one likes this airing our dirty linen in public less than I," she said. "Let's hold our ground. I'll be there Sunday morning with bells on."

Not only was Kathryn there, but more than 20,000 others showed up also. Billington had, unwittingly, given Kathryn and the Humbards more publicity than they had money to purchase.

Back in Pittsburgh, Kathryn was lining up her defense. Maggie Hartner, who was now working full-time, was being helped out by two sisters, Maryon Marsh and Ruth Fisher. Like many others, Ruth and Maryon had been marginal Christians when they attended their first miracle service in 1950. However, after Ruth was healed of a severe spine condition which had kept her in and out of hospitals for half her life, the two of them got serious—with God and with the Kuhlman ministry. Ruth began helping Maggie minister among the people during the miracle services and Maryon went to work in the office as a typist. (Ruth later joined her as a staff member.)

Besides the Sunday services in Akron, Kathryn was holding intermittent miracle services in New Castle, Youngstown, and Butler, as well as a regular Tuesday night Bible study in Pittsburgh and her big miracle service at Carnegie Hall on Friday. Ruth and Maryon were both musical and sensed a need for a choir during the services. They organized a group of single women in Ruth's basement and sang at a few of the services. Seeing the need for a choir, Kathryn then made contact with Dr. Arthur Metcalfe, the distinguished director of the Mendelssohn Choir in Pittsburgh. She persuaded him to come with her as her choir director. It was one of the best moves she ever made. Dr. Metcalfe, dedicated more than twenty-three years to the ministry before he succumbed to a heart attack exactly a year—to the day—before Kathryn died.

Another member of her "Pittsburgh team" was her accountant, Walter Adamack. Already nearing retirement age, Adamack was, in many ways, like Kathryn's papa. He distrusted preachers and religious institutions. When he heard of Billington's attack against Kathryn he knew he had lined up on the right side. He was a fighter and thought nothing of using colorful language when someone attacked those to whom he was loyal, he represented much of what Billington opposed. Kathryn liked him, however. She liked him because he was outspoken, and a little bit arrogant. He became the watchdog over her finances. Later he helped her with the formation of her foundation and several side corporations. He was one of Kathryn's most trusted friends

127

and advisors—and an invaluable aide when she waded into her fight with Billington.

Thus fortified by a good staff and thousands of friends who were writing letters and making telephone calls, Kathryn girded herself for the next inning of the battle between the tent and the temple.

Returning to Akron for the Sunday service, she brought with her a number of people, all of whom had volunteered to testify of physical healings. Two of these, she told the newspaper reporters who crowded around the platform before the service, more than met Dr. Billington's tests for cures from faith alone. The test cases were Jacob Hess and his wife Sarah, both sixty-six years old, who had been born deaf mutes. Mrs. Hess's hearing had been partially restored and she could speak, although not distinctly. Mr. Hess was beginning to make voice noises. Through their thirteen-year-old adopted daughter, who acted as an interpreter before the crowd which numbered again in excess of twenty thousand, the Hesses claimed that God had healed them through a miracle service in Pittsburgh. Mrs. Margaret Richardson, a seventy-one-year-old friend of the Hesses, said she had grown up with them and could testify of their former condition and their healing.

Kathryn's other test case was Priscilla Boyko, a thirty-eight-year-old Pittsburgh clerical worker, who said she had been crippled from birth. She said she had been examined by the staff of a Pittsburgh hospital and was now walking normally.

Then, after asking the giant congregation to join hands while she led them in a special prayer for Billington, Kathryn said she was asking the pastor to "put his money where his mouth was." Her proposal was that Billington place his $5,000 in a special escrow account and that an impartial board of clergymen and laymen be appointed to decide the issue on the basis of the evidence. If she won, she would donate the money to the United Fund of Akron.

Billington, on the other hand, made some counter proposals. Backing off from some of his strongest statements made in the beginning, he said he wanted the people of Akron to know that he believed in divine healing. It was the divine healers he could not go along with. Therefore he insisted that Kathryn had to swear in an affidavit that the healings were caused specifically by her prayers.

That put Kathryn on the spot, for she never claimed her prayers healed.

Then, just as the contest was about to hit its crest, a front page story appeared in the Akron paper revealing that a team of reporters had dug into Kathryn's past and discovered she had married a divorced evangelist a number of years before.

Kathryn exploded. That just wasn't fair play. For almost seven years she had been free from that old scandal, now here it was, raising its ugly head again just when she felt she had won a victory.

When Robert Hoyt of the Akron *Beacon Journal* interviewed her, she denied having ever been married.

"We were never married. I never took my marriage vows," she said, her eyes flashing. "Do you know what happened? I'll tell you what happened. I fainted—passed out completely, I tell you—right before I was to take my vows."

Shaking her finger in the face of the young reporter, she shouted, "That's the truth, so help me God."

Hoyt was insistent. "We have a photostatic copy of your marriage application."

"If I signed an application for a marriage license, it was brought to me for my signature. I do not remember signing any such thing. Besides, I don't believe it should make any

129

difference whether I was married or not. And that's all I am going to say."

It was sad enough that Kathryn and Billington were doing their fighting in public, to the utter glee of an unbelieving world. But infinitely more sad was the fact the battle had no ethical boundaries. It had now shifted from issues to personalities—namely Kathryn's. That old shadow of the past, which she wanted so desperately to leave behind, kept reappearing. Haunting her.

Years later Kathryn told me a little story which helped explain, to some degree, why she so vehemently denied her marriage to Waltrip. She had long before determined, it seemed, that the best way to face an unpleasant situation was to simply pretend it didn't exist—and move on.

"I was preaching in a small church in New Jersey," she said, "and was staying in the home of one of the church members. I remember it so vividly because it was election week the year Franklin Roosevelt was running for his third term as president. [1940, ed.]

"Miss Anna, my hostess, had a close friend who was several years older than herself. She was a large, portly woman who was absolutely dead set against Mr. Roosevelt's reelection to a third term. In fact, she had embarked on a one-woman campaign to try and stop him. Her husband was wealthy and she had spent thousands of dollars on her campaign.

"Well, election night rolled around and she was absolutely exhausted from the mental strain and physical effort. About 7:00 P.M. her husband said, 'You go to bed. When the last returns come in, I'll call you.'

"She retired, feeling confident that Roosevelt would be defeated and she would awaken to a great celebration.

"Of course Roosevelt swept into office on a landslide vote. The telephone rang at Miss Anna's house. It was the husband of the other woman who was still asleep. He said, 'Anna. Come quickly. Mr. Roosevelt won, and it will kill my wife when I tell her. She'll suffer a heart attack and die. Come quickly and help me tell her.'

"Miss Anna said, 'Kathryn, I'll be back in a little bit. I don't know how long this will take.'

"She later told me what happened. It was 2:00 A.M. and Miss Anna tiptoed into the room with the smelling salts. She had taken every precaution to keep the older woman from suffering a complete collapse.

"She awoke and saw Miss Anna by her side. 'Anna? What happened? Did we win?'

"Miss Anna, with the smelling salts in her hand, came close to her old friend and said, 'I'm sorry, but Mr. Roosevelt is in for the third term.'

"The portly woman sat up in bed. With her chins in the air and her nose higher than ever she said, 'Anna! Anna! We'll just act like it never happened.'

"And to her dying day she never discussed it with anyone. She never acknowledged the fact that Mr. Roosevelt was in office. She just acted as though it never happened. Her heart kept right on beating and not a nerve in her body was affected."

Kathryn finished her story and then leaning close to me, made her point. "That is one of the greatest lessons I have ever learned. Never a week goes by, believe me, without something happening that could upset me terribly. I could go into a thousand pieces. When you deal with human lives as I do, it is the hardest work in the world. Believe me! But over and over again I have done what that portly woman did. I have said to myself, 'Kathryn, just act as though it never happened.' It's the best way in the world to accept hurt and disappointment. It's just like that."

Armed with insight, I was able to understand, to some

degree, why Kathryn felt justified in pretending she had never been married—and in pretending she was younger than she actually was. (She also told the Akron reporters she was in her early thirties, when actually she had already celebrated her forty-fifth birthday.) Somehow, to her, she *was* in her thirties. And somehow, using the same logic, she never had been married. Like Miss Anna's friend, she just acted like it never happened.

Even though Billington had mentioned Kathryn's divorce from his pulpit, he did not dwell on that issue. To his credit, he was not a dirty fighter. He felt he was right and felt he could win the battle without striking below the belt. On August 28 he set a Friday deadline for his offer to give $5,000 to anyone who could prove that Kathryn's prayers had healed anyone.

"After twelve noon, Friday, August 29, I withdraw the offer and rest my case with the public as to who has been the honest one and who has been the faker in the subject of divine healing," he said in a press interview.

Kathryn realized that the rules of the game had somehow changed. She never claimed that her prayers healed. All she did was report on what the Holy Spirit was doing in her meetings. She talked the matter over with the Humbards and decided she had no choice but to go ahead and play her ace card.

On Friday, August 29, at 11:05 A.M., she played a tape recording made by Mrs. Hess over radio station WCUE in Akron. Bill Burns of radio station KQV in Pittsburgh conducted the interview with Mrs. Hess. The older woman testified that she had been mute all her life until 1948 when she began attending services conducted by Miss Kuhlman. After the third miracle service, she found she could hear and speak.

At the same time, Maggie Hartner had been busy in

Pittsburgh. She went to the office of Dr. B. E. Nickles to pick up a handwritten letter addressed to Robert Hoyt of the Akron *Beacon Journal* in which he said that Miss Priscilla Boyko had been born a cripple, had a series of operations over the years, and walked with a built-up shoe until she received a healing at one of Kathryn's miracle services. The doctor said he had examined Miss Boyko at intervals since September 9, 1950, but had never treated her leg condition "due to the physical impossibility of treating the limb with its constant spasmodic, involuntary muscle spasms that left the patient in a most weakened condition. However," he said, "I have watched her limb change from one of no movement in the foot, ankle, leg and knee into one that now has motion. Her circulation in the foot and leg has increased remarkably."

For professional reasons, Dr. Nickles asked that his name not be used in the paper, but he did agree to verify his claims in person if necessary.

Maggie hand-delivered the letter to the Akron paper prior to Dr. Billington's noon deadline.

The following day Billington declared that Kathryn had defaulted. In a front page article he said: "Mrs. Kuhlman (he insisted on calling her Mrs. Kuhlman) proved conclusively, when she grabbed at the $5,000 offer, that she had assumed the role of a divine healer. I set a deadline on my offer just to call her out in the open."

The pastor concluded that he had accomplished his purpose and was now withdrawing his offer. "I set out to prove to the public that divine healers were more racketeers than numbers writers."

Nobody won. Billington walked off the field and Kathryn was stranded on the mound. It was, as it always has been when Christians try to settle spiritual matters before an unbelieving public, a fiasco.

133

"I did not want the money," Kathryn told Rex Humbard. "I only wanted to convince Dr. Billington that the gospel he professes to preach is real and the God he professes to love is miraculous and wonderful."

The following week, realizing the futility of what she had tried to do, Kathryn attempted to make amends. On Sunday afternoon she made a special visit to both the Akron Baptist Temple and to Dr. Billington's home to try to find him and express her love and regret over what had happened. He was not available to see her.

"So far as I am concerned, there never has been a feud between Dr. Billington and me," she said. "He challenged me and all I did was protect my ministry."

In a called press interview she told John Waters of the Akron paper, "This whole business never should have happened. It is now ridiculous. For the man or woman established in the faith, it is just good reading. But for those weak in the faith, I'm afraid this may cause someone to lose faith entirely and be damned eternally. It is very un-Christian for two people who profess to be ministers of the gospel, who preach the same Bible, who believe in Jesus Christ as the Son of the living God, to conduct themselves in the manner in which this thing has been carried on."

When Waters asked Kathryn why she accepted Billington's offer, she hesitated and then said, "I am reluctant to open the issue again since we have already done so much damage. But in answer to your question, I had to accept that challenge for it was not only Kathryn Kuhlman being challenged but thousands and thousands of Christians and denominational churches who believe in and practice divine healing. Had I not accepted the challenge, Dr. Billington would have made the claim that I was a fake and that I could not produce any evidence of healing."

Then she added her coup de grace. "You know, the same

miracles that take place at my services would happen at Dr. Billington's if he would instill faith in the hearts of his people."

Despite all her mistakes throughout the unfortunate battle, Kathryn's conclusion remains unchallenged. That Sunday more than four hundred persons answered the altar call in the Humbard family tent, declaring they wanted to give their lives to Christ. Four came forward at the Akron Baptist Temple.

All was not lost, however. One of the Billington remarks which struck home was his criticism of the Humbard family. "I have observed that all divine healers operate away from home and never establish a permanent work anywhere." Rex and Maude Aimee Humbard decided to stay on in Akron, founding Calvary Temple and later the Cathedral of Tomorrow. Recognizing the power of the Holy Spirit to heal as well as save, their church has grown to become one of the largest and most dynamic churches in the entire world.

CHAPTER IX

BEHIND CLOSED DOORS

Very few public figures have managed as well as Kathryn Kuhlman to keep her business affairs secret, while maintaining with such grace that her life was an open door.

"I answer every question that is asked of me," she often said. "I do not believe there is anyone in the religious field today who is more honest in answering questions than I am. I bare my soul to you."

Yet when she was asked about her age, her health, her private devotional life, or her personal wealth, she would just laugh and give an answer like: "Everybody knows me. They know all about me. I get into a taxi and the driver turns around and says, 'Aren't you Kathryn Kuhlman? My wife and I watch your show every week.' Just last week the captain of the airliner came all the way back to my seat just to tell me that his wife had been healed in one of our meetings at the Shrine. I have no secrets. Everybody knows me."

And so the questioner would smile, nod, and go his way. And it wouldn't be until much later, when he stopped to examine just what she had said, that he would discover she had purposefully said nothing—and made him feel like a king while she said it.

In the end, however, it became apparent that while the entire world knew of her, very few knew any facts about her, and no one really knew her. Even her closest and most intimate companion for the last thirty years of her life, Maggie Hartner, who had even begun to look and talk like Kathryn during the latter years, admitted that in many areas Kathryn was a stranger.

And that's probably the way she wanted it. Despite her proffered naivete—"I have no secrets"—she evidently had many. She was a shrewd businesswoman when it came to revealing personal or financial information to even those close to her. She knew human nature like few others, and realized that most curiosity grows out of impure motives. Thus she usually hedged in her answers. She learned, early in her ministry, that few people object to a smokescreen as long as it is perfumed.

Yet, the way she ran things at the foundation office forever baffled even her strongest supporters.

On my first visit to Kathryn's office in the Carlton House in Pittsburgh, in late 1968, I was aghast over what seemed to be the "inefficiency" of the office procedure. For instance, although she was receiving thousands of letters each week (the Pittsburgh postmaster once said her mail volume in the city was second only to that of U.S. Steel), she refused to use an automatic letter opener. Her secretaries sat at desks, surrounded by huge piles of mail, slicing open envelopes with hand-held letter openers. It took me more than a week to discover that behind one huge stack of letters piled on a hexagonal table in the far corner of the room sat a pretty secretary named Connie Siergiej. Connie was the one who usually answered the incoming phone calls, and one day in the office I just happened to recognize her voice coming from the corner of the room. Peering over the stack of mail, I spotted her busily opening envelopes with a stainless steel knife, sorting the contents and placing them in neat piles on the floor beside her.

When I naively suggested that Miss Kuhlman needed an automatic letter opener, Connie grinned and said, "Everyone in the office is an automatic machine. We don't think, we just do. Miss Kuhlman pushes our button and we perform."

It was a confession which I later realized was far more accurate than most cared to admit. I talked with a number of people who had visited the foundation offices and many said the same thing: "Robots! They are all robots in there. They talk like Miss Kuhlman. They laugh like Miss Kuhlman. They're not allowed to have personal problems, or even live personal lives. They are so programmed they don't even need her around to give orders. They don't think. They just follow the behavior pattern which she has programmed into them."

Whether her critics were able to distinguish between automated servitude and extreme loyalty is known only by those who worked for her. There was never any doubt concerning the loyalty of those who managed her office. Her wish was literally their command. When Maggie Hartner once considered changing her hair style, it took only one negative word from Kathryn, and Maggie's hair stayed in the bun she had used for twenty years.

The same loyalty was evidenced even after Miss Kuhlman died. "We must change nothing," Maggie said regarding the work of the foundation. "We'll carry on as though she's still here."

One of her secretaries tearfully told me they had been following the same procedures for so many years that they felt guilty doing anything other than what Miss Kuhlman would have done had she been there. "In fact," the woman said, "we all expect Miss Kuhlman to walk through that door any minute. And we don't want to be caught doing something that she would not approve."

This was six months following her death.

Therefore, after her death, those in the office—Maggie, Maryon, Walter Adamack—all continued with the work of the foundation. To all outward appearances, though, it was like a locomotive without an engineer. Rushing down the track, crossing bridges and trestles, going past grade crossings while the automobile traffic obediently waited behind clanging safety gates, lights blazing and wheels biting at the rails—but with no concept of where it was going, what it was going to do after it got there, or where the fuel was going to come from in the meantime. All because the engineer had neglected to leave instructions before she stepped out of the cab.

David Verzilli, Kathryn's "associate pastor," who preached in Youngstown when she wasn't there, discerned there was no hand on the throttle and unbuckled the remaining passenger cars made up of those who had gathered weekly at Stambaugh Auditorium. The heartbreak that accompanied this final separation of these loyal ones who had called Miss Kuhlman "pastor" from the remnant of the foundation was, in the end, a necessary move. In fact, it was one Kathryn anticipated while she was still alive. The one factor that seemed to characterize the work of the foundation was "rutted unchangeability." It could indeed be likened to a powerful train roaring down the tracks with

Kathryn at the throttle. Its course of direction was planned and there was no time to turn aside to smell the flowers, or even stop and visit with the folks who stood alongside the tracks waving in appreciation.

Kathryn once told me she maintained her office like she did her theological position. "I've found something that works, and I'll never change."

In her earlier ministry she was known as a person who was open to change. Several of her early co-workers used to remark that the earmark of her greatness was her ability to keep her theology flexible. "She always wanted to learn new things about God," one man told me. But in her later years her theology grew more conservative. "I haven't changed my theology in twenty years," she once told me. "Why should I?"

It was a good question, but one that I felt unqualified to answer since I was not nearly as far down the tracks as she.

When I remarked that I had attended a mini-miracle service in the living room of Richard and Rose Owellen in Baltimore which was indistinguishable from a Kathryn Kuhlman miracle service except in size and intensity, she just laughed. "Everything Dick and Rose know about the Holy Spirit they learned from me. And that's the reason their theology is straight. It's just like that."

David Wilkerson once likened Miss Kuhlman to General William Booth, founder of the Salvation Army, a bellowing bull of a man who had no patience with those who did not believe the way he did or were unwilling to do the work of God the way he wanted it done. It was with this same unyielding intensity that Kathryn conducted her ministry and ran her office. "I won't change my theology nor will I change my methods," she said dogmatically.

"I want to keep the personal touch," Miss Kuhlman told me when I asked her about the automatic letter openers.

141

"In the early days I opened all the mail myself. Now I don't have time for that. But I don't want people thinking that when they write Kathryn Kuhlman (she often spoke of herself in the third person) that their letters are going to be opened by a machine."

Yet there was a strange inconsistency about this, for while the letters were hand opened, most of them were answered by a machine. A back room in the foundation office was filled with IBM memory typewriters. Kathryn had dictated a number of general answers to letters which would take care of most of the questions asked by the writers. These answers were programmed into the computer. If a letter needed some kind of "special" answer—that is, an answer not contained in the memory typewriter—then it would go into a different stack to be answered by Maryon Marsh, Maggie Hartner, or some other person in the office. But always, a number of the letters were personally answered by Miss Kuhlman.

Although many other ministries and organizations use the same procedures, Miss Kuhlman did endeavor to keep the personal touch by having the envelopes hand stamped. And, incredible as it seems, she personally signed all the outgoing mail.

Many were the times when the mail load became so heavy that Miss Kuhlman (or Maggie, if Kathryn was not there) would enlist—better, command—the services of anyone who came into the office to help in opening letters and sticking stamps. Still vivid in my memory is the picture of Dr. Arthur Metcalfe, that warm, personable, yet distinguished musician, sitting on the carpet in the corner of the office, licking stamps and sticking them on envelopes.

"It's a team effort," he grinned. "When the load gets heavy, we all lift."

This same mystical authority over people was evident in

many other situations. The first time she spoke in Charlotte, North Carolina, was at the invitation of the FGBMFI for a regional convention. The meeting was held in the ballroom of the old White House Inn, with more than fifteen hundred people present. One of the host pastors, Alfred Garr, was also the featured soloist at the service. When he finished singing, he took a seat on the front row, almost at Kathryn's feet. Al Garr is the pastor of the largest independent Pentecostal church in the state of North Carolina, a church named after his father who first brought Pentecostalism to the Piedmont section of America. He is a well-known and highly-respected member of the Charlotte clergy. But Kathryn was no respecter of persons. She began her sermon by saying: "Let there not be a sound in this great hall. Not a whisper. Let the Holy Spirit speak." All heads were bowed and Al Garr began to pray quietly, very quietly (in fact, it was so faint that those of us sitting next to the speaker's stand on the platform could not hear him). But Kathryn had no hesitation in stopping the entire service to correct him. Without even looking down, she just dropped her slender arm, pointed her finger directly at him, and said, "You, sir, I said not a whisper!"

And there was silence! Even those in charge were not in charge when Kathryn Kuhlman was present. And even though her methods were unconventional, no one doubted her sincerity nor questioned her authority in spiritual matters.

Despite Kathryn's recognized spiritual authority, there remains to this day a mystery concerning her personal devotional life. No one, it seems, knew anything about this aspect of her life. Although she believed the Bible was the absolute Word of God—and classified herself as a fundamentalist (as well as a Pentecostal: "I'm just as Pentecostal as the Bible")—yet during her later years there was little evidence she spent any time in private Bible study. She had saturated herself with the Book's contents for over forty years and, given the frantic pace at which she lived after 1972, her old friend Dan Malachuk was probably right when he surmised that she did most of her Bible study in public.

"Since she didn't have time to study before she stood to minister," Dan said, "she did it on stage, priming her spiritual pump for the time of ministry which was to follow."

In her earlier years she made extensive notes for her sermons, using a detailed outline which obviously came out of deep and intense Bible study. These outlines were written in longhand and she usually preached directly from them. Later Maryon Marsh typed her notes on 3 x 5 or 4 x 6 index cards which Kathryn kept in her "brain box," a battered old attache case which she carried with her to all meetings.

Kathryn often made public claims that she read no books but the Bible. During the last three years of her life this was probably true. However, her desk was filled with underlined copies of books by Andrew Murray and Jessie Penn Lewis on such subjects as prayer, spiritual obedience, and spiritual warfare. Of even greater interest were the printed sermons by Norman Vincent Peale I discovered in the bottom drawer of her desk. Peale and Kuhlman seemed poles apart, yet she obviously admired the famous pastor and at one time or another in her life probably drew from his excellent storytelling ability.

Even Maryon Marsh, though, conceded that during the

last several years of her life Kathryn prepared almost no new material—using the same outlines over and over, often desultory, repeating herself and meandering down well trodden paths. This was quite a contrast to the earlier years of her ministry when her preaching was dynamic, often electrifying, and her Bible studies attended by even the best-educated in the community.

Her lengthy discourses seemed to bother very few. And if, as Dan suggested, she needed to use the first hour of the service in order to get herself spiritually ready, then no one complained. It was worth the price.

This theory, which Malachuk and others projected, was confirmed by the fact that during the last two years of her ministry, Kathryn's "sermons" (actually they were not sermons in a true homiletical sense) grew longer and longer— sometimes lasting an hour and a half. A classic example was the last sermon she ever preached. It was at the huge Shrine Auditorium in Los Angeles, just three days after she had returned from Israel. She was physically exhausted and there had been no time for sleep, much less prayer.

"I'm not going to preach today," she assured the crowd. "I'm only going to speak ten minutes and then we're going to move right into the miracle service."

But after making her announcement, Kathryn proceeded to speak for more than an hour. Of course no one present knew she was, even at that time, deathly sick. In fact, she was dying. But they did discern—many of them— that Kathryn dared not start the miracle service until there was an anointing from God. Until that anointing arrived she had no choice but to keep on speaking, preaching to herself about the power of God and praying that power would soon manifest itself. She was using the time to prepare herself spiritually.

Not only did there seem to be a void of Bible study during

Kathryn's later years, the same was true concerning her prayer life. She told those few who dared ask her about it that she stayed "prayed up" all the time.

"I have learned Paul's secret of praying without ceasing," she told a newspaper reporter who had the nerve to ask why she never withdrew in prayer. "I've learned to commune with the Lord any time, any place. I take my prayer closet with me on the plane, in the car, or walking down the street. I pray always. My life is a prayer. Don't you understand?"

Few understood. One of those who did, however, was Ruth Fisher, one of Kathryn's longtime associates. A deeply spiritual woman who spent much time in disciplined prayer and Bible study herself, Ruth was nevertheless sensitive to the fact that Kathryn simply did not fit the conventional mold of personal devotions. She told me a story that Kathryn had once told her, a story which gave me some deep insight into Kathryn's reasoning.

"I dreamed once," Kathryn had said, "of three kneeling figures. All were waiting for Jesus to pass by. As the Lord came down the path, He stopped and embraced the first figure. When He came to the second figure, He gently laid His hand on her shoulder. But when He passed the third kneeling figure, He only smiled and kept on walking.

"Someone said to the Master, 'You must love the woman you embraced more than the others.'

" 'No, you don't understand,' He said gently. 'The one I embraced needs my encouragement. She is weak in the faith. The one I tapped lightly on the shoulder is stronger. But the third one, the one I merely smiled at, is strong. I never need to worry about her, for she is with me constantly.' "

Despite Kathryn's comments that she stayed "prayed up," there were times when she withdrew and literally agonized in prayer. I am convinced she literally prayed herself to sleep each night—going to bed with the Holy Spirit. Anyone who had ever been with her backstage at the Shrine Auditorium, or watched her pacing the hall behind the old Carnegie Hall in Pittsburgh, or seen her in the wings of a hundred auditoriums before she came on stage, knew that she was a woman of intense prayer. According to Maggie Hartner and others, she often returned home, exhausted from a miracle service, to collapse on the floor in tears.

The first miracle service I attended was in 1968. After fighting my way through the more than two thousand people who had packed Carnegie Hall, I squeezed through a stage door and found myself in a tiny backstage hall that ran the width of the building. Kathryn's associates were at each end of the hall, making sure that no one bothered her. She was pacing, back and forth, head up, head down, arms flung into the air, hands clasped behind her back. Her face was covered with tears, and as she approached I could hear her. "Gentle Jesus, take not your Holy Spirit from me."

I turned and fled, for I felt I had blundered into the most intimate of all conversations between lovers, and just my presence was an abomination.

Later, after having been with her on many such occasions, I began to realize that my presence, or anyone else's presence, did not intimidate her. Sometimes she would stop in the middle of her prayer, chat gaily with whoever had need to see her, or give some instructions concerning the choir or lighting, and then, just as quickly, turn and continue her conversation with the Lord.

I was with her in Tel Aviv, Israel, at the giant sports stadium in late 1975. It was to be her next-to-last public appearance. She was sick, and tired, yet she spent more than an hour and a half in a dark tunnel under the platform pacing and praying, eyes open, eyes closed, her face bathed in tears. Above her was the music from the Living Sound—

instruments and voices—all around was the noise of the international crowd, moving, restless, people of many language groups. Above all was the restlessness of Israel itself. A nation in torment and struggle, battling to stay alive in a hostile environment. The night before, a woman from Finland had died in her service and it had shaken her deeply. The Israeli police had asked many questions. Too many. And so she paced and prayed—trying desperately to touch the hem of His garment. Pleading that she would not have to go up on that stage without Him. Knowing, in her deep inner self, that all those things she had said about herself were true. She was nothing. Absolutely nothing.

Perhaps Kathryn's prayer life defied convention, but those close to her knew she lived, breathed, and slept prayer. The fact that she didn't draw aside, as others do, to wait and listen, to fall prostrate or to wait in agony on bended knee, did not mean she was not a woman of prayer. Like everything else, she had to do it her way.

The problems of her prayer concept became critical only when it came to her relationships with her associates—for somehow she seemed to feel that her office staff and fellow ministers should walk with the same depth of commitment as she walked. Like General Booth, she was extremely impatient with those who were unable to keep her pace.

These difficulties were more evident in the foundation office in Pittsburgh than in any other phase of the ministry. Unlike other Christian ministries where the staffs often meet together for prayer, the foundation employees simply arrived at their appointed time and went straight to work. Miss Kuhlman seldom, if ever, prayed with the staff members. Like herself, they were expected to be "prayed up" when they arrived and remain that way throughout the day.

Likewise Kathryn refused to let herself be drawn into the personal problems of her employees. If a secretary was having trouble with her husband, or someone was having financial difficulties (salaries at the Kathryn Kuhlman Foundation were notoriously low)—all these were unmentionables in the office. "I simply do not have time to get involved with the personal lives of my staff," she told me.

Toward the end of her life, in those final weeks before she was forced into the hospital, however, this philosophy began to bear bitter fruit. It almost devastated her to discover that a long-trusted employee was being accused of questionable behavior.

Kathryn, who had always demanded such high standards of morality from her ushers, musicians, and volunteer associates (many times, in the past, she had refused to let a man sing in the choir because his reputation was tainted), was unable to cope with this in-house situation. Her office associates, who were horrified over what was happening (yet paralyzed from making a move without Kathryn's approval), felt that had she not been so sick and preoccupied with all the other problems which seemed to cascade down upon her during the last six months of 1975, she would have stepped in and put a stop to this open and flagrant abuse of all she believed in. But in her weakened condition she was unable to cope. She simply turned her back on the problem and refused to discuss it. ("Anna, we'll just act like it never happened.")

No one seems to have comprehended just how sick Kathryn must have been during the latter part of 1975. She evidently did a lot of things she would not have done had her body been functioning correctly. On the surface she never lost the old "zip"—the demands for perfection at the miracle services—which had been her trademark. Seemingly oblivious to the pain in her chest and the growing weakness in her body, she plunged ahead, lining up more meetings, maintaining her television schedule, and giving

149

every impression that her dying body was as healthy as ever.

Yet at the very end, just before she entered the hospital for the final time, it became obvious she was slipping. The trip to Israel in October drained her physically. And when, in Jerusalem, she discovered that an employee was slipping away from the hotel at night for a clandestine rendezvous, it was more than she could handle. She turned her back and never mentioned it.

As the ministry grew more intense, with more and more demands on her time, Kathryn backed away from personal involvement in the lives of even those closest to her. At the end, she had become a public recluse, losing herself in the public ministry and then, at the end of the day, withdrawing from all but the one or two people she allowed into her presence. At the very end, she even rejected those closest to her, and submitted herself into the hands of people she scarcely knew. It was a sad exit.

The area where the degree of non-involvement was most difficult to understand encompassed the thousands of prayer requests which poured into the office each week. And while it seems incomprehensible, there is no evidence—at least during Kathryn's later years—that she made any effort to grant these requests and pray specifically for the people's needs. Whether Kathryn felt that specific prayer was unnecessary; whether she was too busy; or whether she prayed for those who wrote her *en masse* as she traveled about the nation, remains unknown.

The fact remains that many, many people who sent prayer requests to Kathryn Kuhlman were healed—often within the week. Some may feel there was, indeed, a special aura which surrounded the entire Kathryn Kuhlman ministry, so that even one reaching out to touch the hem of her garment would be healed. Yet Kathryn steadfastly rejected this concept, stating over and over that she had no healing virtue within herself. Others may speculate that it was the faith of the letter writer which was sufficient for healing. Still others cherish the idea that while Kathryn herself did not pray specifically for those thousands of prayer requests, all around people were praying and this produced sufficient overflow to bring healing to those who wrote in. A few ask the bothersome question as to whether prayer is a necessary factor in healing.

No one seems to know.

The only conclusion I can draw is that a merciful and compassionate God, who saw the need and suffering of His people, and knew the inconsistencies of the ministry He had set apart to help meet these needs, often sovereignly intervened and granted His people the desires of their hearts. And, somehow, beyond the realm of man's comprehension, those letters and calls to Kathryn became prayers themselves. So, Kathryn Kuhlman was merely a catalyst to draw out the prayers of the people. And on the basis of their cries, God, not Kathryn, answered.

When Kathryn preached those heart-searching messages on a jealous God who would not "share the glory" with any earthly figure, she was preaching to herself. She knew how desperately she needed to hear that message and apply it to her own life. So she preached it over and over, for no minister in this century, perhaps even since the time of the Apostles, was under more pressure to weaken and accept some of the glory herself.

Thus when some grateful admirer came to the platform following a healing and said to Kathryn, "Oh, thank you! Thank you!" she quickly backed off, waved her hands, and said, "Don't thank me. I had nothing to do with it. Thank God."

Despite all she said, however, the people did thank her. The foundation received millions of dollars. It came from

151

the rich who willed her their estates, and from the poor who put nickels and dimes in the offering plates. All this without any direct appeal for funds. She took up only one offering in each meeting, or, on occasion, she might take up a special offering for the television ministry. But it was all very low-key. There were no spectacular methods to raise money. No direct mail appeals. She abhorred the method often used by some organizations of having people stand to their feet and pledge so much money. "It just feeds the ego," she whispered to me one day while standing backstage and watching such a spectacle at a meeting where she was to later minister. "If they'll leave it in God's hands, He'll do a far better job than they ever could."

Kathryn left it in God's hands, and as a result she had access to more money than most people can comprehend. Many criticized her—often out of jealousy—for receiving so much money. But she knew, better than her critics, that she was God's steward. And if she misused His funds He would one day hold her responsible.

But it wasn't just the money. The people sent gifts. Trinkets. Some woman, walking through a department store, would see some trinket and think "That looks like something Kathryn Kuhlman would appreciate." She received thousands of such items through the mail, or handed to her at various meetings. These lesser gifts were usually put on a table in the office and picked over by members of her staff. Sometimes Kathryn would distribute them to friends in the ministry. For even a Kathryn Kuhlman had no use for one hundred jewelry boxes, or seventy-five dove pins, or thirty rhinestone bracelets.

They sent her Bibles. Her fans, seeing her on television or on the platform carrying a frayed, battered, threadbare Bible with the pages falling out and the cover half torn off, would rush out and buy the finest Bible available. Sometimes they would have her name engraved on the cover. But she was not comfortable with any Bible other than the one she had carried for years, dog-eared and stained. It was placed on the podium by her trusted bodyguard as the final act of readiness before she appeared to hold it aloft, proclaim its truths, and preach its message.

But the gifts were not limited to trinkets and Bibles. Many were extremely expensive. Rare paintings and antiques from Europe. Sculpture from Italy and South America. Rugs from Persia and the Orient. Diamonds and precious jewels from all over the world. Furs and even designer fashions from some of the most famous couturier houses of fashion. Relics from Israel. Her house in Fox Chapel became a museum, filled with *objets d'art* worth hundreds of thousands of dollars. So much came in that she needed a special vault in the basement of the house to store some of her valuables.

All this presented a unique problem. Kathryn loved fine, expensive things, and, at the same time, she always looked for a good bargain. It was not unusual for her to go into an exclusive clothing shop on Wilshire Boulevard and spend $3,000 at one time. Her life style demanded an extensive wardrobe. In fact, after she died I discovered a huge pile of dated invoices from Profils du Monde, an import shop on Wilshire Boulevard in Beverly Hills, for more than a dozen chiffon dresses in colors ranging from champagne and orange to yellow, blue, and mist green. Yet she never forgot her humble beginnings. Antique hunting was one of her few hobbies (she spent great sums of money buying antiques for herself and her close circle of friends), but she always felt guilty about having so much when there were many who had so little. She was not addicted to things. She could literally take them or leave them, and was just as comfortable sitting on the floor of her office with her shoes

153

off as she was sitting on one of the expensive sofas. As far as I could tell, she had risen above the tyranny of possessions. Instead of being controlled by material objects, she controlled them. She saw them as tools to be used rather than items to be sought after for personal gain and worth. Yet she was wise enough to realize that most people did not understand this particular spiritual plateau, and so she was constantly faced with the problem of what to do with the expensive things in her life.

Some of the *objets d'art* went into her foundation office in Pittsburgh; but not many, for she knew the danger of making a show—even with gifts. For instance, when she received two Ming Dynasty vases, she first hid them away in a small closet in her personal office and later took them to her house where only her most trusted friends ever visited. Other items were used to decorate her lavish apartment in plush Newport Beach, California. Yet in her private moments she often wondered if she was, by keeping these items, "receiving her reward now." An answer which only she knows now.

The same was true with the praise and adulation. How does one keep that balance between giving God all the glory and yet not being offensive to the people who don't understand?

"At times," she once confided privately, "in my weakness I just go ahead and accept the praise and thanksgiving. Sometimes I am so weary that if I did not accept some of the praise I would go under. And it seems God allows me to do it, just to keep me going. But at the end of the day, when I am all alone in my bedroom, I raise my hands toward heaven and say, 'Dear Jesus, you know what they said about me today. But now I give it all back to you. I am nothing, and nobody knows that better than me. I have no healing power. No healing virtue. There's nothing attractive in me.

But dear Jesus, you are everything. And today the people got us all mixed up. I didn't have the strength to straighten them out, but I know you understand. And now I give you all they gave me. I ask but one thing—take not your Holy Spirit from me, for without Him I will surely die.' "

CHAPTER X

THE WISDOM OF WAITING

Leadership, in its truest sense, consists of knowing how to utilize other leaders and motivate them to action. Kathryn was a master at this. She waited until God sent the right persons into her life, and then waited again until she had that perfect sense of timing that "now" was the proper time to move. She took great delight in finding the perfect person to accomplish her vision, and giving that person free reign to work. Gene Martin, an Assemblies of God minister was her man for the mission outreach. Dick Ross, who had produced many of the Billy Graham films before he went to work in Hollywood, was her man for the television ministry. And I was turned loose on the books.

Kathryn refused to put her signature on anything—a book, a television show, a radio program, or some kind of mission outreach—unless it was absolutely first class. "God demands our best," she said. "And He deserves it. After all,

157

He gave us His best when He sent His Son to earth. We must not be satisfied with giving Him less than our best in return."

She personally screened every television show in a private viewing room at CBS immediately following the taping. If anything was less than perfect, she scrubbed it and did a retake. The same was true with the books. We spent three days and must have gone through a score of titles before we finally came up with one that "fit" a little book I did for her about a nurse and her three children, all of whom were healed of fatal diseases in the same meeting. Exasperated, I finally threw up my hands and said, "Kathryn, isn't God big enough to give us a title for this book?"

She clapped her hands, gave one of those almost raucous bursts of laughter, and said, "How Big Is God?" It was the perfect title for the book.

This same sense of perfectionism saturated every move she made. Her lipstick was always on perfect. Her nails manicured and her clothing tailored to every detail. In the services the whimpering of a single child would cause her to stop and motion to an usher. A chair out of place, a choir member with a crooked tie, a staff member dressed with the wrong color shirt or blouse—she noticed every detail and was not satisfied until it was corrected. This same drive for perfectionism prevented her from moving ahead too rapidly in a new project, for she was determined it would be complete in every detail before she gave it the green light. Therefore she waited for years before she agreed to expand her ministry into television, before she agreed to hold her first service at the Shrine Auditorium in Los Angeles, before she wrote her second book, before she accepted invitations to preach in other cities. It was as though she actually did not want to expand but preferred to remain relatively cloistered in Pittsburgh. But the combination of the urging of those whom she trusted, and the open door of opportunity which she saw as the direction of God, eventually convinced her to get out of her rut and invest in the risk of change and expansion. However, deep inside she was always convinced it was better to stick with something which was working rather than risk failing with some new venture. And for that reason she often made firm statements which she later had to renounce. For instance, she often said she would never write an autobiography.

"Wait until I'm dead, Jamie," she nodded seriously. "Then you can say it all."

Yet a year before she died she began to talk to me about an autobiography. When we were together in Las Vegas for the fabulous miracle service at the City Auditorium in May 1975, she pressed me even further. Knowing my natural reluctance to keep on ghost writing, especially if a major book was involved, she pulled out all the stops to butter me up and explain how "we need to get to work on this right away."

We were sitting in the plush, plush living room of the Frank Sinatra suite in Caesar's Palace in Las Vegas. The miracle service was over and Kathryn had returned to the room, exhausted. I ran my fingers over the thick, flocked, deep red wallpaper and listened as she unwound concerning the service. Then she wanted to take us through the suite—my wife Jackie, Dan and Viola Malachuk, and myself—and show us the heart-shaped sunken bathtub (big enough for two—or three) and the round bed with the ceiling mirror. "I'm no dummy," she chuckled, grabbing my arm with her tight grip and leaning against my side. "I know exactly why that mirror's on the ceiling."

Back in the living room we sat on the plush red sofa in what must be one of the most lavish hotel rooms in the world and listened while she gave all the reasons why I should write her book. "You're the only one who'll be honest enough to tell it straight." Then looking at me through squinted eyes, she said, "You know, there's a lot of hanky-panky going on in the name of our Lord. Do you know what I mean?" I wasn't sure—at least not then—but I knew that if she knew, I wouldn't be satisfied until I found out exactly what she was talking about. "But we have to do the book for the glory of God. Remember that. No punches pulled, but for the glory of God."

One reason she didn't give why the book needed to be written soon was one which even she didn't know at the time—a reason which would not come to light for another two months. Her pianist and confidant, Dino Kartsonakis, and his brother-in-law, Paul Bartholomew, who was also her personal administrator, had been fired in February. Unknown to Kathryn, they had been preparing a book manuscript called "The Late Great Kate" which they planned to peddle to the pulp book market as an expose. None of this came to light until July 1975, when Bartholomew brought suit against her in Los Angeles Superior Court. Soon after that, Kathryn settled out of court. One of the stipulations of the sworn agreement was that neither Dino nor Bartholomew would be allowed to put anything about Kathryn Kuhlman in writing for ten years. However, back in May she knew nothing of the proposed expose, and therefore I can only conclude that her desires to start to work on the autobiography came as warnings from God that if she didn't tell her own story, someone else was going to do it—and smear both her name and that of the ministry.

Therefore we agreed to go ahead. But both of us were busy with other things. And neither of us knew just how short the time was. Kathryn did get together with her older sister, Myrtle Parrott, and do some talking into a tape recorder about her childhood days. But death interrupted, and in the long run she got her original wish—a biography rather than an autobiography.

The entire affair, however, was typical of her deliberateness—and of her sensitivity to the Holy Spirit, to wait until He prompted her and then to move with dispatch in the direction He was nudging. Kathryn was often accused of being a driving, impatient person. When it came to pushing her associates in the ministry, she was. But when it came to expanding into some new area of ministry, she had well learned the painful lesson to wait until the right person came along—someone she could trust—and then to move only when God told her to move.

Perhaps no situation better illustrates these principles than her expansion into Canada. It began, as most of her ministry began, with a miraculous healing. Kenneth May, a sixty-two-year-old farmer from the tiny community of Forester's Falls, Ontario, had been told by his doctor in nearby Cobden that he was dying of Hodgkins disease—cancer of the lymph glands. His story can be found in full detail under the chapter heading of "Canadian Sunrise" in *God Can Do It Again*. He had been sent to Ottawa for cobalt treatment. But it was ineffective and the lumps on his body gradually returned. He returned to the cancer clinic at the General Hospital for additional x-ray treatment, only to find the lumps were still growing, and spreading. Sensing his time was limited, the doctors allowed him to visit his daughter in Pittsburgh before admitting him to the hospital for radical treatment. However, before Mr. and Mrs. May left for Pittsburgh, one of their farming neighbors came to them and said, "Oh, I do hope you will have an opportunity to visit a Kathryn Kuhlman service while you are there."

In answer to their question about who Miss Kuhlman was, the neighbor gave them a copy of *I Believe in Miracles*. Kenneth May read the book. He began to wonder, for the first time, if it were possible for God to heal someone in the advanced stages of terminal cancer.

On April 1, 1968, Mr. and Mrs. May attended Kathryn's regular Monday night Bible study at the First Presbyterian Church. They were greatly impressed and afterwards lingered in the lobby of the church to talk to some of those who came each week. These people, learning Mr. May was critically ill, urged them to remain over for the miracle service on Friday morning at Carnegie Hall.

"God can heal you, you know," a man told him.

Mrs. May had to return to Canada, but Kenneth stayed over with his daughter. And although he was in great pain, he kept holding onto that slim thread of hope—"God can heal you, you know."

Friday morning his daughter accompanied him to Carnegie Hall, but when they arrived and found such a huge crowd waiting on the steps even though it was several hours before the service was to begin, he almost gave up hope. However, several of the people he had seen on Monday night spotted him and came to him, encouraging him to stay. A woman, a total stranger, approached him and said, "You have cancer, don't you?"

May was amazed over her insight, but before he could answer she reached out, took hold of his arm, and began to pray. Although he was embarrassed, he bowed his head and said out loud, "I am yours, Lord, do with me what you will."

Instantly he felt a strange sensation running through his body—and the pain was gone. He was healed. He stood for the next hour without any pain. After the service started he was approached by one of the workers, asking if he had been healed. May replied, "I think something has happened to me." Then he corrected himself. "I am *sure* something has happened to me."

He was taken to the platform where Kathryn prayed for

him. After the service, standing in the lobby, there was another strange manifestation. Water began to pour from the pores of his skin—a phenomenon which continued for three days. Saying goodbye to his daughter, he returned to Canada and the cancer clinic at the General Hospital in Ottawa, where he was pronounced healed. Even his doctor called it a miracle.

Soon after Kenneth May returned home, he paid a visit to Mrs. Mary Pettigrew of nearby Cobden who was in the final stages of multiple sclerosis. Under his urging, Mary and her husband, Clarence, drove down to Pittsburgh. She, too, was miraculously healed and returned to the little town of Cobden, overflowing with the good news of the miracle power of the Holy Spirit. After that there was no stopping the people. They drove to Pittsburgh in caravans. Many were healed and soon the word of miracles spread throughout that entire region of Canada.

In January 1969, about six months after Mary Pettigrew was healed, a woman from Ottawa, dying from cancer, called a friend of hers in Brockville, Mrs. Maudie Phillips, to inquire if she knew anything about the Kathryn Kuhlman services. Maudie knew nothing of them, had not even heard the name of Kathryn Kuhlman, but advised the friend to go ahead and attend. After all, she was dying, and what could be worse than that? The woman did attend the services in Pittsburgh and returned to Canada—healed. The change was immediate and obvious. Her skin, once the color of copper, was now healthy pink. All the symptoms were gone. Not only that, but the man who had driven her to Pittsburgh, who had a huge growth the size of a grapefruit on his spine, was healed also.

Maudie was a very conservative person and, even though she had known the woman since childhood, still had trouble believing. She talked the matter over with her husband,

163

Harvey, who was a printing broker, and the two of them agreed to drive down to Pittsburgh and see for themselves. The day before they left, the Phillips' daughter Sharon, their son-in-law Grant Mitchell, and their four-and-a-half-year-old grandson Troy asked to go along. Everybody, it seemed, in that section of Ontario was talking about the miracles taking place in Pittsburgh.

Little Troy had been born with eczema and a chronic lung condition similar to asthma. Canada in winter has the worst climate for people with eczema, for many of the warm clothes contain fibers which break down the skin, causing additional irritation. Troy's skin was covered with large, running sores, caked over with scabs and oozing fluid. Besides this, every place skin touched skin—under his chin, his armpits, his elbows, groins, knees, and in between his toes and fingers—there was an itching, burning inflammation with crusted and cracked lesions.

Troy had been under the care of one of the top dermatologists in Ottawa, Dr. Montgomery, as well as their family physician, Dr. Hal McLeod. Dr. Montgomery had prescribed medication which consisted not only of drugs, but four oatmeal baths a day. The oatmeal had a soothing effect on the skin, and the Mitchells were buying it by the hundred-pound sack. The baths were administered, painstakingly, by Sharon, who was also a registered nurse. At night the child had to be wrapped in gauze and bandages to keep him from scratching open the lesions. The only hope the doctors could give was that as he grew older he would learn to stay away from all the things that aggravated his allergies and perhaps learn to adjust to his condition.

After driving the five hundred miles to Pittsburgh and spending the night at the Pick Roosevelt Hotel, the family arrived at six-thirty the next morning at the First Presbyterian Church—where the miracle services were now being held since Carnegie Hall was being renovated. The church was already filling up even though the service was not scheduled to begin until eleven o'clock. Grant, Sharon, and Troy sat in one pew with Maudie and Harvey directly behind them on the aisle. Troy kept himself occupied with a coloring book during the long wait.

But something was happening. At 9:00 A.M. Maudie noticed that Sharon was crying—for no apparent reason. As the time for the miracle service grew closer, she cried even harder—and louder—and continued to weep even after Kathryn arrived to begin the service at eleven.

All this mystified Maudie, the staunch conservative. She wanted to leave and on two occasions turned to Harvey to take her out. But there was no way to make a graceful exit, and so she stayed, determined to tough it out and never again get herself in such an uncomfortable situation.

As Miss Kuhlman often did, she skipped the preaching and moved immediately into the miracle service, calling out various healings and encouraging people to come to the platform to testify. Midway through the service she stopped and said, "Someone is being healed of eczema." There was no response. Neither the Phillipses nor their children seemed to relate this in any way to Troy's condition. Kathryn continued with the service, but ten minutes later she did a very unusual thing, something her associates remember her doing only twice in her entire ministry. She said, "I'm going to have to stop the service. Someone in this sanctuary is grieving the Holy Spirit."

There was a deathly silence that fell over the huge auditorium. People turned and looked at each other much as the disciples must have done in the upper room when Jesus announced that one of them would betray Him. "Is it I? Is it I?"

Then Maggie Hartner, who seemed to literally flow with

165

the Holy Spirit when the anointing of God was on the miracle services, was standing in the aisle beside them. Sharon was still weeping so hard she was not aware of what was going on. Maggie spoke to Grant and said, "What are you praying for?"

"My son," Grant said simply.

"What's wrong with him?"

"Eczema."

"Well, for goodness sakes," Maggie exclaimed. "Haven't you heard Miss Kuhlman? The whole service is stopped. I've been running up and down these aisles trying to find the one who God had touched. Please check the child."

Suddenly Sharon came alive. Without even brushing away her tears, she reached over and pulled Troy's shirt over his head. Every sore on his body—every lesion, every oozing crack in the skin—was healed. The scabs had turned to powder, and as the shirt slipped off his back they dusted to the floor. Maudie, who was sitting directly behind him, gasped, and almost went into shock. Grant reached over and touched the place where an especially bad, draining sore had been on his left arm. The skin was now whole, healthy. Every part of his body was clean.

Maggie insisted that the parents bring the child forward. But none of them could later recall having gone to the platform. It was as though they were all in a trance.

Leaving the service they drove north, still unable to believe what they had seen and experienced. Near Erie they ran into a heavy snowstorm and had to check into a roadside motel. There was only one room available, so all five crowded in together. Troy went straight to sleep, but the adults stayed awake all night, talking and wondering about the miracle. About midnight Harvey could stand it no longer, and he took the lamp from the desk over to the bed so he could examine Troy's sleeping body. Every area where the sores had been was now snow white, in comparison to the normal pink skin on the other areas of his body. In the middle of each white area was a tiny rash, no bigger than the size of a pinhead. By morning, however, despite the fact that the adults continued to inspect him every hour on the hour, even this tiny rash was gone.

Three months later the Mitchells took Troy with them on a vacation trip to Mexico. When they returned, the boy's body was nicely tanned from the Mexican sun—all except the areas where the eczema had been. These areas remained snowy white for the next year, and then became perfectly normal.

They took Troy back to Dr. Montgomery and to Dr. McLeod, both of whom documented the healings—including his lungs. Dr. Montgomery called Maudie "the miracle grandmother"—a name she still cherishes as a reminder of the time when God so vividly invaded her life.

Maudie Phillips was the most excited woman in Ontario. She was determined that everyone in Ottawa should be exposed to the miracle services in Pittsburgh and be blessed as she had been blessed. A natural organizer, she began to think that if she could get the ministers of the city to attend a meeting, they would return on fire for God and all the churches would be filled with the same Holy Spirit that prevailed at the miracle services. However, she figured wrong. Even when she offered to charter a bus and pay for it out of her own pocket (at a cost of $1,000), the ministers, it seemed, were far too busy to get interested. None of them showed the slightest desire to witness a miracle—much less to get involved in one.

Undaunted, Maudie kept returning to Pittsburgh every weekend, driving down and taking anyone who agreed to accompany her. But she could not shake the feeling that she was supposed to charter a bus and take a group, perhaps several groups, to Pittsburgh.

In the fall of that year Harvey became sick. The doctors discovered a lung condition and told Maudie that there was a good chance he would die on the operating table. Prayer was still a very formal function for the Phillipses. As Maudie described it, they prayed "the United Church style"—meaning they listened to prayers on Sunday, said grace at the table, and repeated the Lord's Prayer at night. However, when Harvey's condition was described by the doctors as critical, Maudie found herself—for the first time—talking directly to God.

"Lord, if you save him I'll take a bus to Pittsburgh."

Harvey began to improve immediately, and the day after he came home from the hospital Maudie had her chartered bus filled and ready to go to Pittsburgh. There was only one minister in the group. The rest, as Maudie described them, were handmaids and servants—the very ones upon whom God had promised in the book of Joel to pour out His Spirit.

From that date until the time Kathryn died, almost six years later, Maudie Phillips missed only five services in Pittsburgh. She organized hundreds of charter busses from Canada and saw thousands of people healed and won to the Lord Jesus Christ.

As the number of Canadians at the miracle services increased, so did the amount of Canadian donations to the ministry. Since the donations to the American-based Kathryn Kuhlman Foundation were not deductible on the Canadian income tax returns, it was obvious that Kathryn needed to establish a Canadian office. And who was more natural to head it up than the person God had dropped in her lap, Maudie Phillips.

However, before Kathryn could call to ask her to take the

job, the Holy Spirit spoke to Maudie first. Although Maudie had worked for more than fifteen years in a responsible position at the Automatic Electric Company, she suddenly felt compelled to resign her job—for no other reason than she felt the Lord had something else in store for her. Thus when Miss Kuhlman's call came through, Maudie Phillips was already prepared to start to work immediately, organizing the Canadian branch of the Kathryn Kuhlman Foundation with headquarters in Brockville, near Ottawa.

Immediately Maudie went to work, trying to convince Kathryn that her following was so strong among the Canadians that they needed their own miracle service in the Ottawa area. She suggested the 16,000 seat Ottawa Civic Center. Kathryn, of course, did not convince easily. She felt comfortable with her services in Pittsburgh and Los Angeles and hesitated to move out, especially into that wasteland where so many ministries had starved to death—central Canada.

Kathryn often talked about a recurring nightmare where she would step out on the stage of some strange auditorium and find the building entirely empty. This kind of fear made her extremely cautious, unwilling to move into any new endeavor until she was sure it would be a success. For, other than appearing on stage without the Holy Spirit, nothing terrified her more than the dread of appearing on stage without her audience.

But Maudie was determined that Kathryn should come to Canada. The growing number of Canadians coming to Pittsburgh finally tipped the scales in Maudie's direction, and Kathryn agreed to come. She planned not only to visit Ottawa, but to have a three-night appearance in Peterboro.

Now the burden of responsibility suddenly fell on Maudie's shoulders. She went to bed that night after Kathryn had agreed to come, and she could not sleep. She lay there thinking. "Now look what you've done. You've taken a few busses to Pittsburgh and you've set up the book work for the Canadian foundation, but what do you know about organizing a miracle service? If Kathryn comes all the way to Canada and nobody shows up for the meetings, then her nightmare will become your reality."

It was two in the morning when, after sleeping only in fitful naps, she was suddenly wide awake. Every detail of how to plan and organize the service was pulsating through her mind. Careful not to waken her sleeping husband, she slipped out of bed and came downstairs. She looked around until she found an old Canadian road map, spread it out on the kitchen table, and once again closed her eyes. She remembered the vision she had in her mind when she had been wakened moments before. In the vision she had seen a map with pins on it, and detailed instructions on how to organize a bus brigade from all the outlying cities. Opening her eyes, she began to stick pins in the map and write out her plans for chartering the busses. By the time Harvey came down for breakfast, she had every detail figured out.

It was a brand-new concept. She knew exactly how many busses she would need and could tell, by looking at her charts, how many would be filled, partially filled, how many additional busses she would need, how many people would occupy the reserved seats, how much of an area to reserve for wheelchairs, and how many ushers would be needed.

Kathryn was impressed. And so Maudie Phillips, the Miracle Grandmother, began traveling all over the United States and Canada, setting up the groundwork for the great miracle services to be held in Chicago, St. Louis, Oakland, Seattle, Dallas, Miami, Atlanta, Las Vegas, and a dozen other major cities. It was the beginning of an entirely new ministry for Kathryn—hers because she had the wisdom to wait.

CHAPTER XI

HELLO THERE!
AND HAVE YOU BEEN
WAITING FOR ME?

Everyone, it seemed, at one time or another enjoyed doing a Kathryn Kuhlman imitation. Her unique, raspy voice as she came on the radio saying, "Hell-ooo there, and have you been waaaa-iting for me?" her dramatic gestures with her hands on television; the way she got up on her tiptoes and with tiny, quick steps flitted backwards on the platform while she waved a finger in the air and said, "The Hoooooly Spiii-rit is here," or "I give you gloooory, I give you praise;" her 1940s hair style . . . all lent themselves to the ideal kind of exaggerated caricature people loved to imitate. One Hollywood movie producer, a Jew was a great fan of Kathryn's. He said she had all the makings of a star since she was the only woman in the world who could turn the word "God" into four syllables.

She became fair bait for the television comedians. Entertainers like Flip Wilson and Carol Burnett could bring down the house with a ridiculous Kathryn Kuhlman imitation. Kathryn always seemed to enjoy them more than anyone else. She knew the television and night club entertainers would only pick on those with national stature, and I believe she was willing to tolerate the humiliation of having Carol Burnett make fun of her just for the sake of basking in the notoriety which belongs only to celebrities. After Ruth Buzzi did a really "far out" imitation of Miss Kuhlman on "Laugh In," (laying hands on casaba melons in a supermarket) Kathryn sent her a personal letter which contained one line: "No one enjoyed the satire more than I." Ruth replied by wiring Kathryn two dozen long-stemmed roses. (Incidentally, Ruth never again did a Kathryn Kuhlman imitation on television.)

Even those of us who knew her and loved her could not resist, if the subject around the dinner table turned to Kathryn Kuhlman, from pointing our finger and saying, "And it's just like that!" Or, if the mood at the prayer meeting was light and informal, to growl in a throaty voice, "I beeeeliEEEEVE in meeeericles."

There were a lot of theories concerning just why Kathryn talked the way she did. Some words were always over-accented. "Jesus" always came out "JEEEZusss." And she could not speak of the Holy Spirit without drawing out His name: "the Hooooly Spir-it." The same was true with those dramatic gestures, especially when she would step back, point her finger, lower her chin, look down her arm beyond her fingertip, and say with the definiteness of Boulder Dam: "That's right! And don't you forget it!"

Kathryn enjoyed telling people that as a child she stuttered (like Moses). Her mother was concerned about this and spent hours coaching her in the correct method of speech, saying, "Now, baby, talk slowly. Eee-nun-ci-ate your words cleeer-ly."

"That's the reason I speak so slowly now," Kathryn explained to a reporter from *People* magazine. "A lot of people think my speech is affected, but it's just my way of overcoming my problem."

That made folks feel a lot better. We all love an overcomer but despise a showman. Actually those who knew her in childhood said she had always talked slowly, over-dramatizing her gestures and over-accenting her words, just to capture the attention of her listeners. One old schoolmate told me that when she heard Kathryn on television she could close her eyes and still recognize that voice as a fifteen-year-old redheaded, mischievous girl standing in front of the class, waving her arms, batting her long eyelashes, thrusting out her hip, and reciting, "O Captain! My Captain!"

"When the teacher left the room," the classmate said, "all the kids would begin to clamor, 'Kathryn, tell us a story.' She was a real spellbinder with her stories, and even though we giggled at her dramatics and the way she pronounced her words, we knew that nobody could entertain us the way Kathryn could."

Many years later, during one of the huge miracle services at the Shrine Auditorium, Kathryn's older sister, Myrtle Parrott, was sitting high in the balcony. A couple of young women were sitting behind her and Myrtle overheard their conversation.

"She's just too dramatic," one said. "I can't stand all those theatrics."

"And the way she draws out her words. What a phoney. She must have stood in front of a mirror for years trying to perfect her accent."

It was more than Myrtle could take. Twisting in her seat, with blazing eyes she said, "I've known her longer than you have. I've known her longer than anyone in the auditorium

173

today, and I want you to know she's always talked like that. I mean always."

Did she really stutter as a child?

Or did she begin working at an early age, developing a technique to entertain—a technique she never changed, because it worked?

It's another of the mysteries which will probably remain forever unsolved.

Kathryn began every broadcast with the same "sign-on": "Hello there! And have you been waiting for me? It's so nice of you. I just knew you'd be there."

It may have sounded like pure corn, but it was that homey touch which endeared her to an entire generation of radio listeners long before television dominated the air waves. In fact, many listeners wrote in saying that when Kathryn's voice came through their radio asking if they had been waiting for her they would answer back, out loud, "Oh yes, Kathryn. I'm right here." Like a lot of other things in Kathryn's life, once she found a workable formula, she never changed.

However, her famous histrionics, her deliberate display of enunciation and dramatic gestures for effect, left her vulnerable for hilarious imitations.

My favorite imitator was Catherine Marshall. Perhaps it was because the famous author is basically a serious person, or maybe because her personality is geared to the non-demonstrative, but she could imitate the other Kathryn's television voice so well one would think the evangelist was actually in the room.

One of my fondest memories is of the meeting between the two—Kathryn Kuhlman and Catherine Marshall. Catherine, the author, and her husband Leonard LeSourd, who was at that time editor of *Guideposts* magazine, had asked if I would introduce them to Kathryn. Both the

LeSourds had come into a new dimension of their spiritual lives and were deeply interested in Miss Kuhlman's ministry—especially her emphasis on the Holy Spirit. Besides this, Catherine was working on her book, *Something More*, in which she planned to include a chapter on healing. She thought the meeting with Miss Kuhlman would be beneficial.

Kathryn was equally eager for the meeting. Although I do not believe she had ever read any of Catherine's books, she was impressed by those who had reached the pinnacle of success. And meeting both the famous authoress and her equally talented husband, was just the kind of the fare she enjoyed. So when I called her in Pittsburgh and told her I intended to bring Catherine and Len to the miracle service in Miami the next week, she acted like I was bringing the king and queen of England.

"Just come on backstage as soon as you get there," she laughed. "I've been waiting for this a long time."

A drizzling rain was falling the afternoon Jackie and I picked up Catherine and Len at their Florida home. As we drove south down the Sunshine State Parkway, both of them were plying me with questions. Writers are always curious people, spending more time asking questions and listening than they do telling stories.

"Do you think the phenomenon of 'going under the power' is real?"

"Do you think she has any hypnotic power?"

"Why are some healed and others return home unhealed?"

"Do you think faith plays an important part in the healings?"

"Whose faith—hers or the person being healed?"

"Why would God choose such a person as Kathryn Kuhlman, with all her obvious faults?"

175

The only conclusion I could reach as we pulled off the turnpike towards the Dade County Auditorium was that healing, like birth and death, was God's business. It was the product of His love and mercy, not man's antics, and He could choose whom He jolly well pleased to convey His healing power.

By the time we reached the auditorium, the rain was falling steadily. It was a few minutes before five when we turned off Flagler Street and pulled around beside the auditorium, windshield wipers slapping rhythmically at the chrome side strips of my four-year-old Chevrolet.

"Wow!" I heard Len say from the back seat, followed by Catherine's more earthy, "Good God, look at that!"

The sidewalk, lawn, and street in front of the auditorium were packed with people. A few had managed to squeeze against the wall under the overhanging eaves, but most—perhaps another two thousand—were standing in the pelting rain waiting for the doors to open. Umbrellas of many sizes, shapes, and colors had been raised and some of the folks were able to huddle under them. Others were standing with heads bent under soggy newspapers. Most were just getting drenched. And the crowd was growing in size as the people, having parked their cars, were hurrying from the parking lot to join at the fringes, spilling out over the grass, the flower beds, and into the main street.

Catherine was on the edge of the back seat, her hands gripping the back of the seat just behind my head as she peered through the windshield at the sight. "Two hours before the service starts and they're out here standing in the rain," she gasped. "Can you imagine folks trying to get into our Presbyterian church like that?"

Len chuckled in amazement. "Well, maybe if the same things took place in our church service as they say take place in these miracle services, we'd have the same results."

We parked the car and slipped through a side door near the stage entrance. The choir was already in place and Dr. Metcalfe was putting them through their final paces. The auditorium seemed almost full, occupied by those who had come on the chartered busses, or by the critical cases in wheelchairs and stretchers. We made our way backstage to Kathryn's dressing room. Maggie met us at the door and made it very plain we were welcome.

Kathryn was pacing, as always. She turned quickly when we came in and held out her arms. "Awww, God bless you," she beamed.

All I could do was stare. She was dressed in a sheer black organza dress that had huge lacy fluffs around the bottom of the skirt and at the ends of the elbow-length sleeves. Her dress was accentuated by a dark red belt, at least six inches wide, giving her the appearance that you could reach around her waist with both hands and make your fingers touch. The fluffy lace on the sleeves emphasized her long arms. She was wearing a heavy silver bracelet on her right wrist and her neck was encircled with an expensive ornament that looked like emeralds set against pure silver. She wore black hose to match the black dress, and dark red shoes. But it wasn't the clothes—it was the glasses that took my breath. She was wearing the largest pair of dark glasses I had ever seen. Dark red frames matched her belt and shoes, but the glasses themselves covered the entire top half of her face and extended a full two inches beyond the sides of her head.

She stood for a moment with one hand resting on her waist in that typical hip-out stance much like Betty Grable used when she posed during the 1940s. Even though she was on the other side of sixty-five, she could still get away with it. She held that pose for just a few seconds and then reached out and grabbed Catherine's hand in both of hers.

She repeated that first "Awwww, God bless you," her face all grin and glasses. Then, still holding Catherine's hand tightly in both of hers, she stepped back half a step as though to view and admire the person who had come to see her.

"I'm still amazed," she said, her voice rising and falling like deep water slipping over rocks in a river, "why anyone like you would want to come see me. But," she chuckled in a throaty way, "I'm sooooo glad you did."

Catherine just stood there, transfixed, looking at those monstrous glasses.

Kathryn gave another of her laughs. "Oh," she said in a raucous voice, "I'm just trying to be inconspicuous."

Catherine guffawed and suddenly the two of them were like old sisters.

We didn't stay in the dressing room long and quickly took seats in the auditorium where we could see not only the platform but also get a good view of the action that was taking place in the seats after the miracles began. In fact, Len and Catherine seemed far more interested in viewing the audience reaction as the healings were called out, than they were in watching Kathryn as she moved back and forth about the platform. On several occasions I glanced at the two of them and saw tears. It was a spectacular show, to be sure, but there was more involved than showmanship. The Holy Spirit was there also.

That was the only time the two Kathryns (or should it be Catherines) met. That night, on the way back to the LeSourd home, after we let Len off at the Miami airport to catch a plane to New York, Catherine was quiet and serious. And although I have been with her many times after that meeting, to my knowledge she never again imitated her famous counterpart.

CHAPTER XII

UNTOLD STORIES

Even though there is no satisfactory definition of a miracle, Kathryn did insist on certain standard criteria before a miracle story could be printed. Unless the healings passed these tests, they were not to be included in her books.

1. The disease or injury should be organic or structural in nature—and should have been medically diagnosed.
2. The healing should have occurred rapidly, or instantaneously. The changes would have to be abnormal, and not the kind that could result from suggestion.
3. All healings would have to be medically verified— preferably by more than one doctor. At least one of the doctors must be the patient's private physician.
4. The healing should be permanent, or at least of sufficient duration so as not to be diagnosed as a "remission."

Because we held rigidly to this standard, many of the most spectacular miracles were never reported in her books.

There was the case of George Davis, for instance, formerly a supervisor of Vocational Education Services for the Philadelphia school system. Davis, who held degrees from NYU, Temple, the University of Pennsylvania, and Villanova, was the first black counselor in the Abington Township School District. I interviewed him in his comfortable home in the northern suburbs of Philadelphia and found him to be one of the most pleasant men I had ever met. His healing fell into the category of "classic."

Pushing to achieve—to overcome in a white world—Davis developed a serious heart condition. His cardiologist at Abington Memorial Hospital diagnosed it as a myocardial infarction. The valve, which allowed the blood to flow between the two ventricles of his heart, was malfunctioning. It was a problem very similar to that which contributed to Kathryn's death several years later.

Davis lived with his condition for almost a year—although he experienced several heart attacks and almost died—until the cardiologist decided to regulate the heartbeat by inserting a pacemaker. The stainless steel electronic device was about the size of a Zippo cigarette lighter. It was placed, during surgery, in his left chest in the hollow below the collarbone. A tube extended over his lung and down into his heart. A small battery in the pacemaker provided an electrical charge which sent steady impulses into his heart, keeping the beat regular.

Eight months after the operation, Davis visited his father in Donora, Pennsylvania, a suburb of Pittsburgh. His father, who was ushering at Kathryn's miracle services, urged him to attend also. Davis was reluctant; he was not a very religious man. However, convinced that his father had undergone some kind of genuine change, he finally agreed to go.

At the close of the service, Miss Kuhlman came down the aisle, praying for people. Approaching George Davis, she laid her hand on his head and moved on down the aisle. Davis fell out of his chair and lay on the floor, unable to move. While he was "under the power," he felt a terrific burning in his chest, a pain very similar to what he had experienced during his first heart attack—a year and a half before.

A woman standing nearby leaned down and said, "That's no heart attack. You're being healed. That's the power of God going through you."

All Davis could reply was, "I hope so."

The pain finally subsided, and Davis was able to crawl back into his chair to await the closing of the service. But his life was changed, spiritually, from that moment on.

That night, in his parents' home in Donora, he finished taking a bath and stood before the mirror drying off. Suddenly he realized something was different. The scar on his chest, where the pacemaker had been inserted, was gone. However, he was tired and the light was poor, so he put it out of his mind. The next morning, though, he reexamined himself and the scar was still missing. Not only that, when he pressed his fingers against the tissue of his chest, he could no longer feel the pacemaker.

Davis was hesitant to return to his doctor, but finally, three weeks later, he decided he should go in for a checkup. During this time he had gained weight and felt stronger than he had in years. When the cardiologist checked his cardiogram, it was perfect. Davis then explained what had happened. Surprisingly, the doctor reacted with anger. He quickly called for a fluoroscopic examination. When the pacemaker could not be found, the doctor accused Davis of having had it taken out. Mystified, David replied that "If there was a scar made to put it in, wouldn't there be a scar if someone took it out?" Then he added, "I tell you, the good Lord took it out—and removed the scar also."

The doctor, now in a rage, said he didn't like it when people tampered with his procedures. Davis tried to argue that "God isn't people," but the physician was too angry to listen. He ordered full x-rays at the hospital, starting with the soles of his feet and going all the way to the top of his head. The pacemaker was gone.

The following week, Davis kept an appointment at the hospital where he was examined by a panel of cardiologists, including a professor of medicine from Harvard. All agreed it was the most unusual case they had ever witnessed. However, when Davis asked his cardiologist for a statement to verify that the pacemaker had been inserted, and that later, upon examination, it was gone, the doctor blew up.

"You want to make me the laughing stock of the entire medical profession, don't you? I will not give you a letter and I forbid you to use my name in anything you have to say. If you try, I will take you to court."

Dr. George Johnston, of Philadelphia, a consulting physician during Davis' earlier heart attack, was willing to testify, however. He said, "I can confirm that Davis had a heart attack, that a pacemaker was placed in his body, and that now the pacemaker and the five-inch incision scar are gone. It's all in the record."

Kathryn asked Davis to appear on her television program, but since the story did not meet one of our criteria—the attending physician being unwilling to verify the story—we chose not to use it in one of her books. The story has remained untold. Until now.

Very few doctors reacted the way George Davis' doctor did. Many, in fact, were eager to document the miracles, unthreatened by God's interference with "their" work. One of those was a physician in southern Pennsylvania, a woman, who actually brought one of her patients to a miracle service for a healing. However, because the girl, although healed, was never able to overcome her moral problems, Kathryn decided to omit the story from her books.

The young housewife had contracted multiple sclerosis, a terrifying disease which attacks the muscles and nerves, often bending the body into grotesque shapes and causing violent convulsions. The patient often is confined to a wheelchair and, since there is no known medical cure, eventually dies from the disease. That is, unless God intervenes.

This case was particularly pathetic. Not only did the woman have young children, but her husband took advantage of her sickness to indulge in an affair with another woman. On several occasions he brought his mistress home and into the back bedroom, knowing his wife could not follow them because the door openings were too small to accommodate her wheelchair. Broken in body and spirit, she would have died had it not been for her doctor, a Spirit-filled Lutheran, who stepped in and took a personal interest. The doctor, who had heard of the miracle services in Pittsburgh, finally convinced the young wife to accompany her to Pittsburgh. It was her only hope, the doctor said.

The two of them went on one of the chartered busses. The doctor stayed with her the entire time, helping her climb the steps of the church one by one, her legs locked in heavy steel braces. During the service, the woman's leg began to vibrate. She removed her brace and found she could use that leg. The doctor accompanied her to the platform. While she was talking to Miss Kuhlman, the young woman "went under the power" and crashed to the stage floor. When she came to, she removed her other brace and was able to walk off the platform, normally.

Since this young woman had been paralyzed from the waist down, she had no control over her bladder. For more than a year, she had worn a urinary catheter which was attached to a plastic sack strapped to her inner thigh. The doctor knew the true test of her healing would come when she removed the catheter. On the woman's insistence, they went immediately to the ladies rest room in the First Presbyterian Church where the doctor, using a pair of forceps which she had brought with her "just in case," removed the catheter. The woman was able to void normally and returned to her hometown, healed.

Multiple sclerosis is a strange disease and often goes into remission, allowing the patient to function fairly normally for a short period of time. However, once it reaches the "wheelchair" stage there is seldom any remission. Yet, six years after her visit to the miracle service, the woman showed no signs of MS. Not only her own doctor, but doctors in Baltimore confirmed a total healing.

However, instead of committing her life to God, the young woman, now divorced from her husband, slipped into immorality. Physically she had been healed, but psychologically she was still a cripple. Kathryn and the doctor both agreed the story should not be published. "We must be extra careful not to bring a reproach against the Holy Spirit," Kathryn cautioned.

It was one of the few times I disagreed with her. I felt the Holy Spirit was quite capable of taking care of Himself. Besides, I felt the story illustrated an extremely valid point—that God is no respecter of persons. His mercy and grace—like the rain from heaven—falls on the just and the unjust, on sinners as well as saints. Kathryn agreed with my theory but stuck to her guns. Therefore the story remained untold. Until now.

Perhaps the most thrilling stories were those told by the medical doctors themselves. Dr. Cecil Titus of St. Luke's Hospital in Cleveland said that a ten-year-old girl's club foot "straightened before my very eyes while Miss Kuhlman prayed." Dr. Kitman Au of Burbank, California, a radiologist, told a newspaper reporter, "I have seen healings in Kathryn Kuhlman's services that I, as a doctor, can only say go beyond human power." And Dr. Richard Owellen, the cancer research specialist from Johns Hopkins University, told of holding his infant child in his arms at a miracle service and watching the child's dislocated hip twist, under the power of the Holy Spirit, until it was healed and in place.

One of Miss Kuhlman's most cherished letters came from Dr. E. B. Henry, who practiced medicine in Pittsburgh until his death in 1963 at the age of seventy-three. He wrote:

> This letter is both an expression of gratitude and an apology; gratitude to God and to you (may He bless you always), and an apology to you for not recognizing a healing when it was taking place. I shall try to make this letter as short as possible, so here goes the "blow by blow" account. . . .
>
> Saturday, November 18 [1950], was a hard day for me. Up at six, going hard all day until five-thirty when I arrived home for dinner. Rushed to get ready and drove to Franklin. There in the hotel, I had very little sleep, due to an infected right antrum which caused me no little pain, and an old fracture of the right clavicle (collarbone) which had not healed together but had formed a false joint with a callus around it about the size of a walnut. It had been very painful so that I could

put my coat on only with difficulty and my hand would shake when I endeavored to raise my right arm. I assure you that the pain from my neck down to my wrist was really severe.

Sunday morning: up again at six in order to get breakfast and get out to Faith Temple before nine. I want you to know that I truly had no thought as to any healing for myself. I have always been able to stand pain, so my chief concern was for my wife, who had her left breast removed in April for signet-cell carcinoma (a very malignant type), and my fear that she might have metastases.

During your healing period you began to state that there was a "sinus opening up. Someone is regaining hearing in an ear" (I have been deaf in my right ear for at least fifteen years). You went on to say, "I see a lump the size of a walnut beginning to dissolve." My wife nudged me and whispered, "She means you," but I, just thinking of her, felt nothing but a burning in my right ear which I thought was the result of mental suggestion.

Then you said, "This is a man. I do not want you to lose this healing. Please speak up." I can see you now as you looked earnestly in our direction waving your left hand almost directly at our group and at the same time pounding the pulpit with your right fist. My wife kept nudging me, but even when you said that the man had a burning in his ear, I couldn't believe that I was being healed. After all, I had asked nothing for myself. I was accustomed to the deafness in my right ear and gave it no thought.

I drove the eighty-five miles home through the rain, a condition not conducive to helping sinusitis. On the way home, my wife kept speaking to me in an ordinary tone of voice. She was sitting beside me *on my right.* Then she called my attention to my ability to hear her and we both realized I was not asking her to repeat. Just after we arrived home, all of a sudden I had to blow my nose. My sinus had opened and the pain was gone. The antrum kept draining freely all evening. I slept well all night, and in the morning I was entirely free of drainage and pain.

To add to my amazement, I found that I was able to use my right arm in normal motion without pain. I cannot state that the hearing in my right ear is perfect. But I need not turn my left ear to my wife and ask her to repeat. Perhaps the rest of my hearing will return gradually.

Dr. Martin Biery, who specialized in spinal cord surgery, was a frequent visitor on the platform at the Shrine Auditorium. He was on the staff at the Veterans' Hospital in Long Beach, California.

"With my own eyes," Dr. Biery said, "I have seen the medically impossible happen time and time again. I have seen arthritics whose spines were frozen get instantaneous freedom and move and bend in all directions without pain. A leg which was shortened by polio visibly lengthened before my eyes as Miss Kuhlman prayed. A boy with osteochondritis of the knee—a chronic inflammation caused by a football injury—had not been able to bend his leg for several years. When I examined him on the spot, he had perfect flexion of his knee. As a medical man, I call these healings miracles."

Dr. Viola Frymann from La Jolla, California, was another frequent visitor on the Shrine stage. She related numerous miracles she had seen, including a child with a blood clot on the optic nerve who received sight. Another child, whose

187

arm and leg were paralyzed from cerebral palsy, was healed before her eyes. "My hope is that an awareness of the reality of such spiritual healing will penetrate the medical profession," she told Canadian reporter Allen Spraggett.

In 1969 I sat beside Dr. Robert Hoyt, on the stage at the Shrine Auditorium. Dr. Hoyt, a diplomate of the American Board of Pathology, was on the staff of the medical school at Stanford University and often flew down from San Francisco to attend the services. A long line of people had come to the stage, waiting to testify of healings. Directly in front of us was an old woman, in her late seventies, wearing a pair of wire-rimmed glasses. One lens was frosted over. She told the helper, who was trying to keep the people in a straight line, that she had been healed of a painful bursitis in one shoulder, but her right eye was still blind. While she was whispering to the aide, Miss Kuhlman, who was at least thirty feet away and could not possibly have heard the whispered conversation amidst all the other noise, suddenly turned. Pointing in our direction, she said, "There's someone over here who's being healed. It's an eye healing of some kind. It's happening right now."

There had been so many healings that I was in a state of semi-shock. But I looked up just in time to see that frosted lens, without anyone touching it, suddenly pop from the wire frame and fall to the floor. Dr. Hoyt gasped. "Did you see that!" he whispered.

Too astounded to answer, I could only nod my head. Of course Dr. Hoyt wasn't watching me. He was watching the woman, who, stunned and perplexed, groped for her glasses. Then she realized. She could see. She had regained her sight. Someone picked up the frosted lens and handed it to her. She staggered off the stage toward her seat, too dazed to even come close to comprehending what had just taken place. Kathryn, unaware of the miracle, did not pause long enough to ask if anything had happened, but turned back to the congregation to continue calling out other healings.

Regaining my voice, I started to say something to the physician who was seated beside me. But when I turned, I saw he had his face in his hands, weeping. The story has remained untold. Until now.

One of the most cherished items in my writing studio is a gold-framed shadow box containing an expensive set of surgical forceps, formerly used by a skilled ophthalmologist in Dallas, Texas, in delicate eye surgery. Kathryn gave them to me just a year before she died, along with a letter from their former owner, Dr. Elizabeth R. Vaughan.

"Hold onto these," Kathryn said with great tenderness. "They are precious to me. One day you may want to write a story."

The letter is dated Christmas Day, 1974, five-thirty in the morning.

Dearest Kathryn:

I am writing this before my children awake on this Christmas morning because I want you to be the first person in this house to receive a present on our Lord's birthday.

Three weeks ago I asked the Lord what you would like for Christmas that no one knew about, that would meet the desires of your heart. This 0.12 mm. toothed forceps was His answer. Let me explain what it means.

For the last four-and-a-half years I have used this very instrument on every single cataract operation that the Lord and I have performed. It is indispensable to me. It has three teeth on the end that are 0.12 mm. long. You will need some means of magnification to see these teeth well. They are used to grasp tissue so that a

189

needle can be passed through it while it is being held with firmness but gentleness. The teeth must be perfectly aligned to grasp the tissue properly. If they are malaligned one hair's breadth they might as well be thrown away, for they will no longer grasp in an exacting manner.

The reason this instrument and its function is so crucial, is because it is used for closing the wound after a cataract has been removed. This means that the eye is wide open and there is no margin for error in the surgeon or the instrument. If this instrument is not grasping properly, causing any pressure to be exerted on an open eye, the contents from inside the eye could be pressed out and the patient's vision compromised if not lost completely. All of this surgery is done through an operating microscope under high magnification. These forceps must grasp tissue ½ mm. thick and hold it firmly enough to pass a needle through it, while exerting no pressure whatsoever on the open eye.

I love this precision instrument. It has served me well and been in the middle of many surgical miracles the Lord has performed. It has functioned perfectly for these four and one-half years of use, and now I want you to have it on this Christmas morning. It is intended to serve as a reminder from our heavenly Father to you, that this instrument has been in my hand like you are in His hand.

You are to Him like this 0.12 mm. forceps, grasping with fine, perfectly aligned teeth whatever He wants you to grasp at the time. You began as a chunk of metal with no form or usefulness, and by being yielded to His will and dying to your own will, He has been able to make you into a perfect, precision instrument in His hand. You are exactly what He wants you to be. He did not want you to be a pair of scissors or an instrument for extracting the cataract. He intended from the beginning of time for you to be a 0.12 mm. toothed forceps—holding the tissue so the Great Physician can do the stitching and healing.

Not many people in this world are so yielded that God can make of them *exactly* what He wants them to be, but you are. Our Father wants you to know, on His Son's birthday, that He loves you beyond words and that it gives Him great pleasure to have such a precision instrument as Kathryn Kuhlman available for Him to use as He wishes.

Amen and amen!
Beth Vaughan

That story (written far better than any biographer could pen) about the Father's purpose in using a red-haired, freckle-faced girl from Concordia, Missouri, has also remained untold. Until now.

CHAPTER XIII

WORSHIPING AT
THE SHRINE

There comes a time in every man's career—or every woman's—when he either moves on—or drops back. In the Book of Exodus there is a fascinating story about God leading the Israelites through the wilderness of Sinai by having a cloud rest over the tabernacle. As long as the cloud remained stationary, the people could remain where they were. But when the cloud moved, it was time to roll up their tents, gather their sheep and goats from the wadis and hillsides, and move out under the cloud.

Kathryn's cloud began to move again in 1965. Ten years before, evangelist C.M. Ward, of the Assemblies of God church, had prophesied to Ralph Wilkerson, a young California pastor: "Ralph, two things are going to happen in the kingdom. There is going to be a major re-emphasis on Bible teaching. And second, there is going to be a great woman evangelist who will come to the West Coast."

Ralph hung onto the prophecies. It never occurred to

him that God might want to use him as the instrument to bring one of them to pass.

Ralph's church, Anaheim Christian Center, was a growing, thriving congregation. His healing ministry (he had been holding miracle services for ten years) was well-known in the local area. Miracles were occurring every week. Besides this, they were sponsoring giant rallies and crusades, using the Anaheim Convention Center. David Wilkerson (no relation to Ralph), founder of Teen Challenge ministry, had been the principal speaker at several crusades. At the same time, David was also working with Kathryn back in Pittsburgh, Pa. and Youngstown, Ohio. Kathryn was impressed with the young preacher of *The Cross and the Switchblade* fame and was helping him raise money for his drug rehabilitation projects by letting him preach in Stambaugh Auditorium and in youth meetings at the Syria mosque in Cleveland, Ohio. David began urging Ralph—who had never met Kathryn—to invite her to Los Angeles.

For several years Ralph had been conducting a prayer meeting in the mansion-like home of a Church of Christ elder in nearby San Clemente. In 1964 the men in the prayer group, which numbered upward to two hundred, agreed with Ralph to begin praying that God would send Kathryn Kuhlman to Southern California. Kathryn knew nothing of this, of course.

In the late summer, Ralph felt it was time to meet Kathryn face-to-face. He asked David Wilkerson to make arrangements for the meeting, and, with his wife, Allene, he flew to Pittsburgh. Like Kathryn, Ralph was cautious and felt the need for a thorough investigation. Rather than going directly to meet her when they arrived, they drove to Youngstown to attend one of the Sunday meetings and try to get a "feel" for her ministry.

"I could be wrong about all this," Ralph told Allene as

they parked the car in the crowded parking lot near the huge auditorium. "That's the reason I want to check things out before I say anything. We have enough 'kooks' in California without being responsible for inviting another."

The Wilkersons slipped into the 2,500-seat Stambaugh Auditorium an hour before the service began. The building was already packed with people. The men's choir was rehearsing under Arthur Metcalfe's direction. Maggie Hartner was busy with the Sunday school. The building had a kind of circus quality to it. The hot dog stand was open and people were eating sandwiches and drinking coffee downstairs. It didn't seem like "church" at all—at least not in the sense the Wilkersons were accustomed to.

"But when Kathryn came out and the service started," Ralph said, "I knew we were in the presence of God. We sang the same songs and choruses we sang on the West Coast. The people raised their hands and were free in their worship. They had the same order of service I was accustomed to, using no printed bulletin but just letting the Holy Spirit lead. Kathryn preached the same kind of message I preached. And they had miracles. God was in that place."

Recalling that morning, Ralph chuckled. "I knew I was in the right place when, while we were standing and singing, a three-hundred-pound lady directly in front of me was slain in the Spirit and toppled backwards. She almost crushed me to death."

The next day Ralph walked the streets of downtown Pittsburgh, going from business to business, asking people what they thought of Kathryn Kuhlman. He got the same reports every place he went. "Well, for one thing, she sure has helped a lot of alcoholics . . . . You know that men's chorus is made up of more than a few former drunks . . . . My wife was healed in her service . . . . We close the store on Friday morning so we can attend the miracle service . . . ."

195

Impressed, Ralph and Allene finally arrived at the Carlton House offices. He shared his dream and extended his invitation. He was sure God had spoken.

Kathryn laughed at him. "Why should I come? I have plenty of people here in Pittsburgh. Besides, that's the graveyard out there, all that Hollywood glamour. I'm just a small-time country girl from Missouri. I'm not interested."

Ralph was determined. "I think you will be when you pray about it. I'm going back to ask our men to intensify their prayers."

In early 1965, Oral Roberts called Allene Wilkerson from Cleveland, Ohio, where he was holding a crusade. His organist's mother had died, he said, and he was in desperate need for someone to play the organ at his service. He realized it was short notice, but could Allene drop everything and fly to Cleveland to play for him?

She talked it over with Ralph. He agreed, but insisted she go on to Pittsburgh and once again invite Kathryn to California. "Don't leave until she agrees," he said.

Allene stayed with Kathryn at Fox Chapel. Every night she called back home. "Ralph, she still refuses to come."

Every morning she told Kathryn, "I talked with Ralph last night. He's still insisting that God wants you to come to California."

Kathryn's reply was always the same. "I've got too much to do here. I don't want to expand this ministry."

But the cloud was moving, and Kathryn knew it. To remain behind simply because she was comfortable would mean running the risk of losing contact with the Holy Spirit. She had no choice but to go.

On the fourth day she pulled Allene aside. "Okay. I think this is of God. I'm going to California. But just one meeting. No more. Just one."

That meeting was held at the civic auditorium in Pasadena. Kathryn was virtually unknown on the West Coast, so most of the 2,500 people who attended came from Anaheim Christian Center—including the ushers and choir.

But not all. Many came from other churches and a few came simply because they were curious. As always, there were miracles.

"I was standing beside a woman who was wearing braces on both hands," Ralph Wilkerson said. "Her arms and wrists were twisted with arthritis. During the miracle service she screamed out. I looked down and saw her hands pop into place.

" 'My God,' she gasped in amazement. 'Look at my hands.' "

Ralph later discovered she was an influential leader in the First Baptist Church of Fullerton. She went home and the next day painted the inside of her house—the first time she had been able to use her hands in years. It didn't take long before Southern California was buzzing with talk about the miracle service—and about Kathryn Kuhlman.

Despite her intention of "just one" service in California, Kathryn now recognized God's intention for a continuing ministry there. And by the third service in Pasadena, the convention center could no longer hold the crowds. Hundreds were being turned away. Many more, however, attracted by reports of miracles, were hearing the gospel for the first time—and being born again. Ralph was concerned because Kathryn had no follow-up ministry. She came into town, held her miracle service, gave an invitation to which hundreds responded, prayed for them, and then left town. Acquainted with the ministry of Billy Graham, whose follow-up work was tied closely to the local churches, Ralph began to make suggestions to Kathryn.

"We need to get these new Christians involved in Bible studies," he said. "They need to be in churches where they can have fellowship and hear the Word of God. The miracles are wonderful, Kathryn, but even you say being born again is more important than being healed. It's wrong to create babies and then leave them out on the street. They need nourishment, protection, and guidance which can come only through the body of Christ.

Kathryn was being faced with one of the great frustrations of her life. She wanted to be known as a Bible teacher, not a miracle worker. All her followers in Youngstown called her "pastor."

Those who knew her often heard her say she felt her first calling was that of a Bible teacher. And as long as she had time to study her Bible, to prepare her messages, she was unexcelled. It was only in her later years, when the schedule got so furious that she was flying all over the nation holding miracle services in a different city each week, that her preaching deteriorated. Before then, her radio programs were the kind of meat that fed the hungry. Listeners by the hundreds of thousands tuned in every day, not because they had been to her miracle services—for most of them had not—but because she was feeding them from the Word of God. Her Monday night Bible studies at the First Presbyterian Church in Pittsburgh were attended by some of the most elite Bible scholars in the city, who gladly sat at her feet and learned. Kathryn knew the need to nourish new Christians, but she was frustrated on how to do it so far away from home. Back in Pittsburgh her people tithed their income to what she called "the ministry." They attended the Sunday services in Youngstown, the Friday morning service at Carnegie Hall, and the Monday night Bible study at First Presbyterian Church. She knew them by name. She had baptized many of them in the great outdoor baptismal services at a nearby lake. She had married their children and conducted funerals for their loved ones. She could tell them she needed an extra $100,000 for a mission project in Indonesia, and they would raise it for her. But in California, she was a stranger who came to town once a month for a miracle service. She was frustrated.

She listened to Ralph. Many of those around her had offered advice when actually they were trying to use her—to promote their own program. Kathryn was willing to listen, but not to novices. And there were very few people in her class. However, recognizing Ralph as a successful pastor, she was willing to follow his suggestions. At least she agreed to try.

Ralph introduced her to Dr. Charles Farah, a Presbyterian theologian who had been active with the Navigators, a discipleship-training organization dedicated to teach new converts the Word of God. On Ralph's suggestion, Kathryn employed Dr. Farah to organize her follow-up work on the West Coast. It was a good idea. Unfortunately, Kathryn was unable to carry through her end of the bargain and wound up torpedoing the entire program.

Chuck Farah put together a board of directors made up of some of the most influential evangelical leaders on the West Coast. All were excited over Kathryn's ministry, believing she was God's choice to lead West Coast Christians to a deeper knowledge of the Holy Spirit. All dedicated themselves to the task of making sure the hundreds of new converts who appeared at each miracle service were estab-

199

lished in the Word of God and found fellowship in a local church. Many of those who volunteered to help were local pastors who saw, through the medium of the miracle service, an opportunity to strengthen the churches of Southern California.

Kathryn called the men together for a large breakfast meeting. She listened to their plans, approved, and pledged to cooperate with them on all points. In turn, the men promised to pray for her, promote the ministry, encourage their people to attend, and be present themselves to help during the services. It seemed like an ideal arrangement. Chuck and the others left the meeting convinced that within a few months every church in Southern California would be feeling the effect of the miracle services.

More than four hundred hand-picked counselors had been enlisted to work during the services and in the follow-up meetings. Training sessions were held in many of the churches, using both the material from the Navigators and from the Billy Graham Evangelistic Association. The counselors who were to work in the services were given specific assignments. They were to come forward during the altar calls and mingle with the people. Ideally, each person who answered the invitation would have a counselor. After the service the new converts would be taken to a back room to receive instruction, be given a New Testament, and asked to fill out an information card. Later in the week, they would be contacted by some representative of a local church. Bible study groups were being formed all over the city, specifically for the new converts and those interested in the Kathryn Kuhlman ministry.

It took only one service before Kathryn reacted. Perhaps she was threatened by men who seemed to be moving in to take over her ministry. Maybe it was the change—having all those counselors down at the front during the altar call.

More likely, and this seems to be the most plausible theory, she felt she was being used. She suspected the pastors were cooperating just to build their own congregations—rather than to support her ministry. She even began to suspect Ralph Wilkerson, thinking he had invited her to California just to feather his own nest at Anaheim Christian Center—at her expense. She sensed, mistakenly, the old M.J. Maloney syndrome rearing its ugly head once again as it did in Franklin. She was not able to understand that even though it seemed she was being "used" to increase the attendance or offerings in some church, that it was all God's great ministry.

Despite all she said about unity, and all she did to unite the various segments of the Body of Christ (and perhaps no one in modern times did as much to bring people together across denominational lines), Kathryn had not caught the full vision of the vastness of God's plan for His Body. It was a great riddle, for even though she was the most ecumenical person I ever met, at the same time she was narrow and parochial.

Time and time again she grabbed my arm and said, "Jamie, we must protect 'the ministry.' " For years I thought she was referring to the body of Christ, which included my ministry, Ralph Wilkerson's ministry, the ministry of the denominational churches, the entire body of Christ. But she wasn't. She didn't have that scope. She was referring to the miracle ministry in general, and to her miracle ministry in particular. She saw herself as uniquely related to the Holy Spirit.

And, ironically, she may have been right. Never, since the days of the apostles, was there a ministry like hers. It can only be explained in the light that she *was* unique; that God had chosen her to receive an extra anointing of faith and power. Like John the Baptist, who introduced Christ to the world but later seemed to have no understanding of the scope of His ministry, Kathryn was the world's greatest promoter of the Holy Spirit—yet she was perplexed and confused when faced with the fact that He was bigger than even *she* imagined.

Over and over I am struck by the similarities between Kathryn's ministry and that of John the Baptist. He was a pioneer with strange ways, outlandish clothes, and a penchant for controversy. He had loyal followers who clung to him in a cultish fashion. In fact, years after he was dead there were still people who knew only "the baptism of John." He had tried to discourage this, saying, "I must decrease and He must increase," but very few listened to him. There was "no greater prophet," yet limited by his narrow provincialism, he was never able to shake himself loose from his own traditions.

Those silly Sunday magazine reporters who called Kathryn Kuhlman a modern John the Baptist may have been much closer to the truth than they imagined.

Kathryn deliberately sabotaged the follow-up program the second month it was in effect. Leaving the stage after the service, she went directly to the counseling room. Sailing through the room, she began praying for the people. It was the way she had always operated. She could not change.

After six months of frustration, Dr. Farah saw that the follow-up program was unworkable and he resigned—as did all the counselors. Then, in what seemed to be an open show of defiance against the pastors, she announced that her next service in Pasadena would be held on a Sunday morning. The pastors, who were trying to support Kathryn's ministry and strengthen their own churches at the same time, saw this as a direct challenge. Many of them were forced to withdraw their support. When the smoke cleared, only a handful of pastors remained.

As a parting shot, Dr. Farah wrote Kathryn four pages of caustic advice. She blew up. "I have to do it my way," she blazed at Ralph Wilkerson. "I am the only one who knows the direction of the Holy Spirit in those miracle services. If these men want to see miracles, they'll just have to fall in line, or get out. It's just like that!"

"Working with her was like working with a buzz saw," Dr. Farah said. "The closer you got, the more likely you were to get cut to shreds. She was absolutely inflexible. Yet there was no denying that the power of God was on her. Every time she stepped on that stage, the Holy Spirit came with her."

Ralph Wilkerson, on the other hand, was never threatened by Kathryn. But Ralph's case was different. They had five Sunday services at his church, and he knew his people could attend an early service and still get to the miracle service on Sunday morning. Besides that, he was already established, with a longstanding miracle ministry. Even more important, he was never shaken—not even by Kathryn's antics—from his faith that God had sent her to the West Coast. Even if she did have eccentricities, he still saw her as God's handmaiden and willingly submitted to her leadership in the miracle services.

Unlike Oral Roberts, who built a university and put his name on it, Kathryn built no institutions. She *was* an institution. Yet like all institutions, she was impenetrable, impervious to change, and rutted in tradition. The pastors, saying she was impossible to work with, withdrew, thanked God for her ministry, attended the miracle services, but most never got involved.

By the end of the year it was apparent that the Pasadena auditorium was too small to hold the crowds attending the miracle services. Kathryn made negotiations with the managers of the huge Shrine Auditorium just off the Harbor Freeway south of downtown Los Angeles. The meeting was scheduled for 1:30 p.m. It was packed out the first service, with two thousand turned away at the door. It remained that way for the next ten years. In fact, to millions of people the word "Shrine" and the name Kathryn Kuhlman were almost synonymous—forming a pun which is almost too good to leave behind without comment. Regardless, however, of how mortals viewed her—some worshiping her, others ridiculing her—God's blessing was upon her. And upon "the ministry."

Kathryn, of course, was constantly having to fight her handicaps. When Ralph Wilkerson bought the huge Melodyland complex, she was intimidated. She was intimidated by the Jesus movement, and the thousands of bearded, barefoot kids who started coming to her services. She was threatened by the huge youth ministry at Calvary Chapel in Costa Mesa, where more than twenty thousand people met each week to study the Bible. Yet, despite her insecurities, she tried to adjust, much as a stiff old tree which has been standing straight and true knows it must bend when the hurricane comes—or break. And Kathryn was caught in the middle of a Holy Spirit hurricane. Things were happening so fast all around her that she was unable to keep up.

She tried. She held a series of youth services at the Hollywood Palladium. The kids turned out by the tens of thousands. She loved them; beards, beads, and bare feet. But that simply wasn't her style. David Wilkerson of Teen Challenge and Chuck Smith at Calvary Chapel were far better equipped—they could speak their language. Yet, even though Kathryn felt the Jesus Movement was a move of God, she soon discontinued her meetings and re-centered her ministry at the Shrine.

That which Kathryn had been preaching was beginning
to come to pass—a fresh move of the Holy Spirit. For more
than three decades she had been prophesying that He was
going to return in a great burst of power. She saw it as the
fulfillment of the prophecy given in Joel:

> And it shall come to pass afterward, that I will pour out
> my spirit upon all flesh; and your sons and your
> daughters shall prophesy, your old men shall dream
> dreams, your young men shall see visions. And also
> upon the servants and upon the handmaids in those
> days will I pour out my spirit . . . And it shall come to
> pass, that whosoever shall call on the name of the Lord
> shall be delivered . . . (Joel 2:28-29, 32).

I don't believe there was anyone in the world who believed that was going to happen literally more than Kathryn
Kuhlman. She literally believed that the day would come
when she would hold a miracle service and everyone in the
room who called on the name of the Lord would be delivered of their sickness and bondage. She literally believed
God had poured out His Spirit upon Kathryn Kuhlman—a
handmaid. She literally believed that she was living in the
last days of history, that the next great event would be the
return of the Lord Jesus Christ. She literally believed that
the reason the Holy Spirit was being poured out on all flesh
was in preparation for that. "I'm putting the last stitches in
my wedding garment," she said. As a part of the bride of
Christ, she was looking forward to His return.

But when it became evident that the Holy Spirit was
moving among other ministries as well as in her miracle
services, she became perplexed. And just a little frightened.
Like the prophet Jonah at Nineveh, she had prophesied it,

yet now that it was coming to pass, she didn't know how to handle it.

"You're missing something, Kathryn," Ralph Wilkerson chided her when she turned down an invitation to speak at a meeting of the Full Gospel Business Men's Fellowship. "God's really moving among those men."

"I've seen enough fanaticism in my lifetime," she argued. "I don't want to get involved with any more Pentecostals."

"Things are different now, Kathryn," Ralph said. "It's not like you think it is. The Holy Spirit is not just moving in your miracle services. He's moving in a thousand different places. He's moving in the Roman Catholic Church. He's moving among the young people in the Jesus Movement. He's moving in many denominational churches that used to be dead and dry. And He's moving among the Full Gospel Business Men."

"I'm from Missouri," she smiled. "Show me. Once I see it, you know you can count on me one hundred percent."

Three months later, Kathryn hesitantly accepted Al Malachuk's invitation to speak at the Washington Regional Convention of the FGBMFI. They loved her as a sister and rejoiced over the miracles. A year later she spoke at the international convention. After that she was a regular speaker at many of the larger conventions. Ralph had been right. The Holy Spirit was moving at the FGBMFI meetings. And Kathryn had enough wisdom to know that if her old friend, the Holy Spirit, was there, she should be there too—following the cloud.

Ralph wanted to videotape one of Kathryn's services when she came to Melodyland to hold a charismatic clinic. She had never allowed cameras in her services. Ralph, however, convinced her to make just one tape, which could be kept so those of future generations (in case there were future generations) could see something of her ministry.

She consented and a video tape was made during one of the charismatic conventions at Melodyland. (Kathryn later allowed three other such filmings—two of them in Israel at the 1974 and 1975 World Conferences on the Holy Spirit and one of her miracle service in Las Vegas.)

Ralph later showed his film to a group of ministers in Tulsa, Oklahoma. "There were more people healed—percentage-wise—from watching the tape than there were in the service when the film was made," he said.

When I quizzed him about this, he concluded: "I don't believe the Holy Spirit just anoints a person. I believe He anoints a ministry. The video tape was a part of the Holy Spirit's anointed ministry, therefore it carried with it just as much power as Kathryn Kuhlman herself."

Later I experienced the same phenomenon in our church in Florida. Our church obtained a copy of the film, *Jerusalem II*, made at the World Conference on the Holy Spirit in 1974 and distributed by Logos International, which closed with a long segment of Kathryn's miracle service in Jerusalem. After the film, the people stood quietly for a time of silent prayer. Suddenly there was the sound of scraping chairs and falling bodies. I opened my eyes. Almost one-third of the congregation, it seemed, were stretched out on the floor or slumped in chairs—under the power. It was one of the most powerful demonstrations of the latent power of the Holy Spirit I have ever witnessed.

Videotaping—through the television industry—became the most dominant fact in Kathryn's life during her last eight years. She loved it. She loved the glamour, the excitement, and the challenge.

"Get me some information," she said to Steve Zelenko, her radio engineer in Pittsburgh. "I need to know something before I make any commitments."

Steve compiled a list of figures and then made his recommendation. "You're the one who is always saying 'Go big, think big,'" Steve said. "My advice is to get the best producer available and line up with a big network in California."

The "best producer" turned out to be Dick Ross, who had just finished a fourteen-year stint with the Billy Graham organization. The "big network" was CBS. Both agreed to take her on, and over the almost ten-year period she did five hundred telecasts—the longest-running half-hour series ever produced in CBS studios.

Kathryn had become a world-wide figure, as much in demand in Sweden and Japan as she was in Cleveland or St. Louis.

There were problems however. One of the purposes of the Kathryn Kuhlman Foundation was to support mission enterprises around the world. Kathryn was determined that if she went on television, it should not hamper the mission work which had been continued across the years. The foundation had built twenty churches overseas: five in Africa, nine in Central and South America, and six in Asia and India. Each of these had been built with foundation funds and then turned over to the people free of all debt. While Walter Adamack had invested some of the foundation's money in stocks and bonds as a reserve, nevertheless the yearly expenditures were always about the same as the annual income. Income for television would have to be extra if Kathryn was to keep the balance between missions and ministry.

It didn't turn out that way. For example, the 1972 financial report showed that while the foundation gave about $500,000 to various mission funds at home and overseas, the TV and radio ministry cost in excess of $1,500,000. By the end of 1974, these figures were even more out of proportion. It soon became obvious that in order to keep the

208

money flowing, Kathryn was having to travel all over the nation conducting miracle services. At the same time, she was more and more in demand because of the incredible coverage the television was giving her. It was a vicious circle which would eventually cost her a dreadful toll.

CHAPTER XIV

THE MIRACLE SERVICE

In 1974, twenty-seven years (and perhaps three million miracles) after that first healing miracle took place in Franklin, Pennsylvania, William Nolen, a medical doctor, wrote a book in which he said he was "doubtful" that any good Kathryn was doing "could possibly outweigh the misery she was causing." Criticizing her for "lack of medical sophistication," he concluded:

> The problem is, and I'm sorry this has to be so blunt, one of ignorance. Miss Kuhlman doesn't know the difference between psychogenic and organic diseases; she doesn't know anything about hypnotism and the power of suggestion: she doesn't know anything about the autonomic nervous system. (*Healing: A Doctor in Search of a Miracle*, by William A. Nolen, M.D. Fawcett Publications, Inc., Greenwich, Conn. 1974, pg. 94.)

Unfortunately, Dr. Nolen's research was, at best, sketchy. He visited only one miracle service and interviewed only a handful of people who claimed healings. Although his attitude toward Kathryn was respectful, even sympathetic, he could see no lasting benefit from the miracle services.

I, too, had some of the same reservations when I first met Kathryn. Nevertheless, after interviewing at least two hundred medically documented cases of miraculous healings, I am forced to toss Dr. Nolen's Latin axiom—which he used to rest his case against her—back at him: *res ipsa loquitur*—"the thing speaks for itself."

Nolen's assertions, by the way, drew a response from within the ranks of the medical profession. H. Richard Casdorph, M.D., Ph.D., a Southern California internist and heart specialist who was quite familiar with the results of Kathryn's ministry, met Dr. Nolen on the *Mike Douglas Show* in Philadelphia in 1975. Casdorph was accompanied by Lisa Larios and her mother. Lisa, a teen-ager, had been healed of bone cancer (reticulum cell sarcoma) at a miracle service at the Shrine Auditorium and Dr. Casdorph had x-rays and medical records to verify it. He later documented nine other examples of miraculous divine healing, most of them related to the ministry of Kathryn Kuhlman, and reported his findings in a book, *The Miracles*, which was published by Logos in 1976. Nolen remained unconvinced, but it is important to know that he did not remain unchallenged by his own colleagues.

Dr. Nolen did draw one valid conclusion when he said Kathryn was ignorant when it came to medical knowledge. She kept herself that way on purpose. It was as though she knew the moment she let herself move from the realm of the *spirit* to the realm of *reason*, she would become like her humanistic critics—powerless. Even though she was ignorant, she was also infinitely wise (wisdom being the ability to see things with God's eyes). This is the reason she seldom answered her critics: she was able to see them from God's perspective. Although there were times when she lost her God-perspective and, with both fists swinging, waded in like any other mortal, her reply to Nolen was simply: "I can only feel pity for a writer who is too analytical to believe."

Many people make the mistake of equating the lack of worldly knowledge with foolishness. Kathryn was no fool, although she was admittedly ignorant of many things. She was, for instance, theologically ignorant. I don't think she ever read a book on systematic theology. Nor a book on miracles or healing. She never even had an acceptable definition for the word "miracle." She left that up to those who were not involved with bringing them to pass.

She had a very limited grasp of what was going on in the world around her. Although she greeted scholars, ministers, and heads of state equally well, once she got past the greeting stage she was lost and would quickly make some excuse to move on. On the other hand, as long as she stayed in her field—the field of the Holy Spirit—she was unexcelled and unconquered. I remember the time she was put on the spot at a press conference in Jerusalem. The Jewish press was hostile over her presence and over the presence of a number of Christian leaders who had come to Jerusalem for the First World Conference on the Holy Spirit. When a bearded, orthodox reporter asked her the baited question, "Why did you Christians come all the way over here for your conference? Why didn't you remain in America?" Kathryn was on her feet with eyes flashing.

"I'll tell you why we're here, young man. We're here because this is God's chosen land and you Jews—whether you like it or not—are God's chosen people. We're here because Christians love this land just as much as you love it. We're here because this very hill where we now stand will

213

one day split wide open when the King of Glory, the Messiah Jesus Christ, returns. We're here because the Holy Spirit was here at Pentecost, and is here today."

I looked at the reporter. He was scribbling furiously in his notebook, his face serious. An Arab Christian pastor sitting next to me chuckled softly and touched my arm. "These Jews sit up and listen when a strong woman speaks. They love Golda Meir, and they'll love Kathryn Kuhlman. Just you wait and see."

They did love her. They sat bug-eyed during the four-hour miracle service the next day. Even the conservative *Jerusalem Post* gave her excellent press reviews. Kathryn was on solid ground as long as she was talking about the Spirit.

Kathryn was medically ignorant. She never read even a family medical book, much less studied physiology, psychology, or anatomy. Yet she was wise. Extremely wise. She knew, when she was on the platform during a miracle service and the Spirit of God was upon her, that she had all the authority of God. No one dared question her at those times. Even Dr. Nolen admitted when he attended that one miracle service in Minneapolis, he was almost persuaded (as King Agrippa was before the apostle Paul) to believe. "You didn't want to reason," he said. "You wanted to accept."

But, sadly, he let reason prevail.

Kathryn's gift in the miracle service was not the gift of healing, rather it was the other gifts the apostle Paul listed in his letter to the Corinthian church—"faith" and the "word of knowledge" (1 Corinthians 12:8). Kathryn was not a healer. The "gifts of healing" which Paul talked about, Kathryn believed, came only to the sick. It was the sick who needed the gift of healing. All she had was faith to believe and a word of knowledge concerning where that gift had been bestowed. For this reason she said over and over, "I am not a healer. I have no healing power. No healing virtue.

Don't look to me. Look to God." Yet during those miracle services, when the wave of faith crested and the presence of God actually invaded the building—inhabiting the praises of His people—Kathryn could suddenly begin to recognize healings which were occurring in the auditorium. It was the trademark of the miracle service. Her critics, such as Lester Kinsolving, called her "psychic." Allen Spraggett of the Toronto *Star* said she was "clairvoyant." Kathryn, however, knew it was simply the power of the Holy Spirit which was available to any person who would pay the price.

It was the belief that she was a "spiritual" person—she thought as God thought—which persuaded me, on our first meeting, that she was not a charlatan. We had left her office in the Carlton House about dusk. I drove her Cadillac and, following her directions, crossed the Monongahela River and took the road north along the bluff to a small but elegant steak house overlooking the Golden Triangle of downtown Pittsburgh. After the candlelight dinner, we sat and talked, discussing the terms of our work together in writing *God Can Do It Again.* I finally stopped her.

"May I ask you a point-blank question?"

"Of course. Go right ahead." Her radiance and openness was absolutely disarming. For a second I started to back down, wishing I had said nothing. But I had to continue, for my own satisfaction.

"Why are some not healed in your miracle services? How do you explain the fact that many leave, broken and disillusioned, while others are miraculously healed?"

She never hesitated. "The only honest answer I can give is: I do not know. Only God knows, and who can fathom the mind of God?"

It was in that instant I knew I could trust her. A nonspiritual person would have bombarded me with logical reasons. But Kathryn was not a reasonable person. She was

215

a spiritual person. Even though she had feet of clay, she knew better than to try to define the undefinable, to explain the mysteries of God.

"When I was twenty years old," she laughed, "I could have given you all the answers. My theology was straight and I was sure that if you followed certain rules, worked hard enough, obeyed all the commandments, and had yourself in a certain spiritual state, God would heal you.

"But God never responds to man's demands to prove Himself. There are some things in life which will always be unanswerable because we see through a glass darkly. God knows the end from the beginning, while all we can do is catch a glimpse of the present, and a distorted glimpse at that."

She went ahead to tell me of several people who had come into the miracle services who didn't believe in God, much less in miracles, who had been healed. And of others— undeniable saints—who left unhealed.

"Until we have a way of defining it, all that I can tell you is that these are mercy healings. They have been healed through the mercy of the Lord. The others . . . who knows . . . perhaps God loved them so much He reserved an even greater blessing for them than physical healing."

Kathryn enjoyed telling of the time she held a miracle service in Kansas City. The Kansas City *Star* sent one of their top reporters to cover the meeting. The last night of the service the reporter came to Kathryn's dressing room and they talked about those who were not healed. Three weeks later she received a letter from the reporter, telling her about a friend she had brought to the final service in Kansas City—an attorney dying of cancer who was wheeled in on a stretcher. The reporter said the attorney died within a week of attending the service, but that his wife related how he had felt the service was the greatest thing that had ever happened to him. He was not healed, but he accepted Christ for the forgiveness of sins. Death came easily. Gloriously. The reporter, remembering the way Kathryn had wept in her dressing room as she discussed those who left the meetings unhealed, said she was writing to ask Kathryn to remember this incident when she thought of the numbers who were not healed.

"No, I do not know why all are not healed physically," she commented, "but all can be healed spiritually—and that's the greatest miracle any human being can know."

Few, very few of those who left the miracle service unhealed, ever grew bitter. Most had already outlived their bitterness. They came to Kathryn as a last resort. Many of them returned, again and again. In their wheelchairs. Pushing their crippled children on stretchers. Hobbling along on crutches or in their braces. To curse Kathryn Kuhlman would be like cursing God. Instead they increased their giving and intensified their prayers. For whether they were healed or not, at least the miracle service gave them something that doctors and modern science were unable to give—hope. The one ingredient essential to life. And joy. She gave them joy. Here, in an atmosphere where they were accepted and loved, the people sang and praised God in joy. What hospital or sanitarium offered joy? Often—far too often—they could not even find it in their churches. Joy had been replaced with the artificial happiness of medically induced tranquility. But in the miracle services it was real. She gave them God. Not a God who condemned them for being ill, but whose heart was breaking over their condition. A God who yearned to reach out and touch them. She gave them Jesus Christ as the one who, by His death on the cross, had forgiven their sin and established their position in heaven. What more could they ask? Healing? Yes. But in the light of everything else that was offered at the miracle service, healing often became a matter of secondary priority. Kathryn was right. Spiritual healing was the greatest of all the gifts.

What was the secret of the miracle service?

Glenn Clark, an earlier mystic and founder of Camps Farthest Out (CFO), once wrote of a Russian port in northern Siberia used for whaling vessels in the summer season. But in winter, with the temperatures ranging from fifty to ninety degrees below zero, no vessel had ever been known to enter. The port was there. The wharves were there. All the avenues for ships to come and go were there. But no vessels ever came. Why? Because the climate was wrong.

The miracle service provided the right kind of climate for healing. It is like a great magnifying glass concentrating the sun's rays on a piece of paper and setting it afire. The sunlight was always there. But until the magnifying glass brought the rays into focus, concentrating them on a particular spot, there was no consuming power. So the miracle services concentrated the power of God into a particular place at a particular time. Although healing was certainly not limited to miracle services (Kathryn constantly said that such healings should be taking place in every church in the land), nevertheless it seemed that in this particular "climate" God's power was more concentrated and thus miracles were the norm, rather than the exception.

One of Kathryn's fondest hopes, right up until the time she died, was that one day she would experience a miracle service like the ones Jesus held—where every sick person present was healed. It never happened, but she believed in the possibility of it, and never went out on the stage without hoping, and praying, "Maybe this will be the time."

Frank Laubach, the great literacy expert (and a colleague, by the way, of Glenn Clark) recognized the healing power which was present in the miracle services. He once wrote Kathryn saying: "You are a wonderful person! I wish I could come to your meetings and just stay there while you break the bread of life and bring hope to so many people. . . . My prayer is that God will make it possible for me to be with you again and capture some of the radiant power of the Holy Spirit which emanates from you as from nobody else I know, you wonderful girl!"

Kathryn said she had nothing to do with the healings. In a sense that was true. She was only the catalyst which brought the power and the people together. Yet, in another sense, she had everything to do with the miracles, for she had put together a "workable package" through which the Holy Spirit was able to market His product: miracles.

Music played a great part in the services. Even though everything seemed spontaneous, it was actually the result of meticulous planning based on many years of trial and error. Kathryn was satisfied with only the best. She never had a poor soloist on stage. She used only the finest musicians at the instruments. Her choir, directed by Dr. Arthur Metcalfe, was trained to perfection, and every number was rehearsed until it could be presented with faultless diction and supreme harmony. Jimmy Miller, the choir's accompanist and her pianist for twenty-seven years, was flawless in his work. In Jimmie McDonald she had one of the finest solo voices in the nation. Even Dino, who later turned against her, was proclaimed by music critics as one of the best keyboard artists in the field. Also important was Charles Beebee, her balding little organist who stretched his short legs toward the pedals, feeling not only Kathryn's moods, but flowing in seeming perfect harmony with the Holy Spirit as his talented fingers roamed the organ keys, reflecting the presence of God in the room. Every time someone came forward to testify of a miracle, the organ was undergirding. Beebee, feeling the intensity of the testimony, would push the organ to a rising crescendo as the people applauded—or offer a subdued background for those who tearfully whispered their deepest longings into the microphone. When Kathryn called for silence—"Not a sound in this great auditorium. The Holy Spirit is here breathing on each heart. . . ."—the organ was playing, offering subliminal support to His presence. To have thought of a miracle service without Charles Beebee was unimaginable. The musical climate, or if you prefer, "mood," was inestimably important in creating an atmosphere in which the Holy Spirit could move with freedom and ease.

The mechanics of the service, the preparation, was one of the secrets of creating the proper climate. Kathryn would often go to the meeting place, especially if it was new to her, early in the morning, to roam the aisles and pray. Later, the ushers were always briefed, in detail, often by Kathryn herself. Nothing was left to the imagination. In some of the bigger auditoriums the ushers even used walkie-talkie radios, whispering instructions to one another. The taking of the offerings, which always seemed so spontaneous, was rehearsed and rehearsed until it could be carried out flawlessly. The men, sometimes as many as three hundred of them, were trained days in advance on how to handle problem people, how to spot those in need, how to respond to emergencies, how to discern whether a healing was genuine or merely emotional. Each man had his station. And his instructions. It was part of the "decency and order" which Kathryn demanded as being "worthy unto the Lord."

Kathryn insisted on the presence of luminaries behind her on the stage. In Youngstown it was that vast men's chorus of redeemed alcoholics. In the huge services at the Shrine Auditorium or in various key cities across the nation it was recognized ministers, politicians, and community leaders, and the choir which sometimes numbered 1,000 voices. She had a special love for doctors, and wanted them either on the stage or on the front rows of the auditorium. The same was true of priests and nuns—especially if they were "in uniform." Nothing thrilled Kathryn more than to have thirty or forty Catholic clergymen, especially if they wore clerical collars or, better yet, cassocks, sitting behind her while she ministered. Somehow it seemed to lend authenticity to what she was doing—and helped create the proper climate of trust and understanding which was so necessary for a miracle service.

Perhaps most important, yet least recognized, were those few hand-picked women—led by Maggie Hartner and Ruth Fisher and Pauline Williams from her staff—who roamed the vast audience when the actual miracle part of the service got underway. They were charged with discerning, looking, listening, and encouraging those who had been healed to come forward and testify.

The greatest secret was Kathryn herself. She insisted on being the focus. She never sat down during those four and five-hour meetings, even when Dino was playing, or Jimmie McDonald was singing. In fact, she was always doing just a little something to keep the audience's attention on herself. To the critical eye it seemed she was "upstaging"—raising her hand when Jimmie hit a high note, or turning to the choir and making some grand gesture when Dino finished his playing. It seemed like the epitome of ego, always demanding the spotlight. But the more discerning ones saw it as wisdom. Kathryn knew about the necessity of spiritual focus. She would never allow anyone to take the microphone away from her. She was always at a person's elbow when he was testifying. If he got long-winded, she'd step in, pray for him, and he'd fall to the floor "under the power." If he tried to say something which would break the harmony of the meeting, she would use authority. She knew better than to permit a dozen little healing services going on in the congregation while she was conducting the meeting from the platform. If that kind of thing ever started, and it often would, she would put a stop to it by saying, "What's going on back there in the balcony? Is somebody being healed? You ushers handle that." And the ushers, already cued, would step in and "handle it," drawing the people's attention back to center stage. Kathryn knew there could be but one leader—and she was it. She never relinquished that position of authority. It was one of the secrets of the miracle service.

For the same reason, she was extremely cautious about allowing the "gifts of the Spirit" to be exercised in the audience. If someone stood to prophesy or speak in tongues, she would silence them. "The Holy Spirit does not interrupt himself," she would say with authority.

I was there in 1968 when she returned to Denver for the first time since she left thirty years before. Sam Rudd, a wealthy Denverite and an international director of the Full Gospel Business Men's Fellowship, had encouraged her to conduct a three-day crusade in the old City Auditorium. I expected Kathryn to come in walking on eggshells, but she didn't. She came in with authority.

Midway through the first service an elderly man in the audience stood to his feet and began shouting, "Hallelujah! Praise God!"

Kathryn never flinched. "Sir, please sit down. You're interrupting this meeting."

The man ignored her, continuing to shout and wave his hands. I wondered if he was an old friend from the tabernacle.

"If you don't sit down, I'm going to have the ushers remove you."

He continued, as if in a trance, mouthing gibberish. Kathryn nodded to a couple of brawny ushers who moved quickly down the aisle toward the man. A friend of the shouting man, who was sitting beside him, saw them coming. Although he was glaring at Kathryn, nevertheless he quickly pulled the man back into his seat and calmed him down.

"This is fanaticism," Miss Kuhlman said deliberately. "This is what brings a reproach upon the Holy Spirit. All who agree, hold up your hands."

The audience was with her. It seemed every hand shot into the air. There were no more disturbances in any of the meetings that weekend.

"The Holy Spirit is a gentleman," Kathryn often said. "He does things decently and in order. When He is speaking through me, He will not interrupt Himself by speaking through someone else."

Focus was one of the secrets of the miracle service.

There were other mechanical things, which many did not understand or appreciate but which Kathryn deemed necessary for a successful service. One of them was a full building. As the crowds grew in Los Angeles, for instance, some of her most trusted advisors counseled her to move out of the Shrine Auditorium and find a larger meeting place. "It's not right that we have to turn away thousands of people each time we hold a service," they said. "The Shrine Auditorium seats only seven thousand persons. Why not rent the UCLA stadium?"

Kathryn refused. Her critics said she liked the "good press" of having to turn away thousands each meeting. But it was more than that. She knew it was far better to have a full house, packed to the rafters, than to have a half-empty auditorium. She also knew that even though she was just an "ordinary person" somehow it was necessary for the people to see her on the stage—something which could not be done in a vast outdoor stadium. Billy Graham could get away with it because he depended on his voice to hold the crowds. But Kathryn depended as much on seeing the faces of the audience as they did upon seeing hers. Hers was a ministry of intimacy. Therefore, rather than rent bigger quarters or open up overflow rooms, she preferred (although sometimes overflow rooms were necessary) to stay in the smaller buildings and keep eye contact with her audience. It was one of the secrets of the miracle service.

As a result, things happened. Miraculous things. *Time* magazine, reporting on the miracle services in a 1970 article, said, "But hidden underneath the 1945 Shirley Temple hairdo is one of the most remarkable Christian charismatics in the U.S. She is, in fact, a veritable one-woman shrine of Lourdes." Then, after listing a number of documented healings which had taken place in these services, they concluded: "Kathryn preaches no theology of healing. She no longer believes that faith necessarily earns healing, or that lack of faith necessarily forbids it. She has seen too many nonbelievers cured, too many believers go away still lame or sick. . . . She does see her ministry as a return to the supernatural element in the ancient church. 'Everything that happened in the early church,' she insists, 'we have a right to expect today. . . .' She is so convinced that her role is only that of an intermediary that she has a recurring nightmare about coming out on stage some day and finding the chairs empty, her gift gone."

But that nightmare was always nothing more than a bad dream. The chairs were never empty—and the gift remained to the end.

One of the ways that gift manifested itself was through a phenomenon which became one of the trademarks of the miracle services, the occurrence of having those she prayed for crumpling to the floor in a quasi-catatonic state. She called it "going under the power," and in her latter years, referred to it as the "slaying power of the Holy Spirit." No one knows exactly when this exceptional demonstration of spiritual power first appeared in her ministry, but it seems it was there from the inception. Kathryn readily admitted she had no explanation for it except to say it was the power of the Holy Spirit.

In 1966 she was invited to speak to a ladies' luncheon at the National Convention of the Full Gospel Business Men's Fellowship in Miami Beach. It was one of her first appearances before the FGBMFI and very few of those present were acquainted with her ministry. The luncheon was held on the ground floor of the Deauville Hotel near the swimming pool. The room was packed with more than a thousand women. Rose (Mrs. Demos) Shakarian, the wife of the founder of FGBMFI, introduced Kathryn, and as she stood to speak there was a rustle of noise in the back of the room, like wind blowing through the trees. Kathryn was on the small platform, straining to see what was happening. Suddenly there was the sound of chairs scraping against the floor and women in the far back of the room began laughing and screaming.

"Come on up here," Kathryn said, waving her hand. "Come on, come on, come on. The Holy Spirit is not going to let me speak. The healings have already begun."

And indeed they had. Women began streaming to the front of the crowded room, tears running down their faces, as they testified of healings which had occurred instantaneously the moment Kathryn stood to speak. Kathryn began praying for the ladies and they began toppling backwards, "going under the power."

Rose Shakarian was dumbfounded. Kathryn motioned for her to come and help. Somebody needed to catch those women as they crumpled to the floor. Rose turned to Viola Malachuk, who was sitting beside her, and whispered desperately, "Viola, I can't. My heart won't stand it. I can't help her."

Viola jumped to her feet and moved into the group of people, catching first one woman and then another, lowering them to the floor. Other women began singing in the Spirit and then, all over the ballroom, the women, most of whom were standing trying to see what was going on, began crashing to the floor or back into their chairs. The power of the Holy Spirit seemed to invade the entire room.

The hotel had been having trouble with its air conditioning system for several days and other guests at the poolside, looking through the huge sliding glass doors that opened into the ballroom, saw the ladies crumpling to the floor. They thought the women were fainting from the heat and rushed in to help. Some of them, also, were kayoed by the power of the Spirit and wound up on the floor. Bathing suits and all.

The meeting lasted almost three hours and a number of people later testified they had been healed of various diseases and disorders during the time. No one was hurt from the falling. Kathryn never did get a chance to preach.

Of course, even though the occurrence of people being "slain by the Spirit" is not common in most mainline churches today, it does seem to be an experience that happened often in biblical times. For instance, in Acts 9 Saul had a face-to-face encounter with the Spirit of Christ and fell to the ground on the Damascus Road. In Matthew 17 the writer tells the story of the three apostles on the Mount of Transfiguration who could not stand to their feet in the presence of God. The apostle John talked about being "in the Spirit" and unable to rise from the ground. Further investigation shows that this same phenomenon accompanied many of the great evangelists in history such as Charles G. Finney, Peter Cartwright, and Dwight L. Moody.

In fact, there are recorded instances of pedestrians in Chicago passing the door of the hall where Dwight L. Moody was preaching, and crumpling to the sidewalk under the power. When the Holy Spirit fell on the evangelistic services conducted by the Wesley brothers, John and Charles, and people began going under the power, the two men grew fearful and said, "No more of this." Shortly afterwards, Charles Wesley was approached by one of his contemporaries who scolded him for quenching the Spirit. "Charles, you haven't had any great miracles, not even many conversions, since you discouraged people from going under the power."

Later Charles Price, under whom Everett Parrott received some of his early training, conducted meetings throughout the nation where people were "slain in the Spirit." The same phenomenon accompanied Parrott's preaching—and of course Kathryn's.

As with many of the things of God, the phenomenon was often abused. Many evangelists, preachers, and "healers" began pushing people over in order to give the appearance of having spiritual power. Others, having once gone under the power, mixed flesh with spirit and often rolled on the floor, giving birth to the name "Holy Rollers."

But there was no way anyone could ever accuse Kathryn Kuhlman of being a holy roller—nor of encouraging (even allowing) such behavior in her meetings. Her critics did often accuse her of pushing people over. Others said she hypnotized them. A few even went so far as to say that Kathryn had studied anatomy and knew how to touch a secret nerve in a person's neck which caused them to collapse. But after all the smoke had cleared, it was still apparent that the experience of going under the power was basically spiritual, not emotional.

To her credit, Kathryn never discouraged the phenom-

227

enon—although it could have been one of those things which would have lent credence to the charge she was a fanatic. On the other hand, she never allowed noisy demonstrations as often accompanied the earlier meetings of Oral Roberts and Rex Humbard.

"Much of our noise is a substitute for power," she said. "I had an old Model-T Ford when I first started out in Idaho. If noise was power, that old Ford would have been the most powerful thing on the road. No, some of the greatest manifestations of the Holy Spirit I have ever seen, some of the greatest miracles I have ever seen, some of the greatest baptisms of the Holy Spirit I have ever witnessed, were quiet and beautiful."

In 1974, at the First World Conference on the Holy Spirit in Jerusalem, I watched as a robed Trappist monk went "under the power" four times. He had been sitting behind Miss Kuhlman on the stage, and during the miracle service Kathryn decided to pray for those around her. When she got to this Trappist monk, the hood of his brown robe covering his head, his long gown touching the tops of his sandals, she paused. He stood erect in front of her, his head bowed. His eyes closed.

Kathryn was crying. She seemed to sense something special about him. I noticed that tears were beginning to trickle down his face also. And then slowly his legs buckled, and he fell backwards into the arms of one of the ushers.

Kathryn didn't move. She stood, transfixed, one finger pointed heavenward, the other hand stretched out toward the silent man on the floor, her face uplifted. Glowing.

The ushers helped the man back to his feet and he stood again before her, his hood now pulled back away from his handsome face. Still, Kathryn didn't move. Her hands remained in the same position. Slowly the man sank back to the floor. It happened twice more. Kathryn never touched him, never said a word. She just stood still, her finger pointing toward God, her face lifted, bathed in an unearthly light. The only sound was the gentle music from the organ and the muted gasps from the audience each time the Roman Catholic monk sank to the floor under the slaying power of the Holy Spirit.

It was as though there was surrounding her an aura of power. Anyone inside that aura could hardly stand. I had the feeling that had Kathryn moved a muscle, she, too, would have gone down—so great was the power of God.

This same aura often appeared around her while she was ministering. On occasions it caused her face to actually glow. Sometimes, when it was stronger, she would simply motion out into the audience, or back into the choir, and entire rows of people would fall over. Once in Carnegie Hall in Pittsburgh, a woman stood in one of the side balconies to claim a healing. Many others around her, who knew her and had been praying for her, stood to rejoice as she took off a leg brace and held it aloft. Kathryn walked to the front of the platform and said, "The power of God is all over that balcony." Instantly almost thirty people fell backwards into their seats. I was on the ground floor and caught my breath, waiting to see if anyone would fall forward and tumble out of the balcony onto the seats below. But there were no injuries. In fact, throughout all her ministry there is no record that anyone who fell under the power was ever injured in the fall. Quite the opposite, many were healed of serious injuries they had sustained in the past.

One of the most dramatic illustrations of this occurred when Clifton Harris, a medical doctor, was healed of a fused hip in a miracle service in Monroe, Louisiana, in 1973. Twenty years before, Dr. Harris, who had recently returned from China as a foreign missionary for the Southern Baptist Convention, was critically injured in an automobile accident. His right hip was shattered, the leg bone driven all the way up through the socket. When the hip healed, after many months in a body cast, it calcified with arthritis, leaving the doctor permanently crippled. Unable to return to the mission field, he entered into a limited practice in the little town of Pineville, near Alexandria. Across the years the pain grew more intense as the arthritic spurs and calcium deposits totally fused the hip. His twelve-year-old son often pushed him down the hospital corridors in a wheelchair as he made his rounds.

Then came the miracle service in Monroe, ninety miles away. His wife drove the car while he lay in the back seat, suffering. Ushers helped him with his wheelchair and he finally got inside the building. Dr. Harris came from a long line of Southern Baptist preachers and missionaries, and while he believed in the Bible, he never had really believed in miracles. Yet while he was sitting in the miracle service, he felt intense heat going through his hip. Suddenly he was out of his wheelchair, running down the aisle. He removed his leg and hip brace and found he could climb the steps to the platform with no pain or discomfort. Standing before Miss Kuhlman, he suddenly "went under the power." There was no one close by to catch him, and he crashed heavily to the platform, landing directly on his right hip. Yet he was unhurt. He got to his feet and crashed back to the floor—again striking that same hip. Still no ill effects.

Returning home, he asked his Jewish orthopedic surgeon friend, Dr. Dan Kingsley—who only recently had considered recommending a hip transplant—to examine him. Dr. Kingsley had repaired the damage caused by the wreck and had continued to follow his case over the years. He reacted to Cliff Harris' story with skepticism, but was forced to admit, after viewing the x-rays and watching him walk without his brace, crutches, or wheelchair, that "I would be thrilled with this good a result after total hip transplant."

Dr. Harris never had to return to his wheelchair.

Not everyone who went down was healed, of course. One woman in Tulsa, Oklahoma, went "under the power," then climbed back to her feet shaking her head, saying, "A nice experience, but my back still hurts."

An imponderable mystery.

Exactly what causes it no one seems to know. It is as if the supernatural power of the Holy Spirit passing through a body short-circuits all the body functions for a moment. Muscles and nerves which are usually controlled by electrical currents from the brain are just overpowered, much as if a million volts of lightning were to strike the electrical system of a house which was wired for 220 volts. In such a case, all systems would be short-circuited. The power would leap all relays and fuses, making inoperative every appliance which was plugged in. Just so the power of the Holy Spirit, flooding through a human body, causes the spiritually "plugged-in" person to collapse to the floor.

At the Shrine Auditorium one Sunday afternoon, Kathryn called all the clergymen—Catholic, Protestant and Jewish—to come to the platform. Almost seventy-five answered the call and stood around her. She reached out twice, once to her right, once to her left, and every man was on the floor, stacked on top of each other like cordwood. In Miami, Florida, she started up through the choir to pray for those she could touch, and almost four hundred people went under the power. At another time in her office in Pittsburgh, a local Presbyterian minister brought in a friend who was a theological professor to meet Miss Kuhlman. Before they left, standing at the door of the office chatting, Kathryn offered to pray for the professor. He knew what that might mean and braced his athletic body to resist any effort to knock him down. She reached out and said, "Dear

231

Jesus!" Instantly the professor was on the floor. His friend helped him to his feet. Amazed, the professor asked, "What happened?" Before his friend could answer, he fell to the floor again. Kathryn stepped back, laughing, and told the pastor to take his professor friend home before he got too drunk to walk. They went down the elevator with the professor, still wobbly, mumbling, "I just don't understand. It doesn't make sense."

Even with all this evidence swirling around me, I had a hard time believing until I, too, went under the power. It happened in the Shrine Auditorium in Los Angeles. The miracle service was drawing to a close and the people were all standing, singing. I was on the stage in a line of men, mostly ministers from the Los Angeles area, when I realized Kathryn had started toward us, touching people as she came down the line. Each man fell backwards as she prayed for him, caught in the arms of ushers who were rushing madly to keep up with her so the men would not fall into the chairs. I was impressed, but not impressed enough to want to be touched. I edged backwards, out of the line. Kathryn kept pressing through the crowd, touching people on both sides as she went. I kept edging back, toward the wing, and suddenly I found I had backed into the edge of the seven-foot grand piano. There was no way to get around it. I saw her coming and made a hasty decision. I would not fall down just because every other man had fallen down. To my knowledge, she never touched me. I do remember looking up, seeing the underside of the grand piano, and thinking how silly I must look, dressed in a gray business suit with black shoes and a pin stripe tie, lying on my back under the concert grand piano in front of seven thousand people. Then I was aware of the presence. A sort of euphoria swept over me, and I put my head back on the splintery wooden floor and just basked in the presence of God. Since I was under the piano, no one helped me to my feet. I lay there long after the other men had already taken their seats, preparing for the closing moments of the service. I finally crawled out from my cleft of the rock and took my chair, but I've never again doubted the slaying power of the Holy Spirit.

Certainly one of the secrets of Kathryn's platform greatness was her capacity of concentration—her ability to continue to function despite obvious distractions. Some of these she was able to control. With a simple nod to an usher she could take care of an excited person who was causing a disturbance in the balcony, or a crying child in the center section. Although some of those who attended the miracle services judged her to be harsh, almost cruel, in the way she handled such disturbances, she knew her ability to concentrate on the voice of the Holy Spirit demanded that all distractions be removed. It was not uncommon for her to stop in the middle of a time of reverent worship, gesture in the direction of a whimpering child, "Maggie, take care of that!" and then continue on as if nothing had happened.

Some situations, however, simply could not be handled with a gesture or quick word. It was in these cases that her propensity to ignore problems sometimes demonstrated itself in incredible ways.

In the fall of 1968, Pat Robertson, president of the Christian Broadcasting Network and moderator of the popular television program, "The 700 Club," invited Kathryn to Portsmouth, Virginia. After participating in a telethon during which a number of people were healed, she finished her ministry in the tidewater area with a miracle service in the Norfolk Civic Auditorium.

Jim Bakker, Robertson's associate at the time, was in charge of the service until Pat arrived. Robertson, however, was delayed. Kathryn was agitated. She had little patience with people who did not arrive on time. The arena was packed, with a number of people in the overflow theater behind the building. The audience was restless and after waiting only a few minutes Kathryn turned to Bakker, who was standing beside her in the stage wings.

"When the Holy Spirit tells me to begin a service, I must not wait. I'm going on."

Before Bakker could say, "But Miss Kuhlman . . ." she brushed by him and was on stage, waving her arms and motioning for the choir and congregation to join her in singing "How Great Thou Art."

More than 3,000 had crowded into the main arena, sitting on metal chairs on the main floor and in the folding bleachers around the walls. But tragedy was just a breath away. As the people rose to their feet to sing there was a sound like a loud sigh, followed by a tremendous crash and piercing screams. An entire section of the folding bleachers, under tension by huge springs, had closed up against the wall. More than a hundred people either fell to the floor or were pinched between the board. It was a macabre scene. As the seats, which evidently had not been properly locked in place, snapped back against the wall, those who didn't fall forward to the hardwood floor below, were caught by their legs and suspended, head down, from the bleachers— screaming in terror. Many on the floor were bleeding profusely. Some had broken bones and others were unconscious. Fortunately, no lives were lost, but the meeting was bedlam as the ushers came running from all points in the arena to try to help the injured.

Jim Bakker, fighting back panic, raced to call the emergency squad and the fire department. The ushers quickly untangled the screaming people from the bleachers and stretched them out on the floor alongside the others. Ambulances arrived, sirens wailing, and the injured were carried out on stretchers. The safety officials then emptied the rest of the bleachers, motioning everyone to leave their seats and come to the main floor. Attendants folded the bleachers against the walls while workers scurried about to bring in another thousand chairs for additional seating. The entire chaotic process lasted more than an hour.

Through it all, however, Kathryn maintained her philosophy to act as though it never happened. Despite the bedlam, confusion and disorder, she kept right on with the service. She led the singing, even though few sang. She introduced the choir which tried to sing without watching the people running back and forth before them. Then she was back at the microphone, introducing some dignitaries in the audience, telling a few stories and taking up the offering. By the time the crowd finally got settled she was halfway through her sermon.

Some in the service saw it as a masterful demonstration of self-control and concentration in a time when everyone else was on the verge of panic. Others were puzzled, and some were disturbed, because she never stopped to pray for the injured—nor did she even make reference to the tragedy throughout the service. Yet, many were healed during the miracle service and by the time the meeting was over, the congregation—at least those not in the hospital—had almost forgotten the uproar. Nothing, it seemed, could distract her from her intended course.

In retrospect, reading some of the verbatim transcripts of those services, one must conclude that it had to be the Holy Spirit who did the healing—not Kathryn. Her approach was, as Kinsolving said, "unbelievable corn." Yet it worked. Standing close to the audience, invading what psychologists call a person's "personal space," she almost overwhelmed the people with her presence.

"We're gonna have fun today."

(Applause and some hearty "amens.")

Then she'd toss out some hoary chestnuts from her minister's bag—frayed jokes which she had used time and time before on the same audience.

"If any of you can't hear me, say amen."

(A weak chorus of amens from the top balcony.)

"If you couldn't hear me, how did you know to say amen?"

(Weak laughter.)

"Maybe some of you have already been healed of deafness."

(Louder laughter.)

This vein would continue for a few minutes, and then after presenting Dino and Jimmie McDonald, and perhaps introducing a few dignitaries, she would launch into her preaching.

"I'm only going to talk ten minutes today. No longer."

(Then she would speak for more than an hour.)

But when the Spirit began to move, you could hear a pin drop.

"There is a heart condition disappearing. Wonderful Jesus, I give you praise and glory. There is a case of sugar diabetes . . . the sugar is draining out of the body . . . an ear has been opened completely. Someone hears me perfectly. In the balcony. Check on that, someone. Up there in the top left balcony is a man with a hearing aid. Check that ear, sir. Hold your good ear closed tight; you hear me perfectly. . . . Arthritis of the feet down here to my left.

Go quickly, Maggie, she's in about the fifth or sixth row. Praise to you, wonderful Jesus!"

By that time a line of those who had been healed was forming on the side of the stage. Turning to Dr. Richard Owellen, the cancer research specialist from Johns Hopkins who often traveled with her and was now talking to a pretty young girl at the first of the line, Kathryn said quickly, "What's this, doctor?"

"Bursitis. This girl is Jewish and was sitting near the back when she felt the shoulder loosen."

"And you couldn't do that before?" Kathryn said in amazement, grabbing the black-haired girl by the arm and bringing her to the microphone.

The girl was weeping and moving her shoulder in small circles.

"Go ahead, honey, swing that arm wide. It won't come off."

The crowd roared its approval.

The girl swung her arm in giant circles, scattering tears all over the platform at the same time.

"And she's Jewish?" Kathryn laughed. "Pretty soon the rabbi is going to call and ask me to hold a miracle service in the synagogue."

The organ, which had been playing quietly, increased to a crescendo. Kathryn shouted to the crowd, "Let's give her a big 'God bless you.' " The audience responded with a terrific round of applause as Kathryn reached out and touched the girl on the head. "Dear Jesus, precious Messiah, I give you glory . . ." She got no further. The girl slumped back into the arms of one of the men stationed on the stage.

Kathryn looked on in amazement. Then turning to the audience, she said, "How about that! Jesus loves Jews also!"

This time the roar of the audience was deafening.

Turning to the other side of the stage, she motioned to an assistant who was standing beside an older man holding a hearing aid in his hand. "Here's that hearing miracle from the balcony, Miss Kuhlman."

The routine was the same from meeting to meeting. It never changed. Asking the man to hold his hand over his good ear, she stood behind him.

"Can you hear me now?"

"Yes."

She backed off a step. "Can you hear me now?"

"Yes."

"Can you still hear me?" She was now several feet away, whispering. The fact that the amplifying system picked up her whisper and turned it into a roar made no difference to the crowd. They understood.

Another man was ready, coming to the microphone holding a brown paper sack. He whispered something to Kathryn and then stood quietly while she slapped her thigh with an open hand and bent double with laughter.

"People, I have to tell you something, the funniest thing. God must certainly have a sense of humor." Turning to the man, she said, "Hold 'em up. Show 'em your potatoes. He says he heard that potatoes are good for arthritis and never goes anywhere without them. While he was sitting out there, he was healed of arthritis of the hip. Now he doesn't know what did it—the potatoes or God."

Laughing, she gave the man a little shove and said, "Go on, sir, run across the platform. Look at him go—and he left his potatoes for me to take home and bake."

No one else in the world could do it and get away with it—unless they had the Holy Spirit. Sometimes people wondered if the Holy Spirit was working in spite of Kathryn. It was a good question. But she was unique. No one else was ever like her. Many tried to imitate her platform mannerisms, but failed. They used the same technique, the same methodology. But there was no power. Kathryn may have been just an ordinary person, but there was no way to describe the miracle services as ordinary services.

A young Canadian reporter, who traveled to a miracle service as a skeptic but returned a believer, wrote in 1972:

> There isn't much more to tell, except that hearing three thousand voices singing Kathryn's theme song, "He Touched Me, and Made Me Whole," while six thousand hands reach high in the air—gnarled hands, trembling hands, thin hands, young hands, nail-bitten hands, workmen's stained hands—is an experience that no one can understand until one has been there . . . A miracle service is, to use the current vernacular, "a total thing."

CHAPTER XV

ALWAYS GIVING—
EVER EMPTY

Most religious celebrities adjust their life styles to fit ascending fame. But even though Kathryn's fame mushroomed like an atomic cloud as she moved into the sixties, she always remained a "small-time operator." By the time the Kathryn Kuhlman Foundation was formed in 1957, her annual gross income was in excess of $1 million. Yet she steadfastly refused to do what most big-time "religious operators" do. She never printed a magazine. She seldom solicited funds through the mail, even though nobody could have done better with a mailing list than Kathryn Kuhlman. She seldom talked about money in her meetings. She never had a high-pressure announcer on the stage. She used no gimmicks. She never fit the category as a money raiser. She remained, until the time of her death, straight Missouri cornbread.

Her one extra outreach in the early days was radio. One

day in 1958 while she was struggling with a radio show in the studio of WPIT, a friend introduced her to a young sound engineer, Steve Zelenko, who was working for Channel 11 in Pittsburgh. Zelenko, a marginal Roman Catholic, stood outside the studio for a few minutes listening as she finished her broadcast. When she came out he scowled: "My God, lady, can't you do any better than that?"

Kathryn hired him on the spot.

Steve struggled with her old radio equipment for about six months and finally came back to her. "Listen, Miss Kuhlman, this stuff is a bunch of garbage. Can't you begin to do something a little more professional? It seems if you're going to do something for God, it should be done right."

That was the one line of criticism Kathryn responded to. She gave Steve freedom to set up an entire sound studio in her expanding offices in the Carlton House. Money for broadcasting was short, but he was able to stretch the dollars in the purchase of equipment and, with the new quality programming, was able to expand the number of shows from her original four stations to twenty, thirty, and eventually almost sixty. While most of the people who worked for her took orders, Steve knew how to give them. And even though she cringed at his choice of words, she loved his blunt truthfulness. Sometimes he would interrupt her in the middle of a taping session, storming out of his engineer's booth, and say, "Miss Kuhlman, you can do better than that. You're the greatest. People all over the nation are tuned in to hear what you're saying. Cut the warmed-over stuff and preach the Word."

He'd storm back into his booth, rewind the tape, and give her the "go" sign—she seldom failed to respond to his lashing except by giving an outstanding performance the next time around.

Kathryn, on the other hand, was no slouch when it came

to broadcasting techniques. She liked the way announcer Bill Martin at WPIT had introduced her, and kept his tape, using his voice for years after he died. She was an expert in editing and could tell Steve, almost to the second, where to back up so she could start over. Because of the press of time, especially in the later years of her ministry, she often ran excerpts from the miracle services or used special guests. She was a master at the ad lib and could watch the clock and time the end of her messages to the second. Despite the fact that a few people complained about the way she came on the air—"Hello, there, and have you been waiting. . . ." and the strange, theatrical sound of her voice, Kathryn was a real "pro" and knew it.

Even so, Kathryn still remained "small time." The Friday miracle services at Carnegie Hall always followed the same format—and always produced dozens of healing miracles each week. The Sunday services at Stambaugh Auditorium, where the people called her "pastor," were affecting all of eastern Ohio and western Pennsylvania. Literally hundreds of alcoholic men and streetwalkers had been saved through her ministry. Dr. Metcalfe, of course, directed her three hundred voice men's chorus and he led the concert choir of two hundred young people. Yet Kathryn never changed. She didn't change her hairstyle, nor did she change her methods for conducting the services. She handled it all. She conducted Monday night Bible studies in the First Presbyterian Church. She performed weddings, conducted funerals, instructed the ushers, led the singing, made the announcements, and did most of the praying.

In Cleveland she drew seventeen thousand. In Wheeling, West Virginia, she attracted eighteen thousand in one week, and pictures of those healed in her meetings appeared daily on the front page of the Wheeling *News-Register*. A fifty-six-year-old woman, deaf and dumb since the age of four, attended the services with her daughter who translated Kathryn's messages through sign language. One day, while sitting in front of the radio at home, her daughter heard the mother say slowly but painfully, "I hear-rrd Miss-ss Koool-mannn laugh on the ra-dee-o." From that moment she spoke and heard perfectly.

Even the one thing which Kathryn had been told was impossible, took place. Noted theologians began putting their blessing—their enthusiastic blessing—on her ministry. Among these was Wade Jumper, a Canadian Baptist and an expert in the synthesis of religion and psychology. Writing in the *Toronto Star* on June 6, 1964, Jumper defended Kathryn's ministry.

> The Kuhlman ministry is unique theologically. By that I refer to the kind of God portrayed through the services. He is a generous and compassionate Creator and Re-Creator who gives miracle healings freely. This concept is in sharp contrast to the oft-portrayed God of favoritism who stintingly doles out his miracle works in exchange for man's righteousness.
>
> Some healing services have seemed to me to resemble glorified auctions. God is the invisible auctioneer and the persons seeking healing are the bidders, the currency is man's faith. Only the highest bidders (those with the strongest faith) are able to secure the limited number of healings.
>
> In that kind of healing meeting, healing seems to be primarily dependent upon a touch and prayer from the central figure, the evangelist. In such a service, healing lines and individual preference cards seem necessary.
>
> There are healings; but there are so many casualties. Some holders of preference cards never receive the

wanted personal attention from the healer. Others, who have their golden moment but fail to respond to the healer's command to be made whole are caused to feel rebuked because they are told their faith is not strong enough. Accepting the healer's diagnosis of their spiritual condition and blaming their sustained illness on weakness of their faith they turn homeward, more dejected than when they arrived. Their new emotional and spiritual wounds seem far heavier to bear than their physical affliction.

Some persons observing these broken-bodied and broken-hearted rejects turn their own defiance upon God. If God is like that—causing these people to suffer so for lack of their faith—I want no part of God, nor of any healing service.

God is not like that, Miss Kuhlman declares. The problem is not with God; it is man's mistaken interpretation of him.

I think that the thousands of personal conversions and healings in her ministry prove that she has succeeded in finding and conveying to others the true nature of God—a God whose power is directed by his love for his people.

Proper focus upon God's free love puts healing in its proper frame of reference. Every true healing, regardless of the technique helping convey it, is a gift from God, depending primarily upon God's love rather than upon the strength of the seeker's faith.

It is hoped that others, blessed with a healing gift similarly to that of Kathryn Kuhlman, will follow Miss Kuhlman's example. Until then, I still must contend her ministry to be in a league by itself. For I think that in saying this I am rightly giving God the credit—and not man (or woman).

245

With such approval by both God and man, it would seem that Kathryn could finally move into that circle of security that she had so long hoped for. Yet, like many celebrities, Kathryn was constantly haunted by an inner fear she would be unable to maintain her image before the public. There was that ever-recurring nightmare that nobody would show up, and the deep dread that the Holy Spirit might one day be taken from her, leaving her aging and ugly, powerless to emanate faith and hope. Therefore she built her own closet of compensations out of which, over the years, she pulled various cloaks to disguise her fears and insecurities.

When she died she had more than seventy-five pulpit dresses hanging in her basement, plus scores of other stage dresses for television—each of which cost in the hundreds of dollars. She rationalized her expenditures by saying most of the dresses were designers' models which she asked the sales clerk to lay aside until the price went down. After wearing them just a few times, she often gave her staff— Maggie, Maryon, and Ruth in particular, who were her size—choice of the lot. Some of the happiest remembrances of the women were the times Kathryn would have them out to her beautiful Fox Chapel home to sort through the racks and take their pick—chiffons, knits, and even the flowing pulpit gowns. No one ever doubted that Kathryn Kuhlman loved the very finest in threads.

Kathryn was, in her later years, a frequent visitor in the fashionable boutiques along Wilshire Boulevard and in Beverly Hills. A California reporter, writing in *Los Angeles* magazine, said she knew a lady who swore that one memorable afternoon she found Kathryn twirling in front of a mirror at I. Magnin's—one of the most exclusive stores on the West Coast. "Young lady," Kathryn was reported to have said to the salesgirl, "I could never talk to God in this dress!"

She enjoyed her expensive jewelry and her antiques, all of which helped her compensate for the frustration of being a woman in a man's world—the world of ministry. At the same time, her inordinate attention to clothing gave the impression that she considered herself to be royalty, something like the Duke of Windsor who, it was said, had been brought up differently from ordinary mortals.

(Many years after the duke abdicated the throne of England, he admitted, "I have never in my life picked anything up. When I take off my clothes, I simply drop them on the floor. I know there is always somebody behind me to pick them up.")

Even though Kathryn was born, and remained, a commoner, she always longed to be a duke's duchess—just as paupers dream of princehood. Yet she knew, especially when she was back home among her adopted family in Pittsburgh and Youngstown, that too much show of royalty would destroy her relationship with those she loved—the Poles, the Irish, the coal and iron workers, the streetwalkers, the alcoholics, those gutsy folks who saw in her the reflection of God. Perhaps the reporter misunderstood Kathryn's statement at I. Magnin's. It was not that Kathryn could not talk to God in "a dress like that," rather she constantly feared God would not talk through her to the common folks. But she loved her expensive clothes, precious jewels, luxury hotels, and first class travel. Therefore she had to compensate in the other direction, constantly telling all those stories about sleeping in turkey houses in Idaho and using the public baths for a nickel when she was too poor to afford a room with a shower. It gave her, she hoped, the needed identification with the poor, while allowing her the luxury of living like a queen. Yet one always wondered whether Kathryn was telling those stories to impress the people—or to remind herself: much as the ancient

247

king would commission one of his soldiers to ride behind him in his chariot and whisper in his ear, "Remember, O king, thou art mortal."

Kathryn was obsessed by crowd size. Although it was good psychology to have her meeting halls filled, there was something in her that craved the satisfaction of knowing that "thousands were turned away, unable to get in." It was an insecurity which had its root deep in Concordian soil. "See, mama, I told you I could make it on my own."

As with most insecure people, she was a name dropper, even though most of the names she dropped were people who couldn't begin to measure up to her on the kingdom scale. She enjoyed talking about the movie actors and actresses who attended the miracle services in California— both the sleazy and the strong—who appeared incognito behind dark glasses, seeking, like all the others in the Shrine Auditorium, spiritual reality. One of the established rituals before each service was to have ushers spot the famous personalities and get the word back to Kathryn in her dressing room. She always honored the stars' desire for anonymity, but she needed to know they were there, sitting and waiting, like kings and princes knocking at her door.

When Betty Hutton showed up one rainy Sunday afternoon at the Shrine Auditorium, Kathryn literally commanded, "Make sure she has a seat right up front. If you have to move someone out, I want her up front." Her bidding was performed by helpers who realized it was more important for Kathryn than it was for Miss Hutton.

After her private audience with Pope Paul at the Vatican, she sent out press releases to several major newspapers in the nation—along with a picture of the pope holding her hand—saying, "His Holiness complimented Miss Kuhlman on the 'admirable work' which she is doing and admonished her to 'DO IT WELL!'"

The more staunch Protestants among her followers might not understand, but to millions of people the pope was the vicar of Christ on earth . . . and for an uneducated farm girl from Concordia, Missouri, to have his blessing would compensate for a lot of things that had happened in the past.

The pathetic side was, of course, that Kathryn needed to prove nothing. The entire world knew she was God's handmaiden. Chosen. A daughter of destiny. Yet it seemed she was never able to outgrow the little redheaded girl who used Spillman's Freckle Cream to try to cover her spots to make her more acceptable to those around her.

"Did you see that article in *Movie Life* magazine?" she giggled when I came into the office one day.

I admitted that *Movie Life* was not one of the magazines in my bathroom rack. Kathryn laughed.

"Maggie, get it, that's right. It's right over there someplace. Oh, this is really a knockout. You'll never believe it. That's it. Bring it over here. Boy! This will really knock their eyes out back in Concordia."

She flipped it open, handed it to me, and then stood back for my reaction. I could hardly believe my eyes. The first page was a full page advertisement on how to increase your bust line three inches in fourteen days. Next came a bizarre headline: "FLASH! LIZ LEARNS BURTON HAS OTHER WOMAN." Then came a two-page spread of Kathryn and TV's Dr. Marcus Welby, Robert Young. Across the top of the pulp pages was a garish headline: "ROBERT YOUNG CURED BY FAITH HEALER KATHRYN KUHLMAN!" I looked up at Kathryn. I knew how intensely she hated being called a faith healer. For a brief instant I considered telling her what I really thought. Then I saw her face, her smile frozen, her hands twitching nervously as she awaited my reaction—my approval. I

249

capitulated, slipped back behind my mask, and said, "Wow! That's really something!"

She roared back to life. "What did I tell you," she laughed. "Everybody's talking about me."

Turning to Maggie and Maryon, who had never stopped rattling away at their typewriters even though we were standing inches in front of their desks, Kathryn said, "Do you think they'll take away my honorary degree from Oral Roberts University when they see this?" She slapped her thigh, threw back her head, and laughed again. "You know, even Oral never made it in the pages of *Movie Life*."

I didn't think she'd get much flak from ORU. Somehow, I just couldn't picture *Movie Life* gracing the periodical section of the university library.

In December 1974, *People* magazine did a four-page spread which included a picture of Kathryn stretched out on her bed in her beautiful Fox Chapel home, reading her Bible beneath an antique chandelier. "Dear Jesus," the caption said, "I don't want a mansion in heaven, just see that I get a good bed." Kathryn thought that was hilarious.

She was equally impressed when the theological journal, *Christianity Today*, put her picture on the cover and devoted seven pages to a question and answer interview. Her reaction was the same when *U.S. Catholic* magazine gave her five pages and concluded stating: "Many Roman Catholics in the 1970s are far more open to the idea, once ridiculed, that the Holy Spirit works through a woman preacher named Kathryn Kuhlman and heals people in our day."

She read every review, every article about her that appeared in all those Sunday newspaper magazines across the nation. It was as though she actually drew sustenance from them, even the bad ones. At least she was being recognized, and that human side of her seemed to need it to keep going.

In 1973 I had been invited to speak at the Greater Pittsburgh Charismatic Conference, held at Pittsburgh Theological Seminary. I just happened to arrive at the Pittsburgh airport the same time Kathryn was arriving from Louisville, Kentucky. Seeing me in the terminal, she laughed: "What are you doing here?"

"I'm one of the speakers at the Greater Pittsburgh . . . ."

"I don't know anything about that," she interrupted, "but let me show you something. Where are they, Maggie? They're in that bag over there. Bring them to me. You'll never believe what the Louisville newspapers said this morning. Can you imagine? Last night we packed 'em out in that great Walnut Street Baptist Church. And Dr. Wayne Dehoney, the former president of the Southern Baptist Convention . . . asking a woman preacher . . . would you believe? . . . and miracles . . . by the hundreds. Oh, boy, where are those papers, Maggie? We just couldn't get over it, reading them on the plane. Oh, oh, there's Loesch with the car. We haven't had any sleep in three days. Let's go, Maggie. . . ."

And they were gone. I never did get to see the newspapers. I doubt if Kathryn ever looked at them again. But for the moment, reading them gave her more nourishment than a full-course breakfast.

These same insecurities plagued her when she was thrust into the company of others with healing ministries—especially those who fit the category of "faith healers." For years, even though they had never met personally, she resented the ministry of Oral Roberts—often sniping at him in the press or during one of her impromptu sermons. Oral never answered back, which no doubt kept the pot from ever heating beyond the "simmer" stage. When his ministry changed from healing to education and he opened his multi-million-dollar university in Tulsa, Kathryn commented, "He always was good at raising money."

The one-sided feud continued. In 1970 Kathryn accepted an invitation to hold a Saturday afternoon miracle service in Washington, D.C., at the regional convention of the Full Gospel Business Men's Fellowship. The service was to take place in the ballroom of the Washington Hilton. Saturday night, almost as soon as she was finished, the World Action Singers from Oral Roberts University were to present a concert—followed by a message from Oral himself.

That night, after she had finished ministering, she changed clothes and slipped back into the darkened auditorium to hear Oral. She had done this on several occasions in the past, slipping incognito into one of his tent meetings. But now he had changed, and Kathryn wanted to see what he was like. Viola Malachuk, Dan's wife, had saved her a seat near the back of the auditorium. Easing into the chair, Kathryn put her hand on Viola's arm and chuckled softly, "We had a bigger crowd this afternoon, didn't we?"

In the spring of 1971, however, something happened to reverse Kathryn's attitude. Oral, who had been listening to Kathryn's radio and television broadcasts, and been inundated by recommendations from friends that he should attend a miracle service, flew to Los Angeles for that purpose. Incognito, just as Kathryn had attended his meetings in the past, he slipped into the balcony and lost himself in the great crowd. It was a life-changing experience for the man who had first introduced miracles to the general public.

Recounting that moment, Oral said, "I looked around. It was a different audience then came to my meetings. You could tell this was an audience that had touched the so-called top people as well as the more common like myself.

Then all of a sudden, there was a change which swept over her being. I could see it from the balcony. She said, 'There is someone over on the left who is feeling the presence of God and is being healed. Stand up and come forward.'

"I turned and saw a woman standing with a little child. The child was in braces and crutches. That little thing stood up, and they were helping as he tried to put one foot in front of the other. By the time they got halfway down the aisle, they stopped. They took off the braces and they took away the crutches and the little boy took a step—and took another step. When he got to the big steps which led to the platform, people started to help him up.

" 'Don't touch him,' Kathryn said. 'Let's see what the Holy Spirit has done.'

"I was absolutely broken up," Oral continued. "When the little boy was turned loose, he didn't walk, he ran. By that time I knew Kathryn Kuhlman was God's anointed vessel, and I thrilled because as I sat there I saw things that God hadn't done through me. I saw things God hadn't done through anybody I had seen. I rejoiced because God was so great. He was greater than I could conceive Him. He was greater than she could conceive Him. I looked up on the platform and saw all those Catholic priests and Protestant ministers and a Jewish rabbi. I had never seen that group coming together before. I knew that Almighty God had to do something awfully special to get all those people up there— and have me in the balcony.

"I recognized God was in this woman and she was unique in my eyes because God was using her in a different way. He had always used not only my voice, but my hands. But He didn't use her hands to heal people. She didn't have to touch the people the way God had me touch them. Unless I touched them there were seldom any miracles. But it was the opposite with Kathryn. I began to see that God doesn't use just one method. He has many methods."

After the service Oral made his way out of the balcony and joined a friend, Tink Wilkerson, a wealthy automobile dealer from Tulsa who was on the board of regents at ORU.

Tink, who had become acquainted with Kathryn, said she had heard Oral was in the meeting and would like to meet him.

"Oh, no," Oral said, holding up his hands. "I know what it's like after you finish one of these services. You're so exhausted you can hardly stand. I mean, when the anointing leaves, you are so weak you have to lie down or else you'll collapse."

"Not Miss Kuhlman," Tink said. "She is even stronger when she finishes than when she started—even if she's been on her feet for five hours."

"But I'm exhausted from just watching her," Oral stammered. "How can that weak, frail woman be stronger when it's over than when she began? This I must see."

Making their way down the long corridor along the side of the auditorium, Tink and Oral finally reached Kathryn's dressing room. It was the first face-to-face encounter between the two ministers. Tink stood back, just a little fearful of what might happen.

Oral took the initiative. Before Kathryn could say anything he said, "God has raised you up as His handmaiden. Your work has gone beyond mine, and I can't thank Him enough."

Kathryn was nodding. Something once bitter had gone out of her. She looked deep into the eyes of the man she once regarded as a rival and said, "Oral, I know. I know who I am and I know who you are. I know what I am and I know what you are. I know what I am in the kingdom and I know what you are. I know my place."

They stood looking at one another for just a moment and

then Oral, sensitive, said, "You must be exhausted."

"Not at all," Kathryn laughed. "I'm going out to have a quiet dinner with some friends, but I feel great."

Oral shook his head. "Well, Kathryn, you have something I don't have, and I've never had."

From that moment on, things were different between them. In the fall of the next year, Kathryn came to Tulsa for a miracle service. Oral attended and gave his blessing from the platform. The service made a terrific impact on the city. More than nine thousand people packed into the Civic Center and for the first time ministers of all denominations, Catholic and Protestant, came together. The first person to "go under the power" was a Catholic nun. Later in the service, the pastor of the First Methodist Church, Dr. Bill Thomas, was also slain in the Spirit. The Christian community in Tulsa was electrified for days after she left.

In the spring of 1973 Oral Roberts University, now fully accredited, gave their first honorary degree—Doctor of Humane Letters—to Kathryn. "We did it," Oral said, "because she represented the finest of the healing ministry of Jesus. I wanted the world to be reminded why ORU was established, that it was more than an academic institution. The one person in the world who epitomized all we believed in was Kathryn Kuhlman."

Kathryn, dressed in the cap and gown she had never ever been privileged to wear in high school, received her doctor's hood and then turned to the audience. The tears came, of course. She held her diploma aloft and said, "No one here can imagine what this has cost me. Only God." Then she turned to Oral and said, smiling, "Oral, you know we are one. We are one."

After the ceremony Kathryn pulled Oral aside. "Richard and Patty want to drive me to the airport."

Richard and Patty Roberts were Oral's son and

255

daughter-in-law, the stars of his television show. Both were vocal recording artists and had sung for years with the World Action Singers. However, perhaps because of all the fame, or perhaps because of the liability of having a famous father, their relationship was becoming strained.

Oral took Kathryn's hand. "There has never been a divorce in my family. My life stands for something. But Evelyn and I are helpless in this matter. It's been hard for Patty . . . to marry into a family like ours . . . but there are problems. . . ." His voice broke and the two walked toward the parking lot in silence.

No one knows exactly what went on in the car that day. But when Richard and Patty returned home from the airport, their marriage was different. Saved.

Kathryn came to ORU in the fall of 1975. It was one of the last sermons she preached before she died. Meeting in the new chapel which seats 4,000 people, she talked to the student body about herself—and about the Holy Spirit. "The world called me a fool for having given my entire life to the One whom I've never seen," she said tearfully. "I know exactly what I am going to say when I stand in His presence. When I look upon that wonderful face of Jesus, I'll have just one thing to say: I tried. I gave myself the best I knew how. My redemption will have been perfected when I stand and see Him who made it all possible."

When she gave the altar call, the entire student body responded. Weeping. Falling on their knees around the platform and in the aisles. One of the star basketball players, a boy nobody had been able to reach spiritually, fell on his knees at the altar and "prayed through." In less than three minutes he was praising God in a new prayer language.

Oral later said, "I found out that day what she meant when she said, 'It's not Kathryn Kuhlman, it's the Holy

Spirit.' The Holy Spirit is the living Christ come back in this invisible, unlimited form. The Holy Spirit was as real to her, more real, than any person around her. They were so wrapped up in each other—she and the Holy Spirit—that they talked back and forth and you never could tell when the Holy Spirit started and Kathryn left off. They were one."

It was a strange alliance which existed between these two ministers, each great in separate fields, yet complementing—even blessing—one another. Both had learned from each other, and the mutual affection lasted for the rest of Kathryn's life.

Despite the fact Kathryn's critics tried to lay much of her motivation at the feet of her insecurities, this was not the case. Much—most, in fact—of what she did was born out of positive direction rather than compensations for negative frustrations. I, personally, never knew a more highly motivated person—driving herself to total exhaustion for the sake of her Lord.

"You know," she once told me, "if some of the people who are doing such a sloppy job for the Lord were to do the same kind of sloppy job for their employer—they'd be fired before the afternoon was out."

Although Kathryn had a special love for ministers, she was especially hard on those who were satisfied with second-class performances. She demanded perfection from herself and her staff and expected it from all others who represented the Lord. She often judged by appearances. "I don't want that man ushering," she would say to whoever was in charge of the ushers. "If he doesn't have enough self-discipline to shine his shoes, then I don't want him touching God's ministry."

When Kathryn first moved to Pittsburgh she had a printing job that needed to be done. She sent it out to a local printer, but when the material came back into her office she was infuriated. "The imperfections were unforgivable," she said. She called the printer and demanded he come to her office and pick up his work. She could not accept it.

When the man finally showed up, Kathryn met him at the door and dressed him down. He stood, sheepishly, and listened as she pointed out all the errors.

He finally apologized. "Well, Miss Kuhlman, I figured that since yours is a religious organization the people wouldn't notice a few mistakes."

Kathryn exploded. "Sir, you wouldn't think of doing a poor job for Mr. Harris of the Ice Capades. You know he would have demanded perfection and you would have given him a perfect job. I represent something that's greater than the Ice Capades. You may not look on it as such, but this workmanship that's sent out of this office represents the greatest corporation in the world, and sitting on the board of directors are the Father, the Son, and the Holy Ghost. I've been entrusted with getting their job done, and I want perfection for them."

Of course she had insecurities. We all do. She was so riddled with them that even the most casual observer could see the gaping holes in her armor. But she was not motivated by them, for in her heart of hearts she was the most secure person I have ever met. It was evidenced by her unquestioned authority in spiritual matters. That was not a front. A mask. It was genuine. And when she was cut the deepest, by friends and enemies alike, even though she bled a little, at the deepest point of the incision one would still find Jesus.

No, the motivating force in her life was love. Like the apostle Paul who said "the love of Christ constrains me," she was driven by love—her love for Christ and her love for people.

Vivid in my memory is the time I sat with her in a grubby stage dressing room in Orlando, Florida. The miracle service was over. The people were gone. But she was weeping. Sobbing almost uncontrollably. I wanted to reach out and hold her, as a father would comfort his broken-hearted daughter. But I dared not touch her. The anointing of God was still upon her, and I knew that she had to remain alone in her sadness. There was but one shoulder she was allowed to rest her head upon, but one heart from which she could draw comfort. Her heavenly Father. I knew from past conversations with Maggie and others who were closest to her that she invariably left the miracle services and stood in the darkness weeping. There were so many in so much pain—and so many souls lost in the darkness of their own guilt and condemnation—and she was but one woman. One frail, ordinary woman—with a heart as big as the heart of God. It's no wonder that in the end she died of an enlarged heart, beating and expanding until it tried to claim the entire world for Christ.

I saw her, on dozens of occasions, take a child that was lame, maybe paralyzed from birth, and hug that child to her breast with the love of a mother. I am convinced she would have, at any moment required of her, given her life in exchange for that child's healing. She would hug bleary-eyed alcoholics and mix her tears with theirs. And the prostitutes who came to her meetings, with tears smearing their mascara, knew that if they could but touch her they would have touched the love of God. And those little old women, hobbling along on canes and crutches, some of whom couldn't even speak the English language but were

259

drawn by the universal language of love. No man could have ever loved like that. It took a woman, bereft of the love of a man, her womb barren, to love as she loved. Out of her emptiness—she gave. To be replenished by the only lover she was allowed to have—the Holy Spirit.

CHAPTER XVI

BETRAYED!

It seemed that Kathryn had finally "arrived." Her desk was cluttered with letters from top-name television personalities asking her to appear on their shows—Mike Douglas, Dinah Shore, Merv Griffin. Some of them, like Johnny Carson on the "Tonight Show," tried to bait her. "Most doctors say that up to eighty-five percent of all illnesses are psychosomatic," Carson taunted. "How can you claim these people are healed when they weren't really sick?"

Kathryn was never better with her answer—after all he was on her turf with a question like that. "If the doctors are not able to help psychosomatic cripples, and they come to these great miracle services and God touches them and they leave without their crutches—and stay healed—what difference does it make whether it's psychosomatic or not?"

Carson gave a weak grin, cleared his throat and said it was time for a commercial.

But along with Kathryn's ascending popularity came

dark pitfalls of danger. She was enamored of the Hollywood mystique. Ralph Wilkerson introduced her to Dino Kartsonakis. It was a natural match. The handsome young pianist with the "Greek god" look had come to Wilkerson's Melodyland as a music director. Ralph realized that despite the young Greek's outstanding musical ability, he was not a choir director. He was a keyboard performer. Just what Kathryn needed.

Kathryn hired him on the spot. She had been using a variety of performers for her television show, but Dino was more than she had ever dreamed of. Dark, with flashing black eyes, he could stroke the grand piano like a harp. Even though he was still in his twenties when she hired him, he was already acclaimed as one of the better keyboard musicians in the country. Soon she had him appearing on stage. "And now, DEEEE-noo." The spotlight would pick him up as he came from the wings, dressed in a dark blue velvet tuxedo with a frilly shirt and flashing cuff links and rings. She would hug his arm after he finished and tell the same silly stories about the little girl who wanted Dino on her Christmas tree, and he would stand humbly and drink it in. After all, she picked out his clothes, finer than he could have ever afforded on his own, and taught him how to wear them in style. She sent him to Italy to have his suits tailored, put him up in the finest hotels, and financed his record and sheet music production.

She, in turn, found it pleasant to be in the company of a handsome young man who could escort her to dinner, sit beside her on the long plane rides, tip the porters, and hail the taxis. Her employees in the Pittsburgh office called him a gigolo—Kathryn's paid escort.

Steve Zelenko, Kathryn's gadfly in the Pittsburgh office, saw the danger and tried to warn her. "Look, Miss Kuhlman, it just doesn't look good. Okay, so the guy is fun.

He's light. He's airy. He's someone to cling to as you grow older. But be careful.

Kathryn was sure of herself. "I know what I'm doing. I know it looks like he's using me, riding my coattails. But I know what I'm doing. Don't worry about it."

But Steve did worry. And so did a lot of Kathryn's friends. Things grew worse when Dino convinced Kathryn she should hire his brother-in-law, Paul Bartholomew, to distribute the television programs and work as her personal administrator. He became her highest paid associate. At the peak of his employment, Bartholomew was earning in excess of $130,000 a year in commissions, plus $15,000 for being her personal administrator. In addition Kathryn paid all the rent and utilities for his offices in Newport Beach.

"Watch that guy," Steve Zelenko cautioned. "You don't need him. You've got too much going for you to get involved. You have assets that guy would never dream of. Get out before you get hurt."

Kathryn stormed out of the recording studio and said to Maryon Marsh in the front office, "I don't know why I talk to that man back there. He's paranoid on the subject."

But Steve was right, and had Kathryn been able to listen to him—or to any of the others around her—it would have saved her considerable anguish and pain—maybe even saved her life.

Kathryn learned that Dino had been dating Debby Keener, who was rumored to be a showgirl. Kathryn was furious. She knew Dino had been friendly with June Hunt, the daughter of Texas billionaire H. L. Hunt, in Dallas. She had approved. But dating a former showgirl was something else. She confronted Dino. He denied Debby was a former showgirl, but confessed the two of them were friends. Kathryn was still outraged. Their relationship deteriorated—with momentary happy interludes—after that.

263

In December 1973, Kathryn, Maggie, and Dino were flying from Pittsburgh to Los Angeles. Maggie was glancing through some tabloids, the *National Enquirer*, *National Tattler*, and other gossip papers.

"Look at this!" she exclaimed.

She handed the paper to Kathryn. It contained a story involving Debby Keener. Strangely, Dino remained silent as Kathryn tore out the article and stuffed it into her billfold.

She confronted him again. "Look, you're going to have to make up your mind. If you want this girl then you are out of this ministry. It's just like that."

Dino tried to explain they were only casual friends.

"Drop her!" Kathryn said. "If you don't, you're finished with me."

Dino agreed not to see her again and for a while it looked as if the Kathryn/Dino relationship was patched up. Kathryn took him along when she and Maggie took a Brazilian holiday and flew to Rio de Janeiro in January 1975. Dino said he wanted to do some shopping for things in his house and Kathryn financed him heavily. Later, when she discovered he was actually buying those things to give to Debby, she was deeply hurt. Yet she was wise enough to realize he was ripe for marriage. She did hope, she often told Maggie, that when he married he would not bring a reproach upon "the ministry."

On February 22, 1974, she had signed an agreement with the Hollywood firm of Rullman and Munger for a multi-million-dollar Kuhlman Foundation media account. Immediately Paul Bartholomew insisted he also was under contract. He pressured her to release the other contract, saying that he was the Kuhlman Foundation's sole agent in handling all television and media accounts. Rullman and Munger sued and Kathryn eventually settled out of court.

Dino saw the handwriting on the wall and in February

1975, he had his brother-in-law, Bartholomew, prepare a written contract for Kathryn to sign, demanding that she pay him $20,000 base salary, plus $500 for each personal appearance (including TV shows), plus all expenses. Dino was now seriously contemplating marriage to Debby and wanted to protect his interests. Kathryn was in Los Angeles for a miracle service at the Shrine on Sunday, and then stayed over to tape eight television shows on Wednesday and Thursday.

Tuesday night Bartholomew came to see Kathryn at the Century Plaza Hotel. He called her eighteenth floor room from the lobby and asked if he could come up. Kathryn was suspicious.

"You know, Paul, I have television tomorrow. We get started early."

"I have a letter for you. You have to see it before television in the morning."

Kathryn bit her lip. "Give it to the bellboy and ask him to bring it up," she said. "I'll take care of it."

Within minutes, after reading Dino's demands, Kathryn was on the phone, calling Maggie back in Pittsburgh. The office had already closed but she reached her at home. "We have trouble," she said.

"What's wrong?" Maggie asked.

"Dino's made some outrageous demands and wants me to sign a contract by tomorrow morning. I need a piano player—fast."

"How about Paul Ferrin?" Maggie suggested. Paul Ferrin had married the daughter of Biney Anderson, one of the girls in the Anderson Trio in Denver. He was an accomplished musician, directing the music at Bethel Church in San Jose, California.

"See if you can get him, will you, Maggie," Kathryn said, her voice tired. "Call me back."

Maggie explained the situation to Paul who agreed to fly down early Wednesday morning in order to be at the CBS studio in case he was needed.

The stage was set—literally—for the confrontation the next morning.

Dino arrived early, but was disturbed to see Paul Ferrin in the studio, talking to Dick Ross. Making his way back to Kathryn's dressing room, he wasted no time.

"Well?" he asked, standing in the door.

"Well, what?" Kathryn responded, never getting out of her chair.

"Did you sign it?"

"No, and I don't intend to. You know you can't pressure me like that. You've had things good. Too good."

"What's that guy Ferrin doing out there?" Dino asked.

Kathryn smiled. "You didn't think I would leave myself uncovered, did you? I've been at this a lot longer than you. Now you're through. Finished. Get out and never come back."

Kathryn was on her feet now, her face flushed in anger. Dino slammed the door. Her hands were shaking as she put them over her face and burst into tears. But she was, as one newspaper reporter called her, a "tough old broad." She knew the Hollywood axiom. The show must go on. She rallied her strength and headed for the make-up room. There was work to do.

It had been an unbelievably heavy week. On Sunday, February 2, she had been at the Shrine Auditorium for a miracle service. Monday she taped the Dinah Shore show at CBS. Tuesday she was back at CBS to tape the Larry Solway Show for the Canadian Broadcasting Company. That night she received Paul Bartholomew's note and the contract. The following morning she had her confrontation with

Dino and taped four telecasts at CBS. The next day she was back for four more telecast tapings. Saturday she flew to Pittsburgh to be in the services in Youngstown on Sunday. The next week she had her miracle service at the First Presbyterian Church in Pittsburgh, and then February 16 she was back at the Shrine for another miracle service in Los Angeles. Tuesday she flew up to Oakland for a miracle service at the Oakland Coliseum. That same day she did the "A.M. in San Francisco" TV show. Thursday she flew back to Pittsburgh in order to hold the Friday morning miracle service at First Presbyterian. That same afternoon she was to tape the David Susskind Show and then go to Youngstown again on Sunday.

It didn't seem possible that anything could happen to make things tighter. But it did. For several months Dr. Arthur Metcalfe, Kathryn's choir director, had been having chest pains. His doctors in Pittsburgh had checked him out and given him a green light, suggesting they would test for ulcers when he got home from California. He was with Kathryn at the Shrine and in Oakland, and then flew home on February 19. On the morning of February 20, 1975, he got up and started to drive in from his country home to the office. The chest pains returned and he had to turn the car around and return home. Mid-morning Mrs. Metcalfe called the office and blurted out, "Art just died."

Maryon was speechless. Not only out of grief for her dear friend, but because she knew Miss Kuhlman was on her way back to Pittsburgh, having just gone through the toughest time of her life. Could she stand the shock? Maryon arranged for Loesch to meet the plane and to have him tell Maggie about Dr. Metcalfe's death. Maggie could then break the news to Kathryn.

No one knows how much pressure the problem with Dino put on Arthur Metcalfe's heart. Nor does anyone know how much pressure the two events put on Kathryn. But on the surface she recouped almost immediately—and moved ahead.

The Dino matter was far from settled. On February 15 Kathryn fired Paul Bartholomew as her personal administrator, although she was unable to fire him as her television syndicator. She had foolishly signed a contract stating that she could not release him without ninety days notice—notice which could not be given before December 31. That meant she could not release him from his contract until March 31, 1976—almost a full year away.

In 1972 when Kathryn was in Tulsa for a miracle service, it was D.B. "Tink" Wilkerson who donated office space for Maudie Phillips to handle the pre-meeting details. At that time Tink had offered to help Miss Kuhlman, at his own expense.

"I really feel I can be of value to you," he said. "You are already running a successful operation, but you need a man to act as your business manager, somebody to negotiate your business contracts."

It was common knowledge that Kathryn had been victimized several times. Kathryn, however, was not interested in Tink's offer. She thanked him and passed it off as a friendly gesture.

However, Tink and his wife kept on coming to the miracle services. Kathryn developed an affection for Sue and would often call her on Saturday morning, from wherever she was, just to chat. Sue began to realize that Kathryn was basically a lonely person and she could perform a ministry by just having a listening ear. It was a warm relationship between the two, although not intimate.

In April of 1975, Tink and Sue flew up to St. Louis to attend the miracle service in Keil Auditorium and visit with

Kathryn. Tink went by her hotel after the service and they chatted briefly. He knew that Dino had left, that there were lingering problems with Paul Bartholomew, and he was concerned.

Kathryn told him she was locked into her contract with Bartholomew and she feared he was trying to take advantage of her.

She told him she planned to buy out Bartholomew's contract, and get a new agent. It would cost her more than $120,000, but she felt it would be worth it to have him gone.

"Kathryn, as far as I am concerned, that is probably the very worst thing you can do," Tink said. Although he had no evidence at the time, Tink strongly suspected that Bartholomew would take the money and then turn around and take further advantage of her.

Kathryn shook her head. "I'm going to do it. I've made up my mind. I've already formed a new corporation called Kuhlman Media International (KMI) which will handle my television and other media business."

Tink shook his head. "You are making a terrible mistake. I'm not going to argue with you about it, but I'm telling you it's wrong. Sue and I are leaving for Hawaii, but we'll stop in Los Angeles and see you on the way back to Tulsa."

On Saturday evening, May 3, Tink and Sue arrived in Los Angeles from Hawaii. They called the hotel. Kathryn had just gotten in from the miracle service in Las Vegas.

"I'm worn out now," she said, "but I'd like to see you tomorrow. Maybe I should listen to you after all."

The next day Tink and Kathryn met together to discuss the growing problem with Bartholomew. Tink urged her to get a lawyer. Kathryn was hesitant to use a Pittsburgh lawyer for fear the word would leak back to the home folks. Ironically, she even had a lawyer on the board of directors for the Kathryn Kuhlman Foundation, but refused to let him handle this matter. Wilkerson recommended Oral Roberts' attorney, Sol Yeager. Kathryn seemed mentally tired and told him to go ahead and do whatever he thought best. Wilkerson called Oral Roberts and discussed the matter with him. Yeager agreed to help some, but he was in semi-retirement and could not give full time to the case. Wilkerson then called his own lawyer, Irvine E. Ungerman, to ask him to handle the case. Ungerman reviewed the terms of the contract and then suggested Kathryn fire Bartholomew.

Paul Bartholomew could read the handwriting on the wall. The second week of May, he placed an "urgent" phone call to Myra White, one of Kathryn's West Coast secretaries, asking her to meet him in the lobby of the Century Plaza Hotel. In a statement made to Miss Kuhlman in writing, Myra White related what transpired:

> During the course of this meeting, Mr. Bartholomew solicited my assistance in Mr. Kartsonakis' new Hollywood office, discussed his own personal dismissal from the Kathryn Kuhlman Foundation and advised me that he had written a book about Miss Kuhlman and was carrying it in a briefcase which he had with him. He told me he carried it every place he went and didn't let it out of his sight. I expressed dismay at this and questioned his motive and the outcome for everyone involved. . . . My feeling through the conversation was that he wanted me to be a "go-between" for a "payoff" to assure her that he would not publish this book. He kept expressing to me that he didn't want to publish the book if only Miss Kuhlman would talk to him. He stated that he had someone big with whom to collaborate— bigger than he had anticipated.

Miss White said the conversation reminded her of an earlier conversation she had overheard in Mr. Bartholomew's Newport Beach office in September 1973. He was talking with someone on the telephone and said, "When I am no longer working with and for Miss Kuhlman, I can collaborate on an article."

Several things were becoming apparent. Dino and Paul had been making plans for some time to take over a larger share of the business and were collecting information to write an expose of her life.

It also seemed obvious that Bartholomew intended to try to pressure Kathryn by asking for money in exchange for not publishing his book. It was a sticky affair.

On July 1, 1975, Paul Bartholomew filed suit in Los Angeles Superior Court charging that Kathryn or her associates illegally took personal records from his Newport Beach office, interfered with his business, and breached her contract with him. The suit demanded $430,500 in damages. Since Bartholomew's Newport Beach offices were leased by the Kathryn Kuhlman Foundation, she felt justified by going in, taking the records, and cleaning out the furniture. But Kathryn was now a world-wide celebrity, every newspaper in the nation carried a report of the battle. *People* magazine sent a reporter to interview Dino and Paul. Russell Chandler, religion editor for the *Los Angeles Times*, splashed the report on the front page of the paper.

Dino and Paul did not limit their remarks to the problems surrounding the lawsuit. Chandler reported Dino said he quit the ministry because of alleged inconsistencies he observed between her professional image and her personal life. "Her double standard of living had paid its toll on my conscience," he said.

Why, one wonders, did he want to sign a contract to continue working under such conditions?

271

Kathryn tried to fight back. She defended her firing of Bartholomew the best she could, but her heart wasn't in it. Time and time again she wished she had followed the leading of her heart and paid the contract off. She knew she could have arranged, somehow, to keep his book out of print. But now everything was on the front pages again.

One of the greatest tragedies of Kathryn's life was she had gathered some around her who never knew or understood the work of the Holy Spirit. They didn't seem to understand Him as the character of Jesus Christ, the holiness of God, the prime mover of the universe. He was simply some intangible power that seemed to reside in or around Kathryn. For this reason most of her staff never saw any need to become spiritual people themselves. It was sufficient that Miss Kuhlman was spiritual.

In late September the suit was finally settled out of court. But not before many other charges and countercharges had been hurled. Kathryn agreed to pay Paul Bartholomew $75,000 plus $16,230.70 claimed as commission due him. Other than cash to Bartholomew, both settlements were the same: "(The parties involved) hereby agree never to make any slanderous, scandalous or libelous comments concerning their past relationships with Kathryn Kuhlman Foundation, Kathryn Kuhlman, or KMI, Inc. including without limiting the generality of the foregoing, and for a period of ten (10) years from this date not to cause to be made the preparation or dissemination either alone or in conjunction with others of any manuscript or information relating to or containing biographical or historical material. . . ."

The agreements were signed by Paul and Christine Bartholomew and by Dino and Debby Kartsonakis.

The battle was over, but as it was in Franklin and Akron, nobody had won and the kingdom had suffered a reproach. Only this time Kathryn suffered more than anyone. Her weakened body simply could not stand the punishment. In the middle of the lawsuit she had been admitted to a Tulsa hospital with a severe heart condition. The doctors had warned her then it could be fatal. She refused to listen. She needed to fly to California. There were television programs to be made, and mail to answer, and battles to fight. After that she had one more place she had to go. Like Anna and her friend, she would live just as though it never was.

That same September Kathryn returned for a brief visit to Concordia, Missouri. She wanted to stop by the cemetery. Mama had died in the spring of 1958. She was eighty-six. Kathryn had been good to her mother. On one occasion she had sent a carpenter all the way from Pittsburgh just to fix a sagging front porch and repair some window sashes on the small house on Orange Street where mama had moved.

It was Indian summer when she arrived. The leaves on the elms, dogwoods, and sourwoods were hanging motionless in the afternoon haze as she drove down St. Louis Street, past the large, white two-story house where she had spent so many happy childhood hours. At the end of the street was the cemetery—divided into three sections: one for the United Church of Christ, one for the Baptists, and one for the Methodists. The Lutheran Cemetery was on the other side of town near the big highway.

Kathryn asked the driver to pull the car into the third driveway dividing the sections and to wait. She got out and walked slowly around the front of the car to the place where the headstones marked the graves. *Emma, 1872-1958*. Mama, who had blistered her bottom in the basement. How she needed her.

273

Next to it was papa's stone. *Joseph Adolph*, 1866-1934. She recalled the last time she saw him alive. He was standing in the back yard of the big house, one hand reaching up and holding on to the clothesline.

"Kathryn, do you remember when you·were a little girl and would stand behind me while I read the paper. You'd say, 'Papa, gimme a nickel'? I would tease you, sitting there pretending like I didn't hear you. You'd keep asking and eventually I'd dig in my pocket and hand you a nickel. Do you remember?"

Kathryn, who had just begun her ministry in Denver, smiled and nodded her head. "Yes, papa, I remember."

"There's something you didn't know, baby. I loved you so much that I would have given anything you asked. You just limited yourself because all you wanted was a nickel."

Kathryn stood looking down at the weathered tombstone, her eyes filling with tears. "Papa, how I wish you were here now. I need to lean my head against your shoulder. I need you to make me well."

She turned away from the graves and looked heavenward. The words of the cardiologist echoed in her mind. "You may have another attack in thirty days, you may have it in ninety days. But I can tell you unequivocally that you will have another episode. Your mitral valve is bad."

"Dear Jesus," she sobbed. "Make me well. I don't want to die. I don't want to die."

The cemetery was silent. She was aware of the twittering and singing of the birds. She turned back to the graves. A small vase of faded plastic flowers was next to mama's grave. It was overturned and she stooped to turn it right side up. She could see where the moles had dug around the base of the headstone, the crusted dirt pushing up brown through the green grass. The sun was setting just behind the rolling hills. Directly to the west was a dairy, the sound of lowing cows carried on the breeze as they came in for milking. A small chipmunk with brown and white stripes scampered through the grass and disappeared behind another headstone. All the names were German. Old, familiar names. Heyenbrock, Koch, Deterk, Lohoefener, Westerhouse, Heerwald, Bargfrede, Franke, Schroeder. . . .

Far to the north, extending up beyond the elms and willows, was the steeple of the Lutheran church. In the center of the cemetery stood a huge old fir tree. Gnarled, it stretched more than a hundred feet toward the sky. One of the bottom branches, a huge limb, had broken off—leaving a gaping hole at the bottom of the tree. It looked much like a small grotto one might find in a Catholic church containing a statue and a candle. The branch had probably broken off the winter before, perhaps because it had become overextended and was unable to hold the weight of the ice and snow. Nothing was left to show where it had been except the gaping hole.

Brushing her tears Kathryn walked slowly to the base of the huge tree, staring at the ugly wound. The words of Jesus, those words she had preached so often, came to mind:

> Every branch in me that beareth not fruit he taketh away: and every branch that beareth fruit, he purgeth it, that it may bring forth more fruit. . . . As the branch cannot bear fruit of itself, except it abide in the vine; no more can ye, except ye abide in me (John 15:2, 4).

She closed her eyes and stood silently. Only the gentle sound of the wind blowing through the spruce trees near the road and the chirping of the small birds could be heard. Like the great branch, she was overextended. Perhaps it was her time to break loose, that other branches could bear the burden. She dreaded the thought of leaving an ugly gaping wound behind. There was no one to take her place. Yet, perhaps God did not intend for her ministry to continue. Was it to be picked up by another, dozens of others—just as the higher branches on the old fir would this winter bear the burden of the ice and snow. The thought was too much for her to comprehend. She turned back to the car, too tired and weak to even pray.

CHAPTER XVII

THE LAST TRAVAIL

"If I ever step out on the platform, and the anointing of the Holy Spirit is not there, I shall leave and never again hold a miracle service. Without Him I am nothing."

It was a statement Kathryn made thousands of times over the last years of her life. In the beginning of her ministry she believed it. But as the end came, I am convinced she had to keep making the statement. There was no way she could stop. The television ministry itself required more than $30,000 a week. The fact that she now had the longest-running series ever produced in CBS's expensive studios was part of the image. To stop, to even cut back, would mean she was beginning to fail. The same was true with the miracle services. As the pain in her chest grew almost unbearable, instead of holding fewer services, she increased the number. She had to continue.

In May 1975 she came to Las Vegas for a miracle service.

The Holy Spirit had been present in great power. In fact, it was one of the times when I thought the day might have arrived when everyone in the auditorium would be healed. But her physical condition was poor. After the meeting, when we were with her in her suite at Caesar's Palace, I urged her to curtail her schedule.

"I can't," she said, pacing nervously back and forth. "There is no way. 'The ministry' must continue."

She was an old trouper. The show had to go on, despite how she felt. For to have rung down the curtain would have been an even quicker and more painful death than burning out on stage.

Yet deep in her heart she knew she was not infallible, nor did she have a corner on God. That was one of the reasons she showed a touch of jealousy when she heard that others, such as Ralph Wilkerson, were holding services in which miracles happened almost as frequently as they did in hers. And Kathryn did believe with all her heart that God intended for every church service to be a miracle service, for every pastor, every priest, every rabbi to be one through whom the Holy Spirit would work to bring miracles to the people.

She also believed the day of the great miracle services was coming to a close. She knew she could not live forever. She knew she was dying—and she intended to go out as a flaming torch rather than a smoldering, flickering candle. But when she died "the ministry" would be over. And as the fact of her imminent death grew apparent to her (although no one else seemed to realize how close she was to dying), it seemed to me she had to make sure that others, especially those closest to her, did not try to keep alive what God was allowing to die.

Yet she had little time to consider the future. She was too involved with the present. Thinking ahead, even six months ahead of time, was beyond her ability. At the same time she was caught in the terrible dilemma of believing, on the one hand, that the Holy Spirit and the miracle services were so bound together that it was impossible to hold a service without His presence, and that recurring nightmare that she might do something to displease Him and He would depart from her.

Over and over she prayed, on stage, and in the quietness of her room, as though she was storming the gates of heaven, "Take not the Holy Spirit from me." She preached the same sermons. "God will not share the glory with any man. He is a jealous God who demands all the glory for Himself." She was preaching to herself, for she knew how close she was to "sharing the glory."

In the fall of 1972, Kathryn's friends planned a gala party at the Pittsburgh Hilton Hotel to celebrate her twenty-five years of miracle ministry in Pittsburgh. One of the highlights of the evening was the presentation of Ev Angelico Frudakis, a renowned sculptor, who had struck a gold medal for the anniversary festivities. Kathryn had posed long hours for the artist and was seemingly pleased with the results of her picture on the medal in gold relief.

The following morning I stopped by her offices in the Carlton House before returning to Florida. She graciously gave me one of the medals, about the size of a silver dollar, and then handed me a copy of the press release which had gone out to the nation's papers. In describing the medal it said, "Miss Kuhlman is depicted on the front of the medal in gold relief, hands of healing extended. On the back is a relief picture of Jesus healing the sick."

I read the typed release and then looked back up at Kathryn. She was standing, as I had seen her do so many times, looking intently at my face, searching for some sign of reaction—her smile seemingly frozen into place.

I knew this time I had to give her something more than the approval she was asking for. I said softly, "Don't you think it would be better to say that Jesus was on the *front* of the medal and Kathryn on the back?"

She never hesitated. "You're right! You're absolutely right!" Whirling to Maggie who was busy at her desk she said, "Maggie, we've got to change this release."

But it was too late. The word had already gone out all over the nation. And even though Kathryn shrugged it off, I knew she was disturbed, for it indicated that something was happening to her—something she didn't like but didn't know how to combat.

It was two years later when she came to Montreat, North Carolina, to address a convention of Christian booksellers. Almost three thousand people had crowded into Anderson Hall, the big pavilion on the Presbyterian Conference Grounds, and most of them were hoping to see some miracles. When she arrived I slipped back stage to let her know we were all ready.

She grabbed my arm in that steely grip of hers and whispered loudly, "Jamie, what are we doing here?"

I grinned. "I'm here to support you."

She shook her head. Her face seemed drawn and tired. "We'll not have a miracle service," she said seriously. "I'll just preach. That's all. I'll just preach."

Moments later she was on the platform, going through all her motions. She waved her arms and talked about the Holy Spirit being there. As she rambled on and on, the people began to get restless. Kathryn had only a little over an hour—she was used to four or five for a miracle service— and by the end of the service, she was trying desperately to salvage the meeting. But it was too late.

A former supper club singer, who had been saved and healed in Miss Kuhlman's ministry, was on stage. As the service was ending she moved to one of the stage mikes so it would pick up her voice and began singing "Alleluia." Kathryn was displeased. To put a stop to it she reached over and touched the woman, praying for her. She went down under the power. Then Kathryn turned, gripped my arm, and pushed me toward the microphone. If there was to be any song leading, she wanted it to come from someone with whom she was familiar, not a stranger.

The people were singing, but listlessly, Kathryn was moving back and forth across the stage, saying all her favorite phrases. They seemed empty. The singer had climbed to her feet and Kathryn touched her again. Nothing happened this time. In a desperate move I heard her say, "The Spirit is all over you, Jamie." She swept toward me, putting her hands on my jaw as I sang. There had been times in the past when, if she even got close to me, I would go down "under the power." But that day it was just Kathryn—with her hands on my jaw. I loved her too much to disappoint her. With a sigh of resignation, I fell backwards into the arms of the man behind me. As the man helped me to my feet Kathryn moved in again, "I give you glory. I give you praise." But this time I simply could not. I just stepped back when she touched me. She whirled and moved to the other side of the platform. Moments later she disappeared through the stage door. On the way to the airport she told Dan and Viola Malachuk, who were driving her to the plane, "I wish I had gone ahead with a miracle service, but I have to catch this plane back to Pittsburgh."

The power was slower in coming than in previous years. There were other instances. Ruth Fisher told of being with her in Tampa when a similar thing happened. There she seemed to combine all the sermons she had been accumulating for years and presented them in one package. It was confusing and powerless. The people were restless, milling around, waiting for the miracle service to start. God honored His word and there were miracles, but it was almost as if they came in spite of Kathryn, rather than because of her.

Something strange seemed to be taking place in her ministry. On the surface she was at the peak of her fame. Her crowds were the largest in her career. Television had made her name a common household word. Her books were being read all over the world. Yet, inside, things were crumbling and falling apart. Dino and Bartholomew had left, throwing mud as they went. Several of her longtime employees had fallen into immorality, and she seemed genuinely confused as to what to do. Things were strained between her and Maggie. Tink and Sue were now with her at all times. On top of this her body was just worn out.

Twenty years before she had slipped out of Pittsburgh and gone to a doctor in Washington, D.C. for a physical checkup. He warned her she had an enlarged heart. She needed to slow down. Instead she followed her philosophy with all things that went wrong, she lived as though it never was. But it was there. As she grew older and the pressures grew greater, the heart condition grew worse.

Steve Zelenko told me that one day Kathryn, after just having had an argument with one of her secretaries, walked back into the radio studio in her offices in the Carlton House. She was ashen white.

"Come here," she said to Steve.

Taking his right hand she placed it against her left rib cage.

"I could feel the organ of her heart, beating, trying to force itself out between her ribs," Steve said. "When I removed my hand I could actually see her heart, pulsating between her ribs—under her dress. It seemed as if it would explode."

On some occasions Kathryn would stop dictating letters

and, without warning, get out of her chair and lie down on the floor.

"She did that in the radio studio once," Steve said, "and almost scared me to death." She was getting ready to make a tape. I was in the control booth and looked up. She had disappeared from her desk. I went into the studio and she was stretched out on the wooden floor."

" 'Go right ahead,' she said. 'I'm just resting a few moments.'

"I returned to my control booth," Steve said, "but I was afraid she was dying. I finally came back to the studio and urged her to lie on the sofa. She shook her head and the strangest look came over her face. 'No, I'll just stay here for a moment. I'll be all right.' I realized as I went back to my booth, that she couldn't get up. She had to stay there.

"Then, about ten minutes later, she was back at her desk ready to go. It was as though it had never happened. But it had."

There were other attacks, some more serious. In the summer of 1974, Maggie had a call from California. "Miss Kuhlman's terribly sick. We're putting her on a plane. She needs immediate medical attention."

It was a Saturday afternoon and Maggie met her at the Pittsburgh airport. TWA had always taken special care of Kathryn. The passenger representative in Pittsburgh had been touched in one of her meetings and most of the airline personnel knew her. She got off the plane white as death, but smiling, nodding and speaking to the people in the airport. Maggie got her to the car and picked up her baggage. When she finally got in beside her, Kathryn said, "Get me to a doctor. I'm going to die."

"Okay, will you go to the hospital?"

"No! No hospitals," Kathryn gasped, holding her chest. Maggie drove her directly to the office of a doctor who had agreed to stand by in case Kathryn refused to go to a hospital. He took x-rays and said her lungs were clear but her heart was radically enlarged. He put her on digitalis, but after only one day's rest she was back to her usual routine.

Although her body was failing rapidly, it seemed she was accelerating her activity. Besides her regular services she planned an October series of meetings in the south: Mobile, Tampa and West Palm Beach. She was scheduled to speak at Melodyland in California and then return to Israel for the Second World Conference on the Holy Spirit in November. It seemed almost suicidal.

Then, in a move which baffled even those closest to her, Kathryn, without warning, decided to wade into the biggest controversy to stir the charismatic movement since its inception in the early 1950s. For more than a year Christian leaders across the nation had been debating the pros and cons of the "discipleship movement." Promoted primarily by teachers from Christian Growth Ministries in Ft. Lauderdale, Florida, (yet by no means limited to them) the emphasis called for all Christians—even those in leadership positions—to submit their lives and ministries to other Christian leaders. The call was for all Christians to align themselves with "committed groups" (churches) and to submit to "shepherds" (pastors).

Nobody demanded more loyalty or submission on the part of her followers than Kathryn.

However, the teaching of the Ft. Lauderdale ministers went beyond that. It insisted that even the leaders in the kingdom needed to be in submission to each other. That, to her, was unthinkable.

On September 5, 1975, she received a fat package of material from one of the officials of the Full Gospel

Business Men's Fellowship International. It seems the FGBMFI was fighting the submission and discipleship movement for the same reasons Kathryn opposed it. Many of the people, formerly loyal to the FGBMFI, were now lining up with cell groups under the authority of lay pastors (shepherds). Some of these people were no longer giving their money through the FGBMFI, but were tithing to their shepherd. The stage was set for a battle.

This packet contained all the information Kathryn needed. He enclosed a number of confidential letters which had been passed out by various independent ministers and laymen attacking the Ft. Lauderdale teaching, and, in particular, Bob Mumford, who was a leader of Christian Growth Ministries.

Although Kathryn had been the pioneer in the movement to re-emphasize the Holy Spirit, she never seemed to realize that the Spirit was also moving in many other areas of the kingdom. In fact, during the last fifteen years of her life, Kathryn had attended only a handful of meetings conducted by other ministers. She had not sat under the teachings of any others. She was too busy with her own ministry. As she told me, "The Holy Spirit is the only teacher I need." It was a vulnerable chink in her armor, and into this chink there was thrust a lance, agitating her to take action.

In mid-September, now fortified by the knowledge that others were standing with her, Kathryn entered the battle against those who taught submission and discipleship. Mumford was supposed to be one of the teachers at the Second World Conference on Holy Spirit in Israel in late October. The conference was sponsored by Logos and Kathryn saw her way to exert her influence so that it would be felt. She called her old friend, Dan Malachuk, president of Logos, and said, "If Bob Mumford goes to Israel, I shall not go."

It caught Dan completely by surprise. "The man is a heretic," Kathryn said. "I shall not appear on the same program with him. Take your pick, Mumford or me."

More than five thousand people from all over the world had already registered to attend the conference. Many of them were coming, not only to listen to the teachers (one of which was Mumford), but to attend the miracle service which Kathryn was to conduct in Tel Aviv. Kathryn's edict put Malachuk in an untenable position. Even though he, himself, had serious reservations about many of the concepts of the discipleship teachings, he still believed Mumford was a man of God. Besides, Logos was doing all it could to promote unity in the body of Christ, and he felt that Mumford's presence would help heal wounds.

A strong-willed man, Malachuk's first reaction was to resist Kathryn's use of threats and intimidations. He had known her for many years, as a close friend, but had never known her to react with such violence.

"Something is wrong," he told his board of directors at a called meeting. "This is so unlike Kathryn. I know she is very ill. I fear for her life."

The board of directors of Logos International Fellowship, which contained some of the biggest names in the charismatic renewal—David du Plessis, the Reverend Dennis Bennett, General Ralph Haines, plus others—weighed the matter seriously. Dan had already called Bob Mumford to tell him what had happened and to sound him out about it. Bob immediately offered to withdraw if that was what the board wanted. It was an impossible situation—and it drove the men to fervent prayer. So many things argued for the alternatives that faced them, but none of those arguments pointed conclusively to the will of God. Nonetheless they had to choose, and, in the end, they chose to accept Bob's offer and to submit to Kathryn's demands.

The following Sunday, Kathryn made one of her now infrequent appearances at Stambaugh Auditorium in Youngstown to deliver what she felt would be the death blow to the discipleship movement.

"Timid souls, you may leave now," she began. For more than an hour she preached, hammering on the pulpit as she defended "the ministry" against the false teachers.

"There's a new doctrine called 'the discipleship and submission movement,' " she said. "You may have never heard of it before. But it is so subtle and doing so much harm that if somebody doesn't do something to rebuke Satan and stop this movement, it is going to absolutely destroy the great charismatic movement."

Kathryn also attacked the concept of small groups, saying they were evil. "Not only do they tell you to give your money to the shepherd, but to become involved in cell groups and 'reveal your deepest thoughts.' I'll tell you one thing, I'm not going to tell anybody my inner thoughts."

The crowd laughed and applauded—just the way they did when she told them she had demanded that Mumford be removed from the platform of the World Conference on the Holy Spirit.

It was totally out of character for Kathryn. No single person in history had been used in such a demonstrative way to bring divergent members of the body of Christ together. Her faith was normally steady, but this time she seemed to be deliberately rocking the boat. It was as though she was being driven to protect "her ministry."

When Dino and Bartholomew had rattled their sabers against her in public, she took comfort that God would take care of her—and them. She knew the strict warnings of the

287

scripture against "lifting up a hand against God's anointed." Even when she had her running feud with Dallas Billington in Akron, Ohio, she had never let it degenerate to a personal battle, and never called him a heretic, and in the end had done her best to rebuild the fences. But now, in anger and frustration, threatened by her own insecurity and egged on by men who had given her only partial information, she struck out against others whom many felt were also God's anointed—just as much as she.

In October Kathryn made her swing through the south. Tink and Sue Wilkerson accompanied her. Tink seemed honored and flattered by Kathryn's constant attention. He convinced Kathryn she needed to own a private jet airplane. After all, Oral Roberts had one. Kathryn finally consented to Tink's plan. He would buy the plane, a Lear Jet, for $750,000 and hold ownership in his automobile leasing company in Tulsa. Kathryn would then lease it back from him for $12,000 a month. Although Tink convinced Kathryn the plane would save her money, actually figures indicated that the Kathryn Kuhlman Foundation was spending less than half that amount on commercial air fares for the entire staff—and the Lear Jet would only hold six people—two of whom would be the Wilkersons. Walter Adamack violently opposed the purchase, but Kathryn insisted that she and the foundation were "one," and if Tink felt she needed the plane, she was going to get it. Kathryn used it only twice—both times she was too sick to know what was going on. In the end Wilkerson got stuck with not only the plane, but with the two pilots he hired to fly it.

Tink also bought Kathryn a car and had it shipped from

Tulsa to Los Angeles. It was an $18,000 yellow two-door Mercedes-Benz and as similar to Kathryn's life style of Cadillacs and Continentals as asking her to exchange her pulpit dress for a bikini. She rode in it only once, and then reluctantly.

Despite the Wilkersons' seeming inability to understand Kathryn's life style and companionship with the Holy Spirit, she still gravitated toward them, virtually shutting herself away from her staff in Pittsburgh. Although there were days when she would come into the office, things were not the same. Maggie visited less frequently out at the Fox Chapel house where for years she and Kathryn had gone to relax, sit, talk, and spend the night. Now Kathryn was limiting her intimate conversations to the Wilkersons.

Unfortunately, they had not known Kathryn long enough to sense the subtle changes that were taking place in her life and personality. They had a genuine concern for her health, wanting to protect her from the unfriendly press as well as from those who wanted to use her. From May 6, 1975 until February 20, 1976, when Kathryn died, Tink spent only thirty-one days at his home in Tulsa. The rest of the time was spent traveling with Kathryn. Exactly what his motives were no one knows. Whether he was enamored by her dependence upon him, or whether it was a genuine service unto the Lord, only God and Tink Wilkerson know. But this is certain, even when she was her sickest, Kathryn tried to remain in control, calling the shots and, with an uncanny sense of timing, making plans right up until she died. She seemed to be a woman driven—trying desperately to wrap up all the loose ends and at the same time to catch up with the cloud, which for some reason known only to God, had once again begun to move— leaving her behind.

289

The first of November she was in Tel Aviv for the World Conference on the Holy Spirit. The pressures were unbelievably strong.

Kathryn wanted to preach on prophecy, but the local Christian leaders in Jerusalem and Tel Aviv had come to Dan Malachuk and Ralph Wilkerson, urging them to go to Kathryn and persuade her to choose another subject. The political situation in Israel was too hot for a noted Christian leader to come in and take sides with the Jewish cause. Kathryn, reluctantly gave in to the counsel of those around her.

The night before Kathryn was to speak, she met with the large delegation from Finland in a hotel in Tel Aviv. During the service, a woman, who had come from Helsinki in the terminal stages of cancer, died. In great anguish, Kathryn returned to her hotel room. It was, to her knowledge, the first time anything like that had ever happened. The implications were staggering.

The Sports Stadium in Tel Aviv was a madhouse of confusion the next day. Technicians were busily preparing for simultaneous translation of the service via earphones for the thousands of people who would be in the stadium but who could not speak English. They had enough headsets to serve the eight main foreign language groups, but not for the local, Hebrew-speaking Israelis, about two thousand of whom would be attending that evening. This was a good deal more than had been expected, thanks to exceptional news coverage by the Hebrew press. Of course the leaders of the conference were glad that so many local people—most of whom were probably unbelievers—would be thus exposed to the gospel. But it also put Dan Malachuk in the awkward position of having to go to an already tired and distraught Kathryn to tell her she would have to work side-by-side with a Hebrew-speaking interpreter. He knew she hated the distraction this would cause and that it was hard for her, even in the best of circumstances.

But these were not the best of circumstances. Many who came to the stadium that night felt a strange oppression in the place.

Backstage, while the young singing group, "The Living Sound" were singing on the platform, Kathryn was pacing. Up and down a dark tunnel that ran under the platform. Praying. Weeping. Begging.

"Dear God, please let me live! Let me live! I beg you, I want to live." It was the same prayer she had prayed many times over the past two years. The darkened tunnel resounded with her weeping and praying.

Dan Malachuk, apologizing for having to interrupt her communion with God, explained the situation. She was going to have to use an interpreter if she was to be understood by the Jews. Kathryn balked. Dan insisted. They had an obligation to the Israelis. After all, it was their nation and they had come to hear her.

"Do you have a good interpreter?" Kathryn asked.

Dan nodded and motioned for a man to join him under the platform. It was Dr. Robert Lindsey, a Spirit-filled Southern Baptist missionary who had lived among the Jews for almost thirty years. He was perhaps one of the best Hebrew scholars in the world and had earned the respect of the Jewish community.

Kathryn shook her head. Dr. Lindsey was wearing desert boots. She could not change. There was no way she could minister beside a man wearing desert boots—even though half the Israelis in the audience were wearing the same things.

"I'll tell you what we'll do," she said. "You have Dr. Lindsey come to the platform before I do. He can bring

291

greetings to the Israelis in their language and tell them that I will speak only ten minutes. Then we'll go directly into the miracle service."

But instead of preaching ten minutes—Kathryn preached an hour and fifteen minutes. More than a thousand Jews got up and walked out on her, shouting at the ushers and slamming doors as they went. Kathryn continued as though it never was. She had to. She could not try to start a miracle service until the power of the Holy Spirit was present. After an hour and a quarter, she started. She called out healing after healing. Many of those who came forward were healed, and many of the Christians were encouraged by the miracles. But it wasn't as it had been.

She wept herself to sleep that night in Israel. She was too tired to fight any more. Too tired to live. The next morning she went alone with Dan to a nearby hospital to pray for a bedridden little girl. It was the kind of quiet mission of compassion for which she had not had time in a long while. From the travail of the previous night she emerged, chastened and subdued—softened and ready for one last anointing.

CHAPTER XVIII

ONE LAST ANOINTING

The end, instead of being smooth and dignified as Kathryn liked things, was ragged and confusing. Three days after she returned from Israel she held her last service at the Shrine Auditorium. It was as it always had been. Kathryn was so weak by this time, however, she could hardly drag herself from her dressing room to the stage. But when the choir, under the direction of Paul Ferrin began singing the haunting "Alleluia," Kathryn's face suddenly became radiant. Supernatural strength poured into her body and once again she was a young woman. She flitted on to the stage, waving her hands as she took over the direction of the music. At that moment she stood ageless, a vessel of the Holy Spirit. A channel of God's power.

After the service Kathryn asked Tink, who had flown to

Los Angeles alone after dropping Sue off in Tulsa, if he would call his wife. "Maybe she can come out here and do something for my stomach. I hurt so badly."

Even though she had been back from Israel only a few hours, Sue dropped everything and flew to Los Angeles, arriving about 7:30 P.M. Kathryn had already gone to bed. Early the next morning Tink got up and flew to Denver to check on the Lear Jet, which was almost ready. While he was there he received a phone call from Sue.

"Kathryn's not well. You need to get back here as soon as possible."

It was mid-afternoon when Tink arrived. Kathryn had told Sue to send Maggie back to Pittsburgh. Kathryn was still in bed, complaining of pains in her upper abdomen. Tink tried to get her to call off an apointment with her television producer, Dick Ross, on Tuesday morning. Kathryn refused. Tuesday morning she was up early but told Sue, who was staying in a room nearby, "I don't feel at all sure of myself. I'm going to meet Dick downstairs in the Garden Room, but you sit close by in case I need you."

Sue and Tink took her downstairs for the meeting and then took a nearby table. Halfway through her conversation with Ross, Kathryn rose abruptly from the table and staggered towards the ladies room. Sue rushed to help her. They got to the rest room where Kathryn vomited. Tink and Sue got her back up to her room and while Sue prepared her for bed, Tink went back down to talk to Ross.

"Dick, whatever you need to do, just go ahead and do it. She's in no shape to go on today. Hopefully she'll be okay to tape the shows tomorrow."

Tink thought Kathryn had the flu and would soon recover.

That evening he called the cardiologist who had treated

her in Tulsa in July. He related Kathryn's symptoms over the phone.

"Can she lie flat on the bed?" the doctor asked.

"Yes," Tink said, "and she seems to have no trouble breathing."

"I imagine she has the flu," the doctor said. He suggested some medication which would ease her nausea.

Tink and Sue had taken a room directly across the hall from Kathryn. They had her room key and insisted she leave the night lock off so they could slip in and out during the night to check on her. The next morning she was feeling no better. However, since eight people had flown in from all over the nation for the television taping, she insisted on getting dressed and going to CBS for the shows.

It was a rough morning. Walking down the hall on the way to the studio Kathryn had to stop several times, leaning heavily on Tink's arm. She got through the morning shows but almost fainted on two different occasions.

Sometime during the morning Dick Ross took a phone call in the control booth. It was from Oral Roberts in Tulsa. "Have Kathryn call me during the lunch hour," he said. "Tink called earlier and asked Evelyn and me to pray. I want to talk to her."

Tink returned the call at noon and put Kathryn on the phone. "Kathryn, the Lord has this moment showed me something, just as I picked up the phone. There's darkness all around you."

"Yes," Kathryn said nodding. "I feel it."

"I see a shaft of light, and the shaft of light is blowing the darkness away and engulfing you."

"I know," she said. "I know, I know, I know."

"You are going to get through this telecast, aren't you?"

Kathryn was nodding vigorously. Her strength seemed to

be returning. Oral prayed for her over the phone, commanding the powers of darkness to leave—asking God to give her new strength. Kathryn seemed stronger. She finished the afternoon telecast without any trouble.

However, immediately after the show was over she collapsed into her chair in the dressing room.

"You might as well scrub the screening," she told Dick Ross. "I'm just too weak to get back to the viewing room."

It was the first time in almost five hundred shows she had not reviewed her programs before they were duplicated and sent out to the various stations across the land.

That night Tink and Sue had dinner with Diane McGregor and Jim West in the Gourmet Room of the Century Plaza. Diane, who had been a guest on television, was a former Las Vegas dancer who had been healed in a miracle service at the Shrine. West, a California millionaire, was Diane's date.

During the dinner West said, "Tink, if you ever need any medical help for Miss Kuhlman, call me. I know all the people on the staff at St. John's as well as the UCLA Medical Center."

Tink thanked him and said he hoped Kathryn would improve so she would not need a doctor.

Kathryn struggled through the next day's taping at CBS and returned to the Century Plaza totally exhausted. Saturday morning at five-thirty, Sue slipped in to check on her. She was half off her bed, lying face down, too weak to raise her head.

Sue helped her back on the bed and said, "You know, we're going to have to do something. We need to get a doctor."

Unable to speak, Kathryn just nodded her head. Her stomach was swollen with fluid, which was obviously putting pressure on her already enlarged heart. She was in extreme pain.

Tink tried to call Jim West, but he was not at home. He placed a call to Diane McGregor.

"Where is Jim?"

"He's at his ranch in Elko, Nevada."

"We need a doctor for Kathryn. How can I get in touch with him?"

"That won't be necessary," Diane said. "I know the doctor he used when he had his heart attack. He's Dr. Carl Zabia." She gave Tink the number.

It was almost nine o'clock when Tink finally got in touch with Dr. Zabia. "My name is Wilkerson. I'm an acquaintance of Jim West. I'm with Kathryn Kuhlman at the Century Plaza and she is in extreme pain with a heart condition."

The doctor said he was on his way to the hospital and would stop by the hotel.

Strangely enough Tink had all Kathryn's medical records from Tulsa with him. Dr. Zabia arrived, checked Kathryn and then pulled Tink into the hall.

"She needs immediate hospitalization. I'll call an ambulance. Give me the records and I'll have them looked over by the time you get her to St. John's Hospital."

The doctor called the ambulance from Tink's room and then drove on ahead to the hospital. Tink returned to Kathryn's room.

"We need to get ready. An ambulance will be here in just a few minutes."

"A what?" Kathryn said, her eyes flashing. This was the first she had spoken except for a few mumbled replies to the doctor. She sat straight up in bed, pushing back the covers. "I'm not going in any ambulance and don't you mention it again. Everybody in this hotel will know it and that means the entire world will know it. I'll walk before I go in an ambulance."

While Sue helped Kathryn get dressed, Tink went downstairs, met the ambulance, got directions to St. John's hospital, and paid them $40.00 for their trip. He returned to Kathryn's room and they started the long walk down the hall to the elevator and then out to Tink's car.

She almost died in the car. In fact, Tink thought she had died. By the time they got her to the hospital she was in and out of consciousness. There was additional confusion at the hospital since Dr. Zabia expected her to arrive by ambulance. It took him almost fifteen minutes to find out where she was, laid out on a stretcher in an emergency room. By that time her blood pressure had dropped far below the point of life and she was rushed to the cardiac unit where the doctors worked feverishly for almost five hours until she was revived and her vital signs stabilized.

Tink and Sue stayed with her constantly. Tink called Maggie every day, giving her progress reports.

"She wants to come home for Christmas," Tink said. "She wants you to go ahead and plan the big Christmas party like you've always had."

Dr. Richard Owellen of Johns Hopkins flew out and spent almost a week, in and out of Kathryn's room—more as a friend than a physician. Maggie flew out, but it was an unhappy experience. They hardly spoke. Maggie stood silently at the end of the bed. Heartbroken, she withdrew to a small lobby at the end of the hall and said, "I'll just sit here. At least Pastor will know I'm here, and that I love her." It was as though forces were trying to break the relationship that had existed for more than thirty years.

Maggie returned to Pittsburgh on Thanksgiving Day. Dr. Owellen flew back to Baltimore that weekend. Kathryn did seem to be making some improvement.

In January 1974, Kathryn had revised her will. In it she bequeathed to Jerome and Helen Stern of Portland, Oregon, a valuable painting "in appreciation for the kindness evidenced by Mr. and Mrs. Stern to my sister, Myrtle Parrott, at a time when she desperately needed such kindness."

The balance of her tangible articles were left to Marguerite (Maggie) Hartner "to be retained by her absolutely or distributed as she deems fit, she knowing my general wishes with respect to the same." (Kathryn had given Maggie detailed information on who in the organization was to receive what items from her house and collection of jewelry.)

In a characteristic manner she included: "During my lifetime I have amply provided for and assisted my sister, Geneva Dickson, and her sons, Gary and Robert, and my niece, Virginia Crane, and her children, Paul, Collene and Theresa, and for that reason I am not making any direct provisions for them herein."

The remainder of her estate was to be divided five ways, among her sister, Myrtle Parrott, Marguerite Hartner, Charles Loesch, Maryon Marsh, and Walter Adamack. They were to receive five percent of the "net fair market value of the trust estate" on an annual basis. If there was anything left over after all five died, the remainder would be distributed to the Kathryn Kuhlman Foundation. William Houston and the Pittsburgh National Bank were appointed trustees to distribute the funds to the five persons mentioned.

The doctors in California kept pressing Kathryn to let them do a heart catheterization. She refused, saying there were "personal things" she needed to do first. One of these "personal things" was to draw up a new will.

There is confusion surrounding the actual facts of the new will. Tink Wilkerson told me that even though Kathryn asked him to call his attorney, Irvine Ungerman, and ask him to fly from Tulsa to Los Angeles for a conference, that he never asked her why. "I had feelings that they might be talking about things of this type," he said, "but I didn't have any knowledge of what was going on. In fact, I found out there was a new will when I talked to Maggie on the Sunday after Kathryn died on Friday."

"Was that the first you knew about the new will?" I asked him.

"That's the first I knew," he replied.

(Maggie, however, told me tearfully that she had no idea Kathryn had even considered drawing up a new will. She knew nothing about it until she arrived in California for the funeral. The discovery at that time fell as a sledgehammer on her already shattered spirit. I believed her when she said she had not talked to Tink on Sunday, or any other day, about the will.)

Ungerman flew to Los Angeles and talked to Kathryn in her hospital room. "I stayed out of the room," Tink said.

Ungerman drew up a rough draft and then returned to Tulsa. On Wednesday, December 17, he returned again. Kathryn had been dismissed from the hospital and was in her room at the Century Plaza with round-the-clock nurses. The new will was signed by Kathryn and witnessed by Ungerman, Dr. Carl Zabia, and Jim West. According to Tink, Kathryn asked him to call West to come to the hospital as a witness, but Tink still maintained he did not know she was making out a new will. "I suppose I sensed it," he admitted, "but like I say, I made it a point not to become a party to it. I thought that was her business."

The new will was entirely different from the one she had made almost two years before. In it she bequeathed specific and substantial amounts to fourteen people who were either relatives or employees in the Pittsburgh office.

Among them were Myrtle Parrott, Geneva Dickson, Agnes Kuhlman, Marguerite Hartner, Maryon Marsh and Steve Zelenko. Smaller amounts went to ten other employees. The total cash distribution was $267,500.

Thereafter the will reads, "All the rest and residue of my property, real and personal, of every kind and wheresoever situated, whether vested or contingent at the time of my death, I devise and bequeath to Sue Wilkerson and D.B. Wilkerson, Jr., jointly, absolutely free and clear of any conditions or restrictions whatsoever."

Irvine E. Ungerman, of Tulsa, Oklahoma, was appointed as the sole executor of the will.

Whether Kathryn intended for "the ministry" to continue or not may have been settled in her will. She did prepare taped messages to be used after her death, but she knew that Kathryn Kuhlman was the ministry. Did Tink exert pressure? Was he an opportunist? Was he working for someone else? Did he really engineer the will and take advantage of Kathryn's weakness? It's hard to say. Could it have been Kathryn's intention to allow "the ministry" to phase out?

Some have already surmised that, had she been thinking clearly, she might have done differently. But who can know?

Four days later Tink had his pilots bring the new Lear Jet to Los Angeles. They flew Kathryn back to Pittsburgh. Maggie and Steve Zelenko helped get her home. Two nurses were traveling with her. Tink took the plane back to Tulsa, picked up Sue and flew out to Vail, Colorado, to spend Christmas in their ski cottage.

Christmas Day he called Kathryn. He could tell by the sound of her voice she was failing. The nurses were there, along with Maggie and a few others.

The next day Tink flew back to Tulsa, picked up a heart surgeon, and flew on to Pittsburgh. It was obvious she was going to have to have heart surgery.

Tink called Maggie at the office from Kathryn's Fox Chapel home. "Maggie, you had better come on out. I'm taking Miss Kuhlman to Tulsa."

Maggie was shocked. She got in her car and drove as fast as she dared. They were getting ready to leave when she arrived.

"Miss Kuhlman wants you to stay and take care of the office," Tink said, "Sue and I will handle everything."

The Tulsa surgeon was along as they carried Kathryn from the house to the car and then on to the airport. Maggie was crying.

"Trust me," Tink said. "They are going to operate Wednesday. I'll send the plane back so you can be there when she goes into surgery.

The following day, Saturday, December 27, Maggie got a phone call from Tink. "They are taking Miss Kuhlman into surgery right now."

"You can't be serious," Maggie said. Angry, then shocked. "You told me you'd give me time to get there."

"The doctors said there was no choice. She must have the operation right now, or she won't live."

Kathryn's private nurse at Hillcrest Medical Center had called Tink at his home in Tulsa at six o'clock on that Saturday morning.

"You had better get up here. Miss Kuhlman's respiration is really slowing down. I am concerned about her."

Tink hung up the phone. He wanted to call Oral Roberts, but he knew Oral stayed up late and then slept late in the morning. He hesitated, then picked up the phone and dialed Oral's unlisted number. Evelyn Roberts answered the phone.

"I'm sorry to bother you," he started, then told her the situation.

"Oral will be up and ready in fifteen minutes," she said. "You can pick him up."

The two men walked into Kathryn's room and stood looking down at her. She was dying. Oral laid his hand on her forehead, prayed a brief prayer, and then the two men left the room.

"Whatever you do for Kathryn do it in a hurry. I've never felt death any stronger on a person in all my life."

Evelyn Roberts and Sue Wilkerson joined their husbands at the hospital while the team of surgeons finished their preparation. Five physicians were involved, including a Spirit-filled cardiologist from Canada who had recently joined the faculty of the new medical school at ORU. At 10:00 A.M. the doctors came into the cardiac care unit where they were joined by the Wilkersons and the Roberts. Kathryn had already been prepared for surgery and was lying on the bed nearby. The Jewish surgeon looked at Oral, "Why don't we all join hands while you pray for us."

Moments later the orderly wheeled Kathryn into the operating room where the team worked for almost five hours in open heart surgery, repairing the mitral valve. At the end of the ordeal, the entire medical team came back down to the waiting room.

"I didn't do the operating," the chief surgeon said. "Someone else was in charge, guiding my hands."

The cardiologist from ORU said he had spent most of his time with his hands on Kathryn, praying in the Spirit, while the others did the work. All were pleased with the results.

But the following Friday she developed an abdominal obstruction. It required emergency surgery. During the next two weeks they had to do three bronchostomies because the size of her heart impeded the drainage from her left lung. There was a great deal of confusion from that point on. Tink called Pittsburgh every day, telling Maggie to go ahead and make plans for the monthly Shrine services and the miracle service in Oakland in April. He released news reports that Kathryn was making fine improvement and would soon be out of the hospital. However, the reports that came from the nurses (before they were forbidden to speak any longer) were just the opposite. There were reports from valid sources that Kathryn actually died on at least two occasions and had to be resuscitated through mechanical means.

Oral returned to pray for her twice.

Myrtle Parrott arrived from California. After one of her visits she pulled Tink aside.

"Tink, Kathryn says she wants to go home."

Her will to stay and fight was gone. She was ready to submit to a far higher call. In the end she stood alone, like the aging Moses when God put His arm around his shoulders and led him from the top of Mt. Nebo on to higher ground.

And so Kathryn, her dream of that day when every church would see miracles still unfulfilled, stepped back into the mist and watched as the kingdom marched on. Her task was complete. She had introduced them to the Holy Spirit. She had shown them that miracles were possible. Despite all her failures and shortcomings, she had proved that God could take even the most imperfect of creatures and use her as an instrument to reflect His glory. In death, as in life, she gave Him the glory.

On February 20, 1976, her face once again began to shine as the Holy Spirit settled upon her for one last anointing. The nurse in the room turned and looked as the glow enveloped the bed. An indescribable peace seemed to fill the room. And she was gone.

Glad did I live and gladly die.
And I laid me down with a will.*

* Robert Louis Stevenson, *Requiem.*

CHAPTER XIX

AN AFTERWORD: LOOKING BEYOND

At the funeral service at Wee Kirk o' the Heather in Forest Lawn Memorial Park in Glendale, California, Oral Roberts told what happened to him when the news came that Kathryn had died.

"My whole concern was about the healing ministry. Then I remembered her words and they hit me like thunder claps. 'It is not Kathryn Kuhlman. She cannot heal anybody. It is the work of the Holy Spirit.'

"Then I saw seven lights and I saw twelve people. I said to God, what do the lights mean? He revealed to me that the light came to people . . . they were not choosing, they were being chosen. There will be special people raised up out of this. These seven lights will shine out across this land, and in her death her ministry will be greater than in her life."

Two months later I visited her grave and then, driving across town, I slipped into the regular Thursday morning miracle service at Melodyland in Anaheim. Ralph Wilkerson was presiding. There were almost two thousand people present—at ten o'clock on Thursday morning.

It wasn't like the meetings at the Shrine or in Pittsburgh. There was no choir. The ushers were not dressed uniformly. Ralph was unpretentious, informal, as he wandered around the front of the huge circular auditorium speaking to people, praying for them, laying hands on them. Some fell backwards in the Spirit. Some were healed. Others were not. All seemed to sense it was God's business, not Ralph's.

He started a song: "Surely goodness and mercy shall follow me, all the days, all the days of my life." It was pitched too high and everybody had to squeak to sing. He smiled and kept on going. He wasn't trying to impress anyone, just wanting to please God.

I looked around. There were more than two dozen people, businessmen and housewives, moving up and down the aisle, praying for the sick, calling out those who had been healed. Kathryn would have never allowed it this way. Yet as I closed my eyes and listened, I realized it was the same Holy Spirit who was present that morning that I had felt at Kathryn's miracle services. He was honoring "the ministry," the ministry of miracles.

But it was not just in Melodyland this was taking place. In St. Louis, in Tulsa, in Detroit, in St. Petersburg, in Ft. Lauderdale, in Denver . . . in thousands of churches and prayer groups all over the world, the Holy Spirit was moving. For the same Spirit that raised Christ from the dead now dwells in us, quickening our mortal bodies.

I thought of Oral's vision. As the Bible came to an end the number seven was used to represent all the churches, for there were seven great churches to whom the risen Christ spoke. The number twelve, of course, represents perfection—and infinity. It's not that twelve persons will succeed Kathryn; rather all churches, everywhere, who are open to the move of the Holy Spirit are destined to see miracles. Kathryn's dream will be fulfilled. The axiom of Jesus remains true, even paraphrased to this generation: *Greater things shall they do than she did.*

Kathryn was not able to enter this promised land. She was of a different generation. She was the pioneer, showing us the way, taking us to the shore of Jordan. She was the John the Baptist of the ministry of the Holy Spirit. Now it is up to us to see it come to pass—in all the churches of the land.

Kathryn's gone. But the Holy Spirit is still alive.

And it shall come to pass afterward, that I will pour out my spirit upon all flesh. . . . And also upon the servants and upon the handmaids in those days will I pour out my spirit. . . . And I will shew wonders in the heavens and in the earth. . . . And it shall come to pass, that whosoever shall call on the name of the LORD shall be delivered. . . .

Joel 2:28-30, 31